Island Musics

Island Musics

Edited by Kevin Dawe

BERG

Oxford • New York

First published in 2004 by
Berg
Editorial offices:
1st Floor, Angel Court, 81 St Clements Street, Oxford, OX4 1AW, UK
175 Fifth Avenue, New York, NY 10010, USA

Berg is the imprint of Oxford International Publishers Ltd.

Library of Congress Cataloging-in-Publication data
Island musics / edited by Kevin Dawe.
  p. cm.
Includes bibliographical references and index.
ISBN 1-85973-797-8 (cloth) — ISBN 1-85973-703-X
1. World music—History and criticism.
2. Ethnomusicology. 3. Islands. I. Dawe, Kevin.
II. Title.
ML3545.I85 2004
780'.914'2—dc22

                                                              2004006546

British Library Cataloguing-in-Publication data
A catalogue record for this book is available from the British Library.

ISBN 1 85973 797 8 (Cloth)
     1 85973 703 X (Paper)

Typeset by Avocet Typeset, Chilton, Aylesbury, Bucks
Printed in the United Kingdom by Biddles Ltd, Kings Lynn

www.bergpublishers.com

Contents

Contributors

Andy Bennett is Lecturer in Sociology at the University of Surrey. Before studying for his PhD he spent two years in Germany working with the Frankfurt Rockmobil project. He has published articles on youth and music in journals such as *The British Journal of Sociology*, *Sociological Review*, *Media Culture and Society* and *Popular Music*. He is author of *Popular Music and Youth Culture* (2000, Macmillan) and *Cultures of Popular Music* (2001, Open University Press) and co-editor of *Guitar Cultures* (2001, Berg). Andy is Chair of the UK and Ireland branch of the International Association for the Study of Popular Music and co-convenor of the British Sociological Association Youth Study Group. Contact: a.bennett@soc.surrey.ac.uk.

Kevin Dawe is Lecturer in Ethnomusicology in the School of Music at the University of Leeds where he is also a member of the Centre for Mediterranean Studies and the Centre for African Studies. He has degrees in music and biology, a MSc in anthropology, and a PhD in ethnomusicology. He teaches mainly on the BA and MMus courses in popular and world musics at Leeds. Kevin has worked as a professional musician and ethnomusicologist in a variety of cultural contexts and has conducted field research in Greece, Spain and Papua New Guinea. He has published articles in journals such as *The British Journal of Ethnomusicology*, *World of Music*, *Popular Music*, *Popular Music and Society*, and the *Galpin Society Journal* and has written several book chapters. He is the co-editor of both *Guitar Cultures* (2001, Berg) and *The Mediterranean in Music: Critical Perspectives, Common Concerns, Cultural Differences* (2004, Scarecrow Press) and is currently writing a single-authored book entitled, *Kritika: Essays on Cretan Music*. Kevin is a member of the editorial board and currently reviews editor for *Ethnomusicology Forum* (formerly, the *British Journal of Ethnomusicology*). Contact: k.n.dawe@leeds.ac.uk.

Ron Emoff is Assistant Professor of Music at Ohio State University-Newark where he also has an appointment in the Department of Anthropology. He received his PhD in ethnomusicology from the University of Texas at Austin. While a graduate student in Austin, he actively performed various musics on, among other things, *kora*, accordion, violin, *'ud*, and *valiha* (a stringed instrument from Madagascar). At OSU-Newark he directs an Afropop ensemble. He has performed ethnographic research in Madagascar, Southwest Louisiana, and the French Antilles. Ron's publications include two books: *Recollecting from the Past: Musical Practice and Spirit Possession on the East Coast of Madagascar* (2002, Wesleyan University Press) and *Mementos, Artifacts, and Hallucinations from the Ethnograper's Tent* (2002, Routledge). Contact: emoff.1@osu.edu.

Jan Fairley is a freelance who has sung since the age of four (the gamut from Gilbert and Sullivan, Bach, Opera to musicals, acapella and sacred). With a first degree in literature and languages she first became interested in music writing through meeting members of the 'new song' movement when teaching in Chile between 1971–3. She returned to do a MPhil in Latin American studies at Oxford and then a PhD in Ethnomusicology at Edinburgh on Chilean exile musicians. She has researched extensively in Latin America and Spain since the 1970s particularly with political singer-songwriters and in flamenco. From the late 1980s she has worked as an editor notably for Cambridge University Press's *Popular Music* journal and *The New Grove Dictionary*. In her guise as a music writer and critic she contributed chapters to *The Rough Guide to World Music*, has written for *fRoots* since the mid-1980s and *Songlines* since the first edition. As a broadcaster she contributed regularly to BBC Radio 4's *Kaleidoscope* in the 1980s, presenting their first world music features as well as documentaries. Her latest documentary (September 2003) was made to commemorate the 30th anniversary of Chilean coup. She has made documentaries for BBC World Service, notably on Finland in the early 1990s and the 12-part world music series *Ports of Call*. As an independent she made the six part series *Songs From A Country Called Spain* for Radio 3. In the 1990s she pioneered world music in Scotland through her weekly BBC radio programme *Earthbeat* and by writing for *The Scotsman, Herald* and *The List*. She has compiled various compilation CDs, written liner notes, tour managed and worked as a club DJ in Scotland since the 1980s while enjoying dancing flamenco, tango and salsa. An occasional lecturer she is a Fellow at the Institute of Popular Music at Liverpool University. Contact: jan@chile.demon.co.uk.

Werner Graebner has conducted research on East African popular musics and popular culture since the mid-1980s. He works as a freelance journalist and record producer. Werner is currently affiliated to the University of Bayreuth's Humanities Collaborative Research Centre project: 'Local Action in Africa in the Context of Global Influences' with a research project on *taarab* music (SFB/FK 560). Publications include *Sokomoko: Popular Culture in East Africa* (1992, Amsterdam: Rodopi) as well as numerous CDs of music from East Africa and the Comoros. Contact: WGraebner@aol.com.

Keith Howard is Reader in Music, School of Oriental and African Studies,

University of London, and Director of the AHRB Research Centre for Cross-Cultural Music and Dance Performance. Author and editor of *Korean Musical Instruments: A Practical Guide* (1988, Se-Kwang, Seoul), *Bands, Songs, and Shamanistic Rituals: Folk Music in Korean Society* (1989, Royal Asiatic Society, Seoul), *The Sounds of Korea* (1990, Korean Overseas Information Service, Seoul), *True Stories of the Korean Comfort Women* (1995, Cassell, London), *Korean Musical Instruments* (1995, Oxford University Press, Hong Kong), *Korea: People, Country and Culture* (1996, School of Oriental & African Studies, London), *Korean Shamanism: Revivals, Survivals, and Change* (1998, Seoul Press/Royal Asiatic Society, Seoul), *Korean Music: A Listening Guide* (1999, National Center for Korean Traditional Performing Arts, Seoul). He is the author of more than 100 articles on Korean music and culture, shamanism, and ethnomusicology. Contact: kh@soas.ac.uk.

Chris Lawe Davies is Director of Studies in the Faculty of Social and Behavioural Sciences at the University of Queensland. He is a graduate of Canberra University (BA, professional writing) and Griffith University (MPhil). Formerly, a journalist on *The West Australian* newspaper and AAP (radio), he worked as a freelance writer and journalist in Australia and Scandinavia. Chris was Course Co-ordinator for journalism, Curtin University, 1990–1. He has been President and Vice-President of the Journalism Education Association and researches and publishes in the areas of journalism, policy and popular culture. Contact: c.lawedavies@mailbox.uq.edu.au.

Richard M. Moyle is Associate Professor of Ethnomusicology and Director, Archive of Maori and Pacific Music, University of Auckland, New Zealand. He is the author of twelve books on the music and history of the Pacific and Aboriginal Australia, where he has spent some nine years of fieldwork. The research on the Polynesian Outlier of Takū, on which this article is based, is ongoing. Contact: r.moyle@auckland.ac.nz.

Karl Neuenfeldt is Senior Lecturer in the Faculty of Informatics and Communication at Central Queensland University. His current research concerns historical and contemporary popular culture in indigenous cultures and in regional Australia, and music media and cultural production. Karl has many edited works to his name including the books: *The Didjeridu: From Arnhem Land to Internet* (1997, John Libbey/Perfect Beat Publications and Indiana University Press), and *Bundaberg: A Regional Perspective* (with Alex Grady and Linda Hungerford) (2000, Centre for Social Science Research: Rockhampton). He was special issues editor for *The World of Music* (Old instruments, new contexts, 40/2, 1998) and the *Journal of Intercultural Studies* (Music-based research, 22/2, 2001). He was for two years co-editor of *Perfect Beat* (*The Pacific Journal of Research into Contemporary Music and Popular Culture*) and has written numerous articles, book chapters and encyclopaedia entries. Karl is active as both music producer and performer. Contact: k.neuenfeldt@cqu.edu.au.

Tina Ramnarine is Lecturer in Ethnomusicology at Royal Holloway, University of London. She is the author of *Creating Their Own Space: The Development of an Indian-Caribbean Musical Tradition* (2001, University of West Indies Press) and *Ilmatar's Inspirations: Nationalism, Globalization, and the Changing Soundscapes of Finnish Folk Music* (2003, University of Chicago Press). Contact: Tina.Ramnarine@rhul.ac.uk.

Fiona Richards is Lecturer in Music and currently Head of the Department of Music at The Open University. Fiona read music at Durham University. She then spent a postgraduate year as a bassoonist at the National Centre for Orchestral Studies and went on to take a MMus at the University of London, Goldsmiths College. In October 1994 she joined the staff of the Open University. Since then she has completed a PhD on the subject of 'Meanings in the music of John Ireland', and has published *The Music of John Ireland* (2000, Ashgate). She has also contributed to *New Grove II* and *The New Dictionary of National Biography*. Her research interests are based in two main areas: music in Britain in the twentieth century, and the interrelationships between music and the other arts. She has produced articles and broadcasts on the music of William Baines, Malcolm Williamson, Judith Weir and John Woolrich. contact: F.Richards@open.ac.uk.

Acknowledgements

The idea for this book was inspired by the 'Cultural heritage in islands and small states' conference in Malta in May 1997. I wish to thank all colleagues present for extremely stimulating and helpful discussion. Whilst I was a staff tutor at the Open University (1997–2001), Tim Benton, then Dean of Arts brought this conference to my attention and recommended that I propose a paper. I wish to thank Professor Benton for his encouragement and also acknowledge the support of the Open University Arts Faculty Research Committee, which funded my trip to the conference.

Since that time I have had various discussions with colleagues who have provided valuable critical assessments of the project. I wish to thank especially Richard Middleton, Trevor Herbert and Stephen Blum.

This is my second book for Berg. I wish to acknowledge the continued support and guidance of Kathryn Earle and her team. I have, yet again, benefited from the rigorous and insightful comments of their anonymous external reader. I must acknowledge the enthusiasm and patience of the contributors to this volume and thank them for their faith in the project and their very high standard of work. It has been a joy to work with such a team and I have benefited greatly from numerous exchanges with them.

I would like to thank my wife Moira and my parents for all their love and support.

Kevin Dawe

Introduction:
Islands and Music Studies

Kevin Dawe

This book serves as a unique introduction to the rich and exciting musical world
we live in. It is certainly not the only introductory text to the musics of the world
but it is, to date, probably the only introduction composed of a series of case
studies about island music cultures drawn from around the world and not just from
one specific region. In this context, there are numerous discussions of space, place,
community, nationalism, solidarity, territoriality, diaspora, globalization,
hybridity, ethnicity, history, memory, nostalgia and how these are constructed and
played out in and as music, song and dance. The island sounds discussed in this
book display a huge range of musical styles, made up of a unique variety of
musical elements and combinations, providing for the expression of islander identities, issues and concerns. There are, of course, ideological orientations carried in
song and talk about music; for example, a positive ethos of self-sufficiency is
displayed among most of the communities featured whereas, negatively, an ethos
of xenophobic insularity may also be present. What is the effect of island life then
upon the musical imagination of a community? What 'focuses and stimulates the
imagination in a place that you can draw a line around' (Blake, 2000: 80)? What
role does the musical imagination play in the construction and interpretation of
islander life, and in the expression of islander sentiments and sensibilities?

Drawing primarily on perspectives offered by ethnomusicological, anthropological and sociological research, this book is mostly about the ways in which song
and instrumental music are socially constructed and made meaningful within
island societies. We write about the ways in which space and place are evoked in
rhythm and rhyme, how islands are symbolically re-constructed in sound and
image, and discuss how and why musicians and others set about creating music of
the islands. This book adds to our knowledge of music around the world but it also
reveals more about the significance of music, song, dance, ritual and myth in

1

everyday life. The book reveals the ways in which these elements of performance are made to work together by musicians, songwriters and composers in specific localities and cultural contexts in a world that challenges and changes.

Rationale

I have tried to be systematic in assembling this collection. The group of internationally renowned scholars featured offers a detailed study and fine-grain analysis of several distinct island music cultures, and of musicians and composers. The themes of their research provide for a coherent whole although, clearly, we cannot claim to have covered every aspect of the topic in one volume. I have also been fortunate to assemble a collection with a broad geographic spread. Again, given the scope of this volume, choices have been made about what to include and, clearly, there are many other island music cultures that might have been included. This collection encompasses islands in major oceans (Atlantic, Indian, Pacific) and seas (Caribbean, Mediterranean), and at maritime crossroads (Torres Straits, Zanzibar); from the smallest atoll (Takü) to the larger islands (Cuba, Madagascar), from island nations (Britain, Papua New Guinea) to diasporic communities (in Australia, Trinidad). Also featured are studies of several international centres of music making (Cuba, Ibiza Trinidad) and music from islands more locally active (Chindo, Takü, Torres Straits).

Island Musics is intentionally made up of a broad range of research methods and sub-field approaches, as reflected in the various forms and styles of analysis and reportage contained herein. There is critical musicology with an emphasis on textual analysis in relation to cultural history and biography (Richards), ethnomusicology with an emphasis on ethnographic fieldwork and participant observation (Moyle, Emoff, Howard, Dawe) and popular music studies with an emphasis on cultural studies, media and commercial music (Bennett, Fairley).[1] Distinctions such as these though are increasingly hard to sustain.[2] Chapters may have different starting points yet in the end there is considerable overlap (Graebner, Lawe Davies and Neuenfeldt, Ramnarine); this adds to the coherence and completeness of the work as a whole and its comprehensiveness/integrity as a work of current scholarship.

Island Musics has to be broad enough in scope to encompass the increasingly dynamic, mediated, interactive and transnational nature of music making in today's world whilst providing detailed studies of the music of insular cultures held in place, as if bound to the island itself (Takü). One tries to look to the horizon, therefore, without losing sight of land yet one admits that island musics can be hard to draw a line around; defined geographically but also symbolically, their 'edges' are often blurred. As Hesmondhalgh and Negus note in their path-finding examination of recent trends in popular music studies, 'there has been a movement away from the nation state as the prime locus for the understanding of the relationship of popular music to places, and a growing emphasis on both the minutiae of locality, and on international musical movements' (Hesmondhalgh and Negus, 2002: 8).

Here we probe the role of local island music cultures within a 'global economy' where some have more complex roles to play as conduits for transnational popular music culture (Cuba, Ibiza, Trinidad), but all have a role to play. Arjun Appadurai's notion of the 'global cultural economy' is composed of a set of fluid and overlapping culturescapes. These ethnoscapes, mediascapes, technoscapes, finanscapes and ideoscapes emphasise the inter-dependency of the various elements that make modern societies and cultures work (and the nature of those elements). One also notes the inter-dependency of societies and cultures in the modern world of new social formations and technological reconfigurations.[3] In *Island Musics* we acknowledge these processes of transformation at work, for instance, the social, political and economic forces of the world at large now come to bear upon Takü atoll society (Moyle) and radiate in and out of transnational culture hubs like Cuba (Fairley). In Takü, music provides a means of solidarity and resistance (particularly for the elders) as the community faces up to potentially irrevocable changes. Not that Takü has been cut off from the outside world. The community has encountered explorers, colonizers, missionaries and traders for centuries. Takü labourers have travelled abroad to find work. Some members of the Takü community have also actively sought new performance material whilst travelling off-island.

Some musics in this book act as voices for diasporas (Torres Straits islanders song in Australia, Carnival, calypso and chutney in Trinidad). Other musics are negotiated and contested in apparently more local settings as part of nationalist agendas and idealized and nostalgic projects (see Britain, Chindo, Crete, Cuba). Crucially, in each case we need to identify what constitutes the *inside* (the local, inland, onshore?) and the *outside* (the global, international, mainland, off-island, offshore?) of our island music cultures, who is defining these, and for what reasons. This book notes how *island music-scapes* make waves in the global musical economy, how they are constructed locally and in the popular imagination, and how they are analysed within the academic community.

Island Studies

The idea for this collection of papers came to me after attending the 'Cultural heritage in islands and small states' conference in Malta in May 1997.[4] Although I did not start working on this book until 2001, the experience of the conference stayed with me. There were representatives from a variety of disciplines and countries taking part and asking exciting, far-reaching and urgent questions. As an ethnomusicologist working then in the Greek islands, I found that I also had things to say and to add to the proceedings and important debates. As one of three speakers on the inter-relationships of performance, local culture industries and heritage projects, I too had proposals, suggestions and skills to offer that might affect the state and fate of islands and islanders.[5] The music panel was treated as seriously and attended as diligently as any other. I was assured that it was not just the ecologists, hydrologists, medics, demographers, economists, archaeologists, historians, and museum curators who had something worthwhile to say, work to do, or actions to take. The problems and processes of environmental degradation, urbanization, tourism, globalization, and so forth were also registered in music, song, dance and drama, and in the lives of musicians, composers, dancers and their audiences. Music, song, dance and drama were seen as important sources of sustainable income and a tremendous resource for island cultures – as socially cohesive yet also as points of culture contact and the means to negotiate with the outside world. I was reassured that decision taking and policy making could even be affected by the comments of an ethnomusicologist in the context of this conference, a meeting of scores of delegates from around the world that was fronted by INSULA[6] and backed by UNESCO.[7] I was even asked to chair a plenary session in front of some of Malta's top government officials. I was excited by the openness of delegates to my discipline, other disciplines, interdisciplinary problem solving, new ideas and solutions. And this excitement has also been there in my reading of recently published textbooks in popular music studies and fine-grain ethnographies in ethnomusicology, but most of all, in studies that have acknowledged the possibility and potential of collaboration and innovation. Perhaps too, long term, something like an 'applied ethnomusicology' might work even closer than *Island Musics* (and a few other publications mentioned herein) with the aims and objectives of INSULA as clearly outlined in their journal statement:[8]

> to encourage technical, scientific and cultural co-operation; to assist island communities in integrated planning; to contribute to the protection of island environments; and to promote the development of the islands' resources, with a special interest in island cultures and human resources development.
>
> Three main lines of action have been proposed within INSULA: management of island resources, technical assistance, and strategies for sustainable development.

My colleagues (from a range of disciplines) at the INSULA/UNESCO conference did not need any convincing that the study of musical performance could be used to provide unique insights into the ways in which human societies and cultures work. Nor did they doubt that such a study could help contribute to their aims and objectives, as outlined above. Study of expressive culture in any society provides us with an insight into deeply held values and beliefs passed down over generations. Music, song, dance and drama for instance, registering changes, pressing issues and reconfigurations in the social environment are, therefore, also a means by which society and culture can be shaped, in social action as lives lived musically. In various contexts then, how meaningful, enabling and empowering is musical performance, composition, production and consumption? One quickly moves on to ask broader yet deeper questions about the music culture one is working within as musical and social practices coalesce. It is essential to understand the ways in which social and cultural boundaries are put in place, how cultural difference is constructed, how local culture interacts with the world beyond the horizon (the 'world system') with international and transnational process, social movements and new technologies. How are new configurations of time and space affecting a world view? How are people finding a space and a place to live in, in what some commentators have called 'a new world order'? Perhaps, in these respects, this book is itself a sign of the times? I hope it will help us piece together a more complete picture of the musical world at least.

In *Island Musics* we move between text based enquiries to a broader examination of the social and cultural contexts. Therefore we present a range of questions that move from 'how is the music, the song text or dance put together and how does the drama unfold?' to 'how does performance relate to the construction of space, place, identity, ethnicity and gender?' The concerns of INSULA resonate throughout the chapters of this book. What kind of resource is music and performance within island societies? In attempting to put flesh on the bones of this question, we can, of course, draw on questions asked of all musical societies. How do musicians make a living? What changes are taking place in local musical worlds, such as the development and expansion of new repertoires, instrumentation, music industry, music tourism, and cultural heritage projects? Are these developments sustainable? How best should these changes be managed? What effects have they had/are they having on the local community? How has the local community responded? These and other questions form the basis of our approach to the study of island musics too.

Island Approaches

> Thus she brought us to the deep flowing River of Ocean and the frontiers of the world . . .
>
> (Homer)

For once on his travels among the islands of the Aegean, Odysseus, the hero of Homer's Odyssey, had the good fortune to travel on a 'favourable breeze' sent by the goddess Circe. However, Odysseus and his crew spent most of the voyage facing up to innumerable dangers, in constant battle with the elements, assorted terrifying creatures, and gods in human and non-human form. The forces of nature (here controlled by the gods) tossed him this way and that on this epic journey. Since that time, Homer's epic has taken its own course through history as one of the greatest stories ever told, and the Aegean islands and mainland remain forever linked by Odysseus's movements.

Like Odysseus, we face many hazards on a journey that takes us geographically and intellectually to many different places, but also to many different parts of the world, on a voyage of discovery to various island cultures and musical worlds. Numerous accounts in travellers' reports tell of the dangers and difficulties of navigating the world of islands; and various ethnomusicologists and anthropologists, for instance, tell us of the difficulties of negotiating complex island cultures. Physical dangers do not only affect the heroes of literature,[9] the following report made by the anthropologist Raymond Firth in 1936 makes the point clearly and with force:

> In the cool of the early morning, just before sunrise, the boom of the *Southern Cross* headed towards the eastern horizon, on which a tiny dark blue outline was faintly visible. Slowly it grew into a rugged mountain mass, standing up sheer from the ocean; then as we approached within a few miles it revealed around its base a narrow ring of low, flat land, thick with vegetation. The sullen grey day with its lowering clouds strengthened my impression of a solitary peak, wild and stormy, upthrust in a waste of waters. (Firth, 1961[1936]: 1)

Firth's report on the difficulties of landing on the Micronesian island of Tikopia stands in stark contrast to the visions of 'paradise' islands commonplace in the popular imagination. And it is reports by those in similar fields of academic enquiry as Firth that I draw on here. The contributors to this book, like Firth and others, have all been challenged, in one way or another, by the island experience – whether on an atoll in the South Pacific Ocean or in club land, Ibiza town. We have all had to explain ourselves to islanders and to our peers, trying to mirror the clarity of clear waters in the lucidity of our explanations and the integrity of our actions (in often quite small and clannish communities). Our encounters with islands and their musics have varied enormously, reflected in the subject matter of each chapter. Each chapter is a critical assessment of problems, concerns and issues arising, those directly affecting the daily life of islanders and their music, our response to the situation as researchers *and* islanders' responses to us.[10]

How can we remain detached and distant when Richard Moyle tells us that the atoll of Takü (Papua New Guinea) is sinking into the waters of the South Pacific? What will happen to its people and their culture? Ron Emoff reminds us that Madagascar is threatened by environmental devastation. How accurate a picture of the situation is provided by conservation agencies? How do local people (including musicians) fit into the picture? How effective are pop songs as a call for action? Keith Howard tells us how the South Korean island of Chindo has been turned into a 'cultural paradise'. What are the ramifications of this move? What role does Chindo music play within the national soundscape? How is history and culture negotiated and contested in this context? How do these changes effect musicians and music making? In Andy Bennett's chapter, I note that the Balearic island of Ibiza exists as a reinvented playground for north European club goers who visit the island every year. It re-emerges annually from the sea of the mind, so to speak, as the ultimate experience of thrill seekers, engendering an oceanic feeling in the foreign DJs and club goers who go there. The island has played a crucial role in the working out and definition of European youth culture for decades. But has Ibiza finally 'chilled'?

Another Mediterranean island that has had its own special place in the popular imagination of many North Europeans since the early 1960s is Crete. Here *Zorba the Greek* (1964) was filmed and the island was also the setting for the British television series *The Lotus-Eaters* (BBC, 1972/3) and *Who Pays the Ferryman?* (BBC, 1977). Yet Crete has been eclipsed at various times – at least in the popular British imagination – by *The Aphrodite Inheritance* (set in Cyprus, BBC, 1979), *The Darker Side of the Sun* (set in Rhodes, BBC, 1983), and later by the film *Captain Corelli's Mandolin* (set in Kefalonia, 2001). Crete is still well and truly on the tourist holiday map though. In my own chapter on Crete, I discuss the complexities of the local music industry (which is tied indirectly to the tourist industry) and ask the questions: how do musicians make a living in Crete? What range of industries, institutions and practices constitute 'music business' in this context? Jan Fairley tells us how Cuban musicians have responded to various internal and external pressures as evidenced by the emergence and re-construction of *timba* music. What factors have affected the ways in which music making and music business are now carried out on the island? What difference has this made to the life of island musicians? In Werner Graebner's study of the influences affecting the production and consumption of *taarab* music we might ask: 'whose music?' It is a contested musical form supplying a means by which various local identities are constructed but also uniting a diverse range of cultures in an island context. Here too, history is negotiated. In Tina Ramnarine's chapter on Trinidad, Carnival, calypso, and *chutney* music provide the means for the negotiation of identities within a multicultural setting. This is not without its problems or challenges. Karl Neuenfeldt and Chris Lawe Davis discuss the ways in which Australian Aboriginal identity is worked out in songs by two of the most well known musicians from the Torres Strait Islander community based in mainland Australia. The richness and complexity of their lyrics detail the importance of their island homes in constructions of islander identity and in the musicians' sense of belonging.

Our concern, in *Island Musics*, is to show how various cultures have responded to a range of problems and challenges, and how their music, in each case, embodies or has been enabling of, a response; whether the response has come from islanders based on 'the island' itself or 'the mainland'. Environmental problems, for instance, beset all the peoples of the islands featured in this book. Song can act as mediator, sometimes addressing these issues (Moyle), sometimes side-stepping them (Emoff). Cultural identity as musically constructed in relation to notions of space, place, gender,[11] and 'roots' are addressed here through various studies. That is: DJ culture in Ibiza town, diasporic communities in Trinidad and Australia (Torres Straits), musicians and others in multicultural Zanzibar (Graebner), men and music in Crete, women and music in Cuba, and art music composers in Britain (Richards). The island soundscape may be filled with 'natural' sounds as well as those made by its human inhabitants. There may well be a mutualism between environmental sounds and the sounds that we might call 'music' as produced by islanders.[12, 13] Whatever, the results are, of course, culture based.

Edmund Leach, writing in *Rethinking Anthropology* (1961) provides a warning, dare one approach the rocky shores of essentialist, determinist or isolationist thinking. He criticized his teacher Bronislaw Malinowski ([1922], 1935) for writing about the Trobriand Islands as composite wholes. That is, Malinowski apparently considered each island and its people in isolation. This might lead one to conclude that islanders (their behaviour and customs) are completely conditioned by their island environment. One needs to know how particular societies live and work *in relation to* the island and its ecology (although detailed discussion of island biogeography is well beyond the scope of this book; see Macarthur and Wilson, 1967; Krebs, 1985). Through the work of musicians and others, we aim to understand how individuals *respond to life as members of a society* living on 'the island'. The 'island' is treated here both as a physical and a social construction, islanders and their land forming a *symbolic* community (after Cohen, 1989), and that symbolic community providing for the needs of islanders living off-island. As Gladwin and Sarason note:

> because the physical environment stands ready to provide for practically every biological need experienced by the Trukese we may take it for granted that those anxieties – including that over food – which he feels are almost entirely a product of his experience within the *social* environment into which he is born. [sic] (Gladwin and Sarason, 1953: 19)

The type of anxiety identified by Gladwin and Sarason is also, of course, variously expressed in song, dance and drama as noted in this book and, as Jan Fairley notes, song can act as a very effective social barometer.

Islands then are not isolates bio-geographically, nor in terms of their societies and cultures,[14] even if they make tempting and convenient units for study. One can, after all, draw a neat line around them *on a map*.[15] But this line will be continuously breached, eroded and even washed away as the case studies in this book have shown. Many of the island music cultures identified in this book have been for centuries colonized, re-colonized, and at the centre of international social and

economic networks. Some of the island music cultures mentioned have partici-
pated in the formation of international popular music culture for centuries (Cuba,
Trinidad, Zanzibar). These developments have brought their own particular challenges to island cultures. For instance, the way in which islanders and their music
feature in the popular music industry has often led to a gross misinterpretation and
misrepresentation of their (musical) world and to the reinforcement of cultural
stereotypes and fantasies in sound and image. Much of the mythology, romance,
and literature about island music cultures as paradise islands is continually worked
up into a lather and frothed by the tourist industry (Fairley, Ramnarine), not to
mention the work of one or two anthropologists. It is important that one works
through and moves beyond the limits and pretensions of romantic and (neo)-colo-
nialist interpretations here.

Paradise Islands and Musical Tourism[16]

> The isle is full of noises,
> Sounds and sweet airs, that give delight and not hurt.
> (Shakespeare)

Tropical islands tend to feature in visions of paradise that are 'full of delight and
not hurt'; places where even a figure like Caliban might find sanctuary. Writing in
1953, the anthropologists Gladwin and Sarason made astute observations about
the way we tend to perceive islands. Their comments are still relevant and perti-
nent today:

> The exotic tropical island with its sheltered lagoon and sloping coconut palms has,
> since such islands became known to the western world, represented to many the ulti-
> mate in the luxuriance of nature and the freedom of man. This is perhaps because these
> warm and colourful islands with their clean white sand, rich vegetation, and deep blue
> waters are in many ways the antithesis of the urban environment in which many of us
> live. It is hard for us to believe that anyone could live on a Pacific island and be
> anything but happy and carefree. (Gladwin and Sarason, 1953: 19)

It is very difficult to get past this romantic vision. After all, who wants to be
reminded of the realities of island life on a two-week 'get away from it all to paradise'? Indeed, the tourist industry has not been slow to exploit the potential of
islands as holiday destinations; perhaps islands are the most potent of all symbols
of 'the great escape'? The problems of and ways of dealing with the impact of
tourism are noted in two seminal studies: *Host and Guests* (Smith, 1989) and *Last
Resorts* (Patullo, 1996). These studies not only bring one back to shore with a jolt
but discuss in hard-hitting detail the consequences of waves of tourism affecting
local cultures, social cohesion and environment in particular parts of the world

(including Tonga, Bali and the Caribbean). The studies try to ascertain if the relationship between 'hosts and guests' (the ideal model) can go beyond one of exploitation in order to lead to positive regional development, leading to a situation where locals are able to exploit the opportunities at hand. It is certainly a question of balance – sustainable development – and depends on the co-operation of governments as much as tour operators, and the call for local ownership and control. Whatever, one is talking about injections of big money and large capital investment into islands that has been going on for nearly a century with hardly any of it trickling down to the local population. All of this has enormous consequences for local music and musicians, and needs further critical examination here. Take, for example, the development of Paradise Island, off Nassau in the Bahamas, a story that makes for fascinating if not alarming reading:

> from rich man's retreat to transnational investment. The originally named Hog island had become a favourite picknicking spot for the Nassau smart set by the time Axel Wenner-Gren, a Swedish industrialist said to be the world's richest man, bought a slice of it in 1939. He dredged a pond to make a lake, cut canals and christened his estate Shangri-La. In 1961 he sold it for more than £3,600,000 to Huntingdon Hartford, the New York railway tycoon who began a major building expansion by investing US$10 million into Paradise Island.
>
> Twenty years later, there were some 3,000 hotel rooms on Paradise Island. Almost 90 percent of these were managed and/or owned by five foreign companies. These were Holiday Inn, Club Med, Sheraton and Loews and, above all, Resorts International, the former Mary Carter Paint Company, which had bought most of the island from Hartford in 1966 and came to control 42 per cent of its hotel rooms. By 1985 Resorts International owned four hotels on Paradise Island, the Paradise Island bridge, the Paradise Island airport and Paradise Airlines. At one point, it also owned more than 25 per cent of hotel room in the whole of the Bahamas. (Patullo, 1996: 20–1)[17]

In 1994, the refurbished Paradise Island resort included the world's largest outdoor aquarium and lagoon. The needs and every whim of clients are catered for in this sanitized environment. Indeed, guests need only see something of the rest of the island on their way to and from the airport. Resort hotels also provide musical entertainment on a nightly basis. Polly Patullo (1996) discusses the nightly show at the Crystal Place Resort and Casino at Nassau's 'fabled' Cable Beach: 'where white America is urged to "sway to Caribbean rhythms as our Las Vegas-style revue takes on a tropical twist". The backdrop, which had been changed for the finale, was a stretch of blue sea with a cruise ship on the horizon' (Patullo, 1996: 178).

Patullo describes the series of events that make up the Jubilation revue, a medley of 'island songs', a clash of local and non-local musical instruments and costumes, adding up to a performance of 'high class American kitsch'. Patullo is critical of presentations like Jubilation that 'at many levels' threaten to 'overwhelm the Caribbean with its slick otherness and metropolitan tastes' (Patullo, 1996: 179). She notes that, 'In many instances, tourism has bred cultural decline despite the efforts of those who are attempting to take control.' Patullo rather worryingly posits the view that 'Hotel entertainment may well be the only expression of Caribbean culture offered to tourists' (Patullo, 1996: 183).[18] Fairley and Ramnarine explore these and other issues in their chapters on Cuba and Trinidad, respectively. The struggle for control is, of course, not confined to the Caribbean. In my own chapter on Crete I note that the struggle for power is by no means confined to the tourist sector in island societies, small islands having their own share of imploding and catastrophic political power struggles.[19] In Crete, for instance, musicians often turn their back on tourism and seek work with the local recording industry and in clubs, however, they soon find that the tourist industry is not the only industry to exploit the paradise island theme.

The music industry has a long record of appropriating island sounds and using islands as the basis for the construction of a Shangri-La in sound. In many ways, the *exotica* music of the 1950s epitomizes a public infatuation with paradise – the ultimate destination – and makes an interesting and highly relevant case study. *Exotica* received much attention in the 1990s, being referred to as the 'cult of the primitive' and 'lounge music'. Many *exotica* artists were rediscovered with the craze for retro-fashion (you can hear the *exotica* influence in many 'chill out' records and their influence upon 'world music' is clear).[20] Islands feature prominently within this highly imaginative musical landscape that draws on themes that impact on the way we approach island peoples and cultures.

The post-war era up to the late 1950s saw the emergence of some of the first *exotica* productions on long-playing record. This coincided with an enormous growth in travel, tourism, films, television and the establishment of record companies throughout the world (with headquarters in the US, Europe and Japan). These factors started to bring 'the world' closer to home and even into people's living rooms in one form or another. They also helped to foster and rekindle a fascination with foreign and 'exotic' places. The 'exotic' is a term that often has currency when we talk about 'other' cultures in unfamiliar, novel and colourful settings. Many media productions, including those of the music industry, tried to recreate the feeling of warm, colourful, seductive, enticing and 'far away from it all' places (places not spoilt by the war, that is). Many popular songs of the 1950s were 'window-dressed' to give them a tropical feel – a balmy, vacation sound – usually by the inclusion of a little-heard 'ethnic' (that is, non-Western) musical instrument over an unexpected jazz or Latin beat.[21] Although there were a number of artists working with these trends, they are epitomized by the work of American-born, Hawaii-based jazz musician, arranger and bandleader Martin Denny (b. 1911). Denny's heyday was in the late 1950s and early 1960s but he still remains a central figure in the history of North America's fascination with the 'tropical paradise' of Waikiki beach and the cultures of the Pacific Ocean rim and islands.

Quiet Village was a hit-single in North America in 1957, going to number one in the charts. It is from Martin Denny's debut album, *Exotica*. It is also featured on a recent re-release collection of Denny's recordings entitled *Coconut Cream*. Piano and percussion dominate the proceedings, along with a variety of birdcalls and vibraphone. Denny incorporated sounds from a range of sources into mainstream jazz and other popular arrangements using non-Western musical instruments, animal calls and other environmental sounds to create a 'tropical' atmosphere. The Denny sound is colourful, unusual and instantly recognisable. As Sam Szczepanski notes in the liner notes to *Coconut Cream*:

> In 1956 whilst the band were performing at the beautiful open-air Shell Bar, part of the luxurious Hawaiian Village complex owned by millionaire Henry J. Kaiser, Denny hit upon the idea – quite by chance, it seems – of combining impromptu animal calls with various exotic instruments to create a novel variation in popular music. (Szczepanski, 1996)[22]

A Paradise Island set-up seems to be depicted here, providing the context for Denny's musical explorations. From studying the impact of recordings made by artists like Martin Denny, scholars have realized the debt that many 'world music' productions owe to early *exotica* albums with their 'international' outlook and broadly based orchestrations. Joseph Lanza argues that:

> Denny's idea of the ultimate Hawaiian sound was much different from what he encountered among the indigenous peoples. Disillusioned over the extent to which 'genuine' Hawaiian music depended on steel guitar, Denny sought to superimpose a variety of international rhythms to get the 'feel' of the South Seas. (Lanza, 1994: 123)

Scholars now have a considerable body of cultural theory and criticism with which to approach these works. Indeed, current thinking would locate *exotica* (along with most, if not all, 'world music' productions) in a system of colonial and post-colonial power relations.[23] Denny's Hawaiian-jazz-Pacific-world music mix might be considered a prime example – particularly his appropriation and mixing together of a variety of sounds, from a range of indigenous cultures, in a largely America-based musical context. In Joseph Lanza's opinion, *exotica* productions:

> had much in common with Rodgers and Hammerstein's *South Pacific*, which was not so much a South Sea Island romance as a science-fiction celebration of America's power to mould the unknown in the image of reconstructed psychosexual fantasies of G.I.s who had been stationed in the islands in World War II. (Lanza, 1994: 121)

In its 'moulding' of the musical unknown, Denny's jazzed-up-Hawaiian-South Pacific soundscape incorporates the 'natives' of the Pacific area, their music and their lands, in snapshot-like musical pastiche for the pleasure of a Western audience – rather like the grass-skirted *hula hula* dancers who 'welcome' newly arrived tourists to Honolulu. From the very localized context of the Shell Bar and, later, the recording studio, Denny's productions helped fuel a *global* image of Hawaii as 'the great escape' and 'the playground of the American world'. As Joseph Lanza notes, 'Denny became as much of a packaged tourist attraction as Diamond Head or Pearl Harbour' (Lanza, 1994: 122).[24, 25, 26]

The work of Martin Denny is indicative of the way in which islands, jungles and 'natives' feature in the recordings of *exotica* artists. It is also but one instance where the 'cult of the primitive' and the romancing of the Stone God sets the standards for our interpretation of island music cultures. The legacy lives on. Christian Scholze, producer, editor, compiler and commentator of the impressive CD collection *Island Blues: Entre mer et ciel* (2002) aims to take his listeners on what he describes as 'A dream voyage to the soul of the isles' (cover notes). Moving from Haiti to Hawaii, Madagascar to Martinique, Sumatra to Sardinia, and Cuba to Crete, he notes that:

> For many people, including the author, islands have an almost irresistible appeal. Is it because the dream of a different life might come true here? Is it the experience of infinity? Another sense of time and space? Is it the clear air and sweeping views? Or the generally slower pace of life? Is it the comforting embrace of the sea? Or the contrast to our stringently organised industrial society? It may well be a little of all these things. (Scholze, 2002)

As the reader may wish to discover, Scholze's production might be considered an appropriate audio companion to this book – the recordings are mostly very good and certainly far ranging.[27] However, the approach taken here does not quite match the glossy account of island life and musical performance given by Scholze.[28] I share his enthusiasm, but recording projects such as *Island Blues* tend to perpetuate the myths mentioned above. In my interpretation of recordings, liner notes and academic writings I have tried to keep in mind Steven Feld's helpful critique of 'celebratory narratives of world music' (Feld, 2000: 179) such as the one found in *Island Blues*. I have deliberately tried to steer away from the stance depicted therein in this book. For all its uses, *Island Blues* is still musical tourism with a capital T, a 'global' project that never really touches the ground. Hopefully, *Island Musics* is a project with a capital M attached much more firmly to Island Life. Steven Feld usefully critiques the use of the word 'global' in relation to music industry productions and states with force the problems that multiply when:

'global' replaces the previous label international as a positive valence term for modern practices and institutions. This has the effect of downplaying hegemonic managerial and capital relations in the music industry, and bringing to the foreground the ways in which somewhat larger segments of the world of music-making now get somewhat larger returns in financial and cultural capital to match their greater visibility. (Feld, 2000:180)

It is true that some islands as featured in this book are further away from the mainstream (that flow of 'globally' mediated culture) than others. There are few radios on Takü atoll but Cuban music has a very wide audience. Cuban music is highly visible in the international music industry; Cuba's size, geographic position, and local musical infrastructure are plugged into mainstream currents yet retain a degree of autonomy (Fairley). But who is in control of the operation? The music scene in Cuba has attracted much attention recently through Ry Cooder's reconstructed *Buena Vista Social Club*, whilst Bill Laswell's *Imaginary Cuba* works local street sounds and studio recorded backings into a 'globally' accessible ambient mix.[29] Not many people have even heard of Takü. The songs of the people of Takü exist largely in recordings made by ethnomusicologist Richard Moyle. Although 'remote', the giant red island of Madagascar is a world of music marketed as the ultimate exotic (cultural) safari, as a 'world out of time'[30] but very much 'in time' with trends in Anglo-American popular music (Emoff). For most of the island musics featured in this book, one quickly moves with them into regional, national and international networks and contexts of interaction in which they are increasingly embedded, contested, manipulated, and appropriated. Some island musics are a force to be reckoned with on the international music scene but musicians must win control and security by finding niches in an increasingly competitive market. They must have sponsors and backers. However, if they break through the pay-off can be considerable. Island musics, as elsewhere, make musical and other statements that can resonate around the world.

Beyond the Horizon

Music has long been a vital part of the Island Way of Life. Between community ceilidhs and house parties, Island music-makers have kept feet and hearts tapping and humming throughout Prince Edward Island, Canada, and the world.

(collections.ic.gc.ca/island/music.htm)

Jamaica, with the hotel industry, all the people can expose Jamaica, because tourists come and they can ask for reggae. It's just a matter of time now. There are a lot of artists comin' forward and presentin' themselves with good packages – good lyrics, good show – and the world come to hear.

(Willie Stewart of Third World in Jahn & Weber, 1998:242)

The first statement above, from a musician based on Prince Edward Island appears to show that locally based musicians see a place for their music on the island *and* see a role well established for it in the wider world. Local musicians seem able to work with the time-space co-ordinates that put their island on the musical map of the world, acting locally but thinking globally, as it were, cultivating connections and presenting a carefully constructed vision of 'tradition'. The vision of the Jamaican reggae musician in the second statement above complements this approach. He believed that reggae as a complete 'package' would make it big in the 1990s through exposure to foreign audiences in hotels and enter, via tourism, the international music market once again. These are both positive and optimistic statements. They might be challenged by some of the evidence presented in this book and elsewhere as one encounters as many local musicians cynically exploited as exploiting. Clearly, the relationship of island music cultures (as elsewhere) to the world at large is a complex one and difficult to reduce to local-global processes. Musicians are proactive and will explore an indefinite number of avenues, creatively and professionally. In-depth case studies are necessary to reveal the particularities of each case, and detail about the groups and individuals involved.[31] We are only too aware of the sort of questions posed by James Clifford in *Routes: Travel and Translation in the late Twentieth Century*. Clifford asks: 'Why not focus on any culture's farthest range of travel while *also* looking at its centres, its villages, its intensive fieldsites? How do groups negotiate themselves in external relationships, and how is a culture a site of travel for others?' (Clifford, 1997: 25).

Clifford presents an extraordinary case study of the Moe family, an all singing, guitar playing and dancing troupe that toured the world for fifty-six years. Tal Moe's home movies provide what Clifford calls 'a travelling Hawaiian view of the world' (Clifford, 1997: 26). Clearly, the ways in which islanders view the world beyond the horizon are as important as our interpretations of their island based culture. In a study of *exotica* and 'world music', and in a discussion of the ways in which tourism has impacted on island cultures, we have begun to assess the integrity of outsiders' interpretations and the problems of fieldwork. There are no simple answers or solutions. The chapters in this book are indicative of the way scholars are beginning to approach and have even begun to search for a deeper understanding of the complexity of local music cultures and their interaction with international socio-economic forces. It just so happens that a good many of these studies focus on islands, and mostly Caribbean islands. In her seminal study of *zouk*, Creole popular music from the West Indies (an economic, sociopolitical, and cultural force in the Lesser Antilles), Jocelyne Guilbault considers 'zouk as a musical phenomenon in its original locale, but I also connect it with its wider networks: those of regional and international scope as well as those representing economic, ethnocultural, and musical fields' (Guilbault, 1993: xvi-xvii). She takes this analysis much further:

To a much greater extent than imported music – to which small populations are customarily exposed – it can indeed be assumed that a local music that has become exportable and been granted considerable commercial value not only raises a feeling of pride among the local populations but at the same time has also has an increased influence on them. (Guilbault, 1993: xvii)

While the international market in many ways forces regional musical genres to become more homogenous, it does not prohibit unique innovation and development at home. (Guilbault, 1993: xvii)

This research shows that the islands of Lesser Antilles are connected through *zouk*, its popularity throughout the region confirmed by commercial sales registers and several years of fieldwork by Guilbault. She explores the relative meanings *zouk* has acquired in each island in the Lesser Antilles and her work challenges 'traditional' ethnomusicological approaches as 'rarely have they been concerned with understanding how various cultures have responded to the same music' (Guilbault, 1993: xvii). Yet 'traditional' critiques (from some ethnomusicologists) of emerging popular music styles – *syncretic* forms – have reminded us that many forms of 'traditional music' are 'deeply rooted' in their communities. The terms 'deeply-rooted' and 'traditional' can, of course, have many different and hotly contested meanings, from Tukü atoll to Cuba.

In *Caribbean Currents: Caribbean Music from Rumba to Reggae*,[32] Peter Manuel considers the Caribbean region as a major unified force within the international music scene. He identifies five themes in the study of Caribbean music, issues raised directly by Caribbean musics locally and internationally and which add to their relevance and ability to connect the whole region. These are issues of, race and ethnicity, music, sex and sexism, international popularity and diaspora, music and politics, and unity and diversity in a continent of islands. Manuel states that 'Music may yet play a role in forging a new sense of Caribbean unity, which could help the weak and divided islands of the region to collectively to challenge their multinational masters and take control of their own destinies' (Manuel, 1995: 246).

More detailed studies will continue to put this optimistic statement to the test. There is no doubt that local Caribbean musicians are conscious of their role in a world of music and the opportunities this has brought to others playing local music at home and abroad (Ramnarine). Manuel notes that: 'As the media and musical trends transcend geographical distances and borders, a new sort of Caribbean unity may yet emerge, based not on homogeneity but on a cosmopolitan multiculturalism' (Manuel, 1995: 234).

The Chapters

I have applied a simple logic to the layout of the chapters. There are groupings and contrasts but I have tried to allow themes to flow from one chapter to the next. Chapters 1 and 2 focus on questions and problems of physical, cultural and psychological survival among two islander communities as expressed in song. In Chapter 1, Richard Moyle analyses a sample of new fishing songs (*tuki*) that he recorded on Takü atoll. The atoll lies within the territory of Papua New Guinea's North Solomons Province but has close cultural affinities with Polynesia. Moyle notes that 'song poetry idealises interpersonal relationships … it openly acknowledges the dependence on spiritual powers to complement human skills so as to ensure ongoing survival in often-difficult environmental circumstances.' Moyle details a range of songs that show the links between performance and the maintenance of an egalitarian ethic within Takü society. Singing helps to sustain social integrity, and as part of a performance complex (with dance, ritual, and celebration) 'gives public and visible form to social balance of another kind, between maintenance of corporate solidarity and recognition of individual achievement and prominence.' Two problems threaten to undermine this 'balance': the arrival of a 'rival religion carrying the potential for the establishment of a competing form of social authority', and the fact that the island is sinking at the rate several inches per year as the result of tectonic plate movement. These new songs provide a strategy for dealing with the looming crises and the fundamental changes that threaten to destabilize Takü society.

The focal issue discussed by Ron Emoff in Chapter 2 is the relationship between environmental politics and popular song in Madagascar. Ravaged by slash-and-burn agriculture, and deforestation leading to soil erosion, the 'big red island' is a major focus of attention for world-wide conservation agencies and all those interested in environmental issues. The Malagasy people are on the edge of starvation; sickness and disease are rife. Emoff's position and concern come through with force as he examines the work of a number of Malagasy songwriters and recording artists, some of which (Rossy, Tarika) are well known on the 'world music' circuit. He focuses on the work of Mily Clément and in particular his song *Mandrora Mantsilany* (literally, 'spitting on oneself' or 'spitting into the wind') (1993), which received as much airplay on Radio Nationale Madagascar as Bryan Adams's *Everything I Do, I Do For You*. Emoff notes that Clément 'voices an international environmentalist cause' (79) that leaves the survival of local people out of the picture. Reserving his own judgement, he notes local reaction to the song. The song leads one to consider the Catch 22 position that the Malagasy find themselves in: they need the resources of their island to live, yet by carrying on with their current methods of farming they are destroying the land itself; but if they stop they starve. Such is the dilemma facing locals and development agencies. Emoff guides us through the disconcertingly problematic world inhabited by Malagasy musicians. He discusses the connections between popular song and traditional practices (such as spirit possession), how musicians debate these and other connections, and how musicians work with local issues but within a music market that makes increasingly uncertain demands upon them (personally and artistically).

In Chapter 3, Kevin Dawe discusses the ways in which musicians in Crete encounter the problems and challenges of life on a ledge. The island is equidistant from northern Greece and Libya, but there is no doubt in Cretan minds where their identity lies: as a distinct island member of the Greek nation state; namely, as Cretan first, Greek second. Some musicians in Crete can make a good living from their work, others, usually the less skilful, as semi-professionals rely on tourism to eke out a living. Whatever, the fortunes of musicians fluctuate year to year. The virtuosi may turn their backs on tourism but even they rely on the disposable income generated from it, which is invested in their employment at weddings, baptisms and other village and town celebrations (along with money brought back by expatriates in the summer).

Musicians deal in various ways with outsider approaches to their apparent musical exoticism. To tourists and 'world music' *aficianados* they are still marked out by *Zorba the Greek* stereotypes (and some of them play on this) as well as 'Eastern' sounding music played by wild, rugged shepherds dressed in black and carrying guns. The provinciality of musical tradition here is played out in word, action and deed by inward looking Cretan musicians who appear to be xenophobic. However, many of them appear to kick over the traces at one time or another and make the most of the tourist season, playing at Greek nights, club engagements all over the island and in Athens, and 'world music' festivals whilst vying for a record deal. Some have no qualms about adding Middle Eastern instruments to their ensemble even if this ruffles the feathers of 'traditionalists' and draws attention to the island's proximity to the Middle East.

Dawe asks three main questions of musicians. Firstly, 'what makes the Cretan musician?' Here he discusses the ways in which the musical structure relates to social structure and what it means to be a musician based on the island with all the obligations one has within a still insular Cretan society. There is no doubt that *lyra* music plays a very important role in the construction of Cretan identity, in particular, in the working out of gender roles. *Lyra* music (performed on a bowed and plucked lute duo or trio) is essentially men's music. Secondly, 'where does the money come from to finance a music industry and regular musical performances in Crete?' Here the work patterns of Cretan musicians are detailed in relation to the socio-economic infrastructure of the island. Thirdly, 'how does a musician make a living on an island like Crete?' Here the main sources of income, including weddings are discussed, as are the finer points of band leading and musicianship.

Until the 'special period' in the 1990s, Cuban musicians were state employees working for an *empresa de espectaculos,* receiving a monthly salary from a tiered system dependent on their classification grade as a musician. Today the state receives its money from every aspect of the music business. José Luís Cortés, the leader of pivotal *timba* group N.G. La Banda told Jan Fairley: 'Before, we had financial guarantees whether we were working or not and we had money to support ourselves with while we were creating. Today, we have to go out and look for support for our work and any projects. We can make a lot of money but we have to work out how to do so ourselves.' As Fairley notes in Chapter 4, musical changes are driven by both musicians and dancers with the sexualized solo female body (as opposed to that of the couple) becoming the central 'object' focus of dance music. The female body becomes the site of symbolic exchange between 'Cuba(n) and foreign men'. Indeed, *timba* music appears to meet all the criteria one might initially imagine of an island style. As a Cuban style it shares in the historical centrality of Cuban music in the development of popular music styles in the widespread populations that have been touched by maritime-trade relations that include Cuba as a hub. Fairley argues that Cuban musics have always been inextricably tied up with the economy of the island.

Themes of *timba* music in 1990s Cuba voice the impact of dramatic changes in Cuban society as a result of the transformed mixed economy and socially divisive dollar tourism. Fairley charts the impact of such change directly to aspects of Afro-Cuban culture. Dance music and the performances of high-profile groups, hitherto regarded as 'entertainment', challenged the status quo. The lyrics of dance-songs referencing religion and social behaviour within a popular culture context act as chronicles of social change, serving as an important barometer of everyday Cuban life on an island with a fully controlled media.

In Chapter 5, Keith Howard describes the history of dance and music on Chindo, an island county at the south-western tip of the Korean peninsula where a range of opportunities have opened up for professional performers. Here, musicians have been appointed as 'intangible cultural assets' and are supported by the state. Some of the performers involved, for instance, those involved in shamanistic rituals, have made a substantial number of commercial recordings. Howard opens his chapter with 'This then is the story of how music has become the lynchpin in the reinvention of Chindo as a cultural paradise.' Howard, unlike Emoff in his chapter, takes an optimistic view. For all its 'faults' state patronage has 'allowed music that no longer has any links to daily and ritual life to endure' and 'any mention of Hobsbawm's accusative notion of "invented tradition" would be summarily dismissed'. For many reasons the island makes an ideal place for such activity.

Howard reports that, by 2000, 114 intangible cultural assets had been appointed on the island, covering music, dance, dramas, plays and rituals among other items. It is a fact that Chindo has a greater proportion of these than any other Korean county. Musicians, then, as appointed guardians of repertoire and performance practices, are expected to be active in preserving music and in finding new contexts for its performance, a part of festivals, conferences and seminars at Cultural Centres and they remain the subject of much local academic interest. In May 2004, The National Center for Korean Traditional Performing Arts, 'the Seoul-based government-sponsored successor to court music institutes that can be traced back at least 1200 years, and the bastion of traditional Korean music' is due to finish building a new campus on Chindo's southern coast.[27] As Howard notes, 'Chindo is set to become a living museum for Korean music'.

In Chapter 6, Andy Bennett's study of dance culture on Ibiza stands in contrast to the 'cultural paradise' of Chindo and the 'magical islands' of the Torres Straits diaspora. Yet to DJs and club-goers Ibiza might well be a kind of 'cultural paradise', a 'magical island', a non-diasporic community but, nevertheless, a community that belongs to young people, everywhere. Ibiza has drawn younger holiday-makers to its dance club culture since its boom in the 1980s with a 'Balearic beat' that has helped shape new genres of dance music across Europe and the rest of the world. Thousands of young people from across Europe and other parts of the world visit Ibiza 'to sample the island's characteristic blend of vibrant club culture and Mediterranean mystique'. This convergence of cultures seems to offer the young travellers everything they need and desire. It results in 'a seasonal, and primarily hedonistic, trans-national community whose temporal relationships are framed exclusively around the aural and physical pleasures of the club atmosphere as experienced in the exotic setting of a Mediterranean island'. Indeed, club culture has sprung up all over the Mediterranean, particularly in resorts such as Ayia Napa, Cyprus but also in places as far away as Goa, India. To this effect, Bennett notes that 'the transnational and tribal nature of the Ibiza club culture is further accentuated by the global flow of DJs, musicians and producers whose temporal associations with Ibiza ensure an ever-changing soundscape of musical moods and fragments drawn from all over the world'.

The 'neo-tribes' discussed by Bennett contrast sharply with the Torres Strait islander community in Australia. In Chapter 7 Chris Lawe Davies and Karl Neuenfeldt note that

> As an island that is also a continent, Australia provides a unique example of 'island-ness'. It was the colony of an island-based coloniser, Great Britain, and its early migrants were primarily from the island nations of Great Britain and Ireland. Arguably, 'island-ness' was and still is at the core of the Australian worldview.

They go on to consider the island-ness of Torres Strait islander communities in Australia and the role of those islands in islander songs. The focus is upon an analysis of the songs of Getano Bann (born on the Mainland) and Ricardo Idagi (born in the Torres Strait region) as 'songwriters in-between' living for but off the islands 'who celebrate from a physical but not necessarily emotional distance'. These songs are explicitly about their island homes, constructing a particular island identity that is of their time, place and situation. The songs document historical events in the islands and contain themes that epitomize the songwriters' predicament, such as a clash of cultures and comments on the diasporic experience.

In Chapter 8, Tina Ramnarine explores further the theme of diaspora in her study of various musical genres from Trinidad. She makes use of music with transnational appeal to reflect critically on the concepts of community and ethnicity that have formed the ground for political organizations in Trinidad's past where the histories of colonialism, slavery and indentureship have left their mark. She notes: 'Such is the diasporic imagination that musical performances, and the discourses that surround them, serve to demarcate specific spaces that point to the different kinds of histories that shape contemporary Trinidadian sensibilities'. By focusing on the nationally significant music and ritual of Carnival she reveals how performances

> interrogate the notions of 'islander' and of 'home' [...], draw on imageries of other places, reach out to audiences in a global sphere, and are deeply implicated with political processes that relate to the island space but resonate beyond these geographic parameters.

Islanders use this music to engage in self-reflection and scrutiny and it is clear that Carnival and other performance genres are at the centre of a range of conflicting discourses, deliberated as much by tourism officials as the musicians involved. Musicians appear to be striking out against the very concept of ethnicity and the 'continuous, vigilant crafting of difference', appearing to single-mindedly focus on the features of their musical practices. Her interpretation of the situation brings Ramnarine to some challenging conclusions:

> Island boundaries are sonically blurred through the juxtaposition of various musical elements and through the versatile approaches of musicians to a variety of musical traditions and repertoires in which musical and aesthetic considerations override all others. Music in the diasporic imagination and the ambiguities of performing cultural (dis)placement in the island setting of Trinidad offer us another route to questioning the 'place' of 'culture' altogether.

Werner Graebner's history of *taarab* music in Zanzibar in Chapter 9 also identitifes with the phenomenon of where to 'place' music as a travelling culture. Graebner deciphers *taarab* music, as both an acoustic and verbal text that 'occupies a highly contested intermediary ecological niche between the African continent and the expanse of the Indian Ocean and respective musical cultures'. Zanzibar is made up of the islands of Unguja and Pemba and a few smaller islets just off the east African coast, a centre of Swahili culture and Islamic urban culture moulded by tradewinds and contacts across the Indian Ocean. In this setting, the people of Zanzibar, look out across the ocean to the Islamic world rather than to the African coast, an outlook that is mirrored in their music and song where images of seafaring and the sea abound in both Swahili poetry and *taarab* song.

Graebner discusses important episodes in the origins and development of the *taarab* style, its main commentators and its main documents. All of these carry tensions and negotiations as he describes how the present orientation of *taarab* music came to be. As Graebner charts *taarab* history it becomes clear that cultural politics has played a significant role in the cultivation, shaping and performance of this music as it is pulled this way and that by various commentators with quite different ideological positions. Fascinating is the fact that the history of the Ikhwani Safaa club is often generalized as the history of *taarab*. As Graebner notes: 'Most local writers have been associated with this club and have based their histories on the reminiscences of club members. Most of these reminiscences are in turn based on a short written club history, authored by Shaib Abeid Barajab, one of the club's founders.'

Graebner brings us up to date and notes that images of the sea can also be found in the new 'modern *taarab*' as well. *Love in Sea Express* by Abdallah Issa refers to the introduction of the first regular speedboat service between Dar es Salaam and Zanzibar in the early 1990s.[33] There is also the phenomenon of *taa-rap*, a form which attempts to bridge the gap between the classical *taarab* tradition and current youth music. Despite these new developments, which include a tourism industry that has generated new contexts for performance, the economical stalemate after the revolution and the subsequent socialist austerity policy may have generated the right conditions to sustain the old-style 'pure *taarab*' in which there is great interest from 'world music' audiences.

In Chapter 10, Fiona Richards focuses on three British composers whose imaginations have been stimulated by particular British islands that they visited. The work of these composers demonstrates something of a trend among British composers who seem to share a 'desire to visit and create real and imagined island worlds of secrets and adventures' perhaps as 'a deep-rooted part of British culture'. Richards focuses on the work of Judith Weir, John Ireland and Andrew Hugill in whose work nostalgia and memory are constant themes. Some works, through their timbral shape and contour, provide a real sense of topography whereas other works are more impressionist in their depiction of island soundscapes. We might compare their work to the songs of place by the Torres Strait islanders or the orienting orchestrations found in *taarab*, for instance. Richards analyses the structure and form of the orchestral and operatic works in question as well as noting how, when and where they were written and for what purpose.

Intriguingly, Judith Weir has been drawn to the Western Isles of Scotland, attracted by Hebridean folk songs and legends. Weir reworked the myths of South Uist into her music. Richards analyses the three-act opera, *The Vanishing Bridegroom* (1990), which weaves together three Gaelic tales concerned with disappearances. Each act of three acts of the opera takes a version of the vanishing myth as in many folk tales. But the acts together tell a story that goes across the whole opera concerning three episodes in the life of a particular family who live on a remote Scottish island. To enhance the evocations of islands described only through words, Weir drew extensively on elements of traditional Scottish musics such as *pibroch* (piping / *piobaireachd*), traditional *waulking-songs* (songs to accompany work on the island) and the psalm singing of the Western Isles.

John Ireland (1879–1962) repeatedly visited the Channel Islands, creating musical fantasies based around real places. In *The island spell* (begun 1911), Ireland's manner of capturing the essence of Jersey was to focus on its French aspects; hence there is a strong influence of Debussy in terms of the piece's structure, harmonies and stylistic piano writing. *Island Symphony* (1995), written by Andrew Hugill (*b.* 1957) was composed on the tiny St George's Island, which lies off the Cornish coast south of Looe. St George's Island 'appears as the archetypal 'fantastic' island, with a long history complete with medieval chapel site and ancient caves.' This electroacoustic piece uses natural, sampled and synthesized sounds within its four movements.

These examples begin to show how the islander predicament and experience is registered in music, dance and drama, and how variously musicians and composers have responded as islanders and as those passing through but deeply affected by the environment, the people, island lifestyles and legends. The ways in which island cultures are organized and imagined are mirrored in humanly organized sound and highly imaginative musical works. They reflect a unique experience. There is such a thing as 'island music' and it resonates with force through the examples mentioned above. However, I celebrate plurality and polyphony by calling this book, *Island Musics*. Clearly, such a complex, diverse and significant expression of islander-ness in song and symphony as noted above is worthy of further in-depth discussion. We begin to reveal the finer details in the chapters that follow.

Notes

1. See Clayton, Herbert, and Middleton (2003) for an overview of the current state of music studies. Read especially Richard Middleton's introduction.
2. See Hesmondhalgh and Negus (2002) for an overview of the state of popular music studies and its interaction with ethnomusicology and critical musicology. Read especially the editors' introduction.

3. In Arjun Appadurai (1990). See Slobin (1993) for a useful demonstration to how one might apply Appadurai's model to the cultural study of music.
4. International conference: 'Cultural heritage in islands and small states', Valetta, Malta, 8–10 May 1997. The conference was organized by the Islands and Small States Institute at the Foundation for International Studies of the University of Malta in collaboration with Insula (International Scientific Council for Island Development); the Centre for South Pacific Studies, University of New South Wales, Australia; and the Ministry for Education and National Culture of the Government of Malta.
5. In my case, drawing on experience of island life in Greece, Papua New Guinea and the South Pacific (Australia, New Zealand and Fiji), Japan, and attendance at conferences and holidays in Malta, Madeira and Mauritius. I have also been based in Ireland for thirteen years and was, after all, born and brought up in England a part of the British Isles and the country where I currently work.
6. The International Scientific Council for Island Development. www.insula.org.
7. www.unesco.org.
8. *International Journal of Island Affairs*, 2: 1. An example might be the wide-ranging study of eastern Fiji by Bayliss-Smith et al. (1988).
9. More recent than the Odyssey, take, for instance, the reef shipwrecks that marooned Robinson Crusoe in Daniel Defoe's classic tale (1791) and the central characters of R. M. Ballantyne's *The Coral Island*. See also *The Swiss Family Robinson* by Johannn Rudolf Wyss, Jules Verne's *The Mysterious Island* and *Treasure Island* by Robert Louis Stevenson.
10. Like Will Farnaby in Aldous Huxley's *Island*, one soon becomes an interested party in the fate of the people and culture one studies, almost convinced that the way of life one is studying should remain unspoilt. Most of the studies in this book document change and transition in one way or another. Our very presence may be an arbiter of change and any representation of what we see, hear and experience value-laden. See Clifford and Marcus (1986), Barz and Cooley (1997).
11. See Stokes (1994), Feld and Basso (1996).
12. Appropriate here is James Clifford's comment that 'Fieldwork is earthbound – intimately involved in the natural and social landscape' (Clifford, 1997: 52).
13. Steven Feld's work amongst the Kaluli tribe of Papua New Guinea has raised some very interesting questions about the inter-relationship between a people, its music and its environment. The Kaluli have no concept of music, recognizing sounds, arranged in categories, that are, to varying degrees shared by the natural elements, animals and humans. They assume that every member of the community will become a competent producer and maker of the natural and cultural sound patterns in a rainforest environment that demands acute

auditory and perceptual skills (Feld 1982/1990).

14. Despite the dictionary definition of island as: 'A thing that is isolated, detached, or surrounded' (Pearsall, 1999 [1995]), islands are more than 'things' to the people whose musics we are studying. The basic description of an island as 'a piece of land surrounded by water' is the most obvious embarkation point for this book.

15. James Clifford's critique of 'bounded sites' is useful and applicable here (see Clifford, 1997: 21).

16. See Clifford (1997:154) where the origins of the word Paradise are traced 'From old Persian (*pairi*, meaning 'about', 'around' plus *daeza*, meaning 'wall'). *The Oxford Concise English Dictionary* (tenth edition) defines Paradise as 'the Garden of Eden', paradise as 'an ideal or idyllic place or state'. From the 'Latin from Greek *paradeisos* 'royal (enclosed) park'.'

17. See also a revealing article in *Business Life* (July/August, 2001: 85–6) about the purchase of islands entitled: 'Isle have one of those'. Alexander Garret 'investigates the market in personal kingdoms ... it's the ultimate dream'. 'The roll-call of those who have taken the plunge include Tony Curtis and Nicholas Cage ... Malcolm Forbes, Richard Branson ... the Barclay Brothers ... Edward de Bono.'

18. See also Elizabeth Tatar's richly illustrated account of the impact of tourism on Hawaiian music (Tatar, 1987). She notes that 'A better understanding of how tourism has influenced traditional expressions of music and dance would bring the industry and the community closer to a mutual solution to this problem' (Tatar, 1987: 2). See also Philip Hayward's account of the effects of tourism on the music of the Whitsunday Islands (Hayward, 2003).

19. See Averill, 1997.

20. 'World music' is a music-industry designed pigeon-hole category into which popular mixes of indigenous musics can be placed, a category that is often synonymous with 'roots', 'ethnic' and 'world beat' and sometimes 'New Age' and 'folk'. It can also include, for example, Indian or Persian 'classical' musics. In turn, we can detect sub-categories of 'World Music' where the focus is on one particular continent, region, country, or tribal group. Likewise, the category of 'World Music' intersects with various genres and sub-genres whose boundaries are in a continual state of flux. At the time of writing, categories such as *exotica*, ambient, trance, ethno-techno and techno-tribal have been reported (for example, in Taylor, 1997:4).

21. Martin Denny (1996) [1957/1958], *Exotica 1 and 2*. Scamp Records/Liberty Records/Caroline Records. SCP 9712.

22. Martin Denny (1996), *The Coconut Cream of Martin Denny: 20 Pearls from the Exotique*, Carlton Home Entertainment Ltd./Elite 30364 00154.

23. See Stokes (1998: 243) and Negus (1999: 167).

24. See also an extended interview with Martin Denny in Vale and Juno (1993) and a chapter on Denny in Hayward (1999).
25. Readers might find the following mix of Pacific Ocean field recordings and commercial recordings useful: Deep Forest (2001), *Pacifique*, Sony/Epic, BOOOO58ABZ. David Fanshawe (2002), *Music of the South Pacific*, Florida, USA: Arc Music Inc. EUCD1709. Ryukyu Underground, *Ryukyu Underground*, Riverboat Records, TUGCD1028. Te Vaka (1999) *Ki Mua (To the Fore/Future)*, Spirit of Play Productions Ltd/Warm Earth Productions Ltd. WMCD 1002. *South Pacific* (1988) [1958] (Rodgers and Hammerstein), RCA/Victor, BMG ND83681.
26. Composers have been drawn to islands and their music since at least the time of Claude Debussy. See Sorrell (1990), Chapter 1, for discussion of European and American composers' and scholars' ongoing interest in and fascination for Javanese and Balinese *gamelan* (percussion orchestra) music. See also Cooke (1998), for a discussion of Benjamin Britten's trips to Bali and his interest in Balinese music.
27. Christian Scholze (Producer) (2002), *Island Blues: Entre mer et ciel*. Frankfurt: Network Medien GmbH. LC6759. 2 CDs. Liner notes in German, French, and English. 26pp. The reader may also find *The Rough Guide to World Music*, Volumes 1 and 2 (Brouhton et al.) useful as a companion guide to some of the musics mentioned in this book.
28. I remain wary of the content of most liner notes. Take, for instance, this quotation from the liner notes to the 1969 Manos Tacticos LP:
    'There is always an aura of mystique about the music of distant lands. The hot blooded, thrilling sound of Flamenco and the romantic ethereal sound of the Bohemians all create some form of emotional involvement in the mind of the listener. In the same way, music from the Greek islands conjures up visions of idyllic places and people, warm and warm hearted and free from the political distortion of the moment.'
    It seems to try to debunk this romantic vision but instead becomes patronizing: '
    The people of Greece are kind, hospitable, hard-working and aware of the tensions and problems that surround them. Their music to a certain extent reflects this but is even more a mark of their tremendous awareness of the need to live life to the full, even though circumstances are not always in their favour ... music the one true escape from reality.' (Blase Machin? Liner notes, 1969). Tactikos, Manos and his Bouzoukis (1969), *Music from the Greek Islands*. EMI/Music for Pleasure Ltd. MFP1395.
29. Ry Cooder et al. (1987), *Buena Vista Social Club*, World Circuit Bill Laswell (1999), *Imaginary Cuba*. Wicklow Records/BMG Music. CD09026635142.
30. Kaiser, Henry and David Lindsey (1992), *Madagascar: A World out of Time*.

Newton, NJ: Shanachie 64041.
31. See the pathfinding research by Wallis and Malm (1984).
32. See also books by Daniel (1995), Austerlitz (1997), Averill (1997), and Stolzoff (2000).

References and Further Reading

Allen, R. and Wilcken, L. (eds) (1998), *Island Sounds in the Global City: Caribbean Popular Music and Identity in New York*, New York: Institute for Studies in American Music, Brooklyn College, CUNY and New York Folklore Society.
Anderson Sutton, R. (1991), *Traditions of Gamelan Music in Java: Musical Pluralism and Regional Identity*, Cambridge: Cambridge University Press.
—— (2002), *Calling Back the Spirit: Music, Dance and Cultural Politics in Lowland South Sulawesi*, New York: Oxford University Press.
Appadurai, A. (1990), 'Disjuncture and difference in the Global Cultural Economy', *Public Culture*, 2 (2): 1–24.
Austerlitz, P. (1997), *Merengue: Dominican Music and Dominican Identity*. Philadelphia: Temple University Press.
Averill, G. (1997), *A Day for the Hunter, A Day for the Prey: Popular music and power in Haiti*, Chicago: University of Chicago Press.
Ballantyne, R. M. (1993) [1857], *The Coral Island: A Tale of the Pacific Ocean*, Ware, Herts: Wordsworth Editions Ltd.
Barz, G. and Cooley, T. (1997), *Shadows in the Field: New Perspectives for Fieldwork in Ethnomusicology*, New York: Oxford University Press.
Bayliss-Smith, T, Bedford, R. Brookfield, H. and Latham, M. (1988), *Islands, Islanders and the World: The Colonial and Post-colonial Experience of Eastern Fiji*, Cambridge: Cambridge University Press.
Blake, Q. (2000), *The Laureate's Party*, London: Red Fox.
Broughton, S., Ellingham, M., Muddyman, D. and Trillo, R. (eds) (1999–2000), *The World Music: The Rough Guide*. 2nd edition, Vol. 1, *Africa, Europe and the Middle East*, Vol. 2, *Latin and North America, Caribbean, India, Asia and Pacific*, London: The Rough Guides.
Clayton, M., Herbert, T. and Middleton, R. (eds) (2003), *The Cultural Study of Music: A Critical Introduction*, New York and London: Routledge.
Clifford, J. (1999) [1997], *Routes: Travel and Translation in the Late Twentieth Century*, Cambridge MA and London: Harvard University Press.
Clifford, J. and Marcus, G. F. (1986), *Writing Culture: The Poetics and Politics of Ethnography*, Berkeley and Los Angeles: University of California Press.
Cohen, A. P. (1989) [1985], *The Symbolic Construction of Community*, London and New York: Routledge.
Cooke, M. (1998), *Britten and the Far East: Asian Influences in the Music of*

Benjamin Britten. Aldeburgh Studies in Music, Volume 4, Woodbridge: The Boydell Press.

Cowley, J. (1996), *Carnival, Canboulay and Calypso: Traditions in the Making*. Cambridge: Cambridge University Press.

Daniel, Y. (1995), *Rumba: Dance and Social Change in Contemporary Cuba*, Bloomington: Indiana University Press.

Defoe, D. (1994) [1719], *Robinson Crusoe*. London: Penguin.

Erlmann, V. (1998), 'How Beautiful is Small? Music, Globalization and the Aesthetics of the Local', in *Yearbook for Traditional Music*, International Council for Traditional Music, New York: Columbia University.

Feld, S. and K. H. Basso (1996), *Senses of Place*, Santa Fe: School of American Research Press.

Feld, S. (2000), 'Sound Worlds', in P. Kruth and H. Stobart (eds), *Sound*, Cambridge: Cambridge University Press.

Firth, R. (1961) [1936], *We, the Tikopia: A Sociological Study of Kinship in Primitive Polynesia*, London: George Allen & Unwin.

Firth, R. and Mclean, M. (1991), *Tikopia Songs: Poetic and Musical Art of a Polynesian People of the Soloman Islands*, Cambridge: Cambridge University Press.

Fischer, H. (1983) [1958], *Sound-producing Instruments in Oceania*, Boroko: Institute of Papua New Guinea Studies.

Gladwin, T. and Sarason, S. B. (1953), *Truk: Man in Paradise*, New York: Wenner-Gren Foundation for Anthropological Research Inc.

Guilbault, J. Averill, G., Benoit, E Rabess, G. (1993), *Zouk: World Music in the West Indies*. Chicago and London: University of Chicago Press.

Hayward, P. (ed.) (1998), *Sound Alliances: Indigenous Peoples, Cultural Politics and Popular Music in the Pacific*, London & New York: Cassell.

Hayward, P. (ed.) (1999), *Widening the Horizon: Exoticism in Post-War Popular Music*. Sydney: John Libbey/Perfect Beat Publications.

Hayward, P. (2003), *Tidelines: Music, Tourism and Cultural Transition in the Whitsunday Islands (and Adjacent Coast)*, Lismore, Australia: Music Archive for Pacific Press, Southern Cross University.

Hesmondhalgh, D. and K. Negus (eds) (2002), *Popular Music Studies*, London: Arnold.

Huxley, A. (1994) [1962], *Island*, London: Flamingo/HarperCollins Publishers.

Jahn, B. and T. Weber (1998), *Reggae Island: Jamaican Music in the Digital Age*. New York: Da Capo Press.

Krebs, C. (1985) [Third Edition], *Ecology: The Experimental Analysis of Distribution and Abundance*, New York: Harper & Row.

Lanza, J. (1995) [1994], *Elevator Music: A Surreal History of Muzak, Easy-listening and other Moodsong*, London: Quartet Books Ltd.

Lortat-Jacob, B. (1995), *Sardinian Chronicles*. Chicago and London: Chicago University Press.

Macarthur, R. H. and Wilson, E. O. (1967), *The Theory of Island Biogeography*. Princeton: Princeton University Press.

Malinowski, B. (1983) [1922], *Argonauts of the Western Pacific: An Account of Native Enterprise and Adventure in the Archipelagos of Melanesian New Guinea*, London: Routledge & Kegan Paul.

Malinowski, B. (1935), *Coral Gardens and Their Magic: A Study of the Methods of Tilling the Soil and of Agricultural Rites in the Trobriand Islands*, London: George Allen & Unwin Ltd.

Manuel, P. Bilby, K. and Largey, M. (1995), *Caribbean Currents: Caribbean Music from Rumba to Reggae*, Philadelphia: Temple University Press.

Mitchell, T. (1993), *Popular Music and Local Identity: Rock, Pop and Rap in Europe and Oceania*, London and New York: Leicester University Press.

Negus, K. (1999), *Music Genres and Corporate Cultures*, London and New York: Routledge.

Patullo, P. (1996), *Last Resorts: The Cost of Tourism in the Caribbean*, London: Cassell.

Pearsall, J. (1999) [1995], *Concise Oxford English Dictionary*, tenth edition, Oxford: Oxford University Press.

Plastino, G. (ed.) (2003), *Mediterranean Mosaic: Popular Music and Global Sounds*, London and New York: Routledge.

Smith, V. L. (ed.) (1989), *Hosts and Guests: The Anthropology of Tourism*, 2nd edition, Philadelphia: University of Pennsylvania Press.

Sorrell, N. (1990), *Guide to the Gamelan*, London: Faber & Faber Ltd.

Stevenson, R. L. (1883), *Treasure Island*, London: Dean.

Stokes, M. (ed.) (1994), *Ethnicity, Identity and Music: The Musical Construction of Place*, Oxford and Providence: Berg.

Stokes, M. (1998), 'Review of *World Music: The Rough Guide*, by Simon Broughton et al, London: Penguin (1994)', in *Popular Music*, 17 (1): 243–5.

Stuempfle, P. (1995), *The Steelband Movement: The Forging of a National Art in Trinidad and Tobago*, Philadelphia: University of Pennsylvania Press.

Tatar, E. (1989), *Strains of Change: The Impact of Tourism on Hawaiian Music*, Honolulu: Bishop Museum Press.

Taylor, T. D. (1997), *Global Pop: World Music, World Markets*. Routledge: New York and London.

Schumacher, E. F. (1974) [1973], *Small is Beautiful: A Study of Economics as if People Mattered*, London: Abacus Edition/Sphere Books Ltd.

Slobin, M. (1993), *Subcultural Sounds. Micromusics of the West*, Hanover and London: Wesleyan University Press.

Stolzoff, N. C. (2000), *Wake the Town and tell the People: Dancehall Culture in*

Jamaica, Durham and London: Duke University Press.

Sullivan, P. (2003), *Waking Up in Iceland: Sights and Sounds from Europe's Coolest Hotspot*, London: Sanctuary Publishing Limited.

Toop, D. (1999), *Exotica: Fabricated Soundscapes in a Real World*, London: Serpent's Tail.

Vale, V. and Juno, A. (1993), *Incredibly Strange Music,* Volume 1, San Francisco, Re/Search Publications.

Verne, J. (1986), *The Mysterious Island*, New York: New American Library.

Wallis, R. and Malm, K. (1984), *Big Sounds from Small People: The Music Industry in Small Countries*, London: Constable & Company Limited.

Wyss, J.R. (1999), *The Swiss Family Robinson*, New York: Yearling Books.

–1–

Don't Rock the Boat – Sing!
Maintaining Balance within a Coral Atoll
Community

Richard M. Moyle

One of the world's smaller island communities, Takū maintains its largely traditional lifestyle through a combination of geographical isolation, economic invisibility in terms of Papua New Guinea's gross domestic product, discouragement of casual visitors, and a determination to continue traditional forms of social authority. The community itself, which has existed for possibly as long as 2,000 years, and which has survived multiple demographic disasters even within the historical period, has developed a set of social strategies designed to maximize survival chances through the exercise of the twin principles of egalitarianism and reciprocity. The means by which the community as a whole gives verbal expression to the approved means by which those principles are enacted is group singing. Song poetry idealizes interpersonal relationships, maintaining relevance by contextualizing specific references to both the living and the recent dead and to both human and ancestral identities, and it openly acknowledges the dependence on spiritual powers to complement human skills so as to ensure ongoing survival in often-difficult environmental circumstances. Singing, thus, is used as an instrument to sustain social integrity in a broad sense. Singing and dancing also give public and visible form to social balance of another kind, between maintenance of corporate solidarity and recognition of individual achievement and prominence. To this end, egalitarianism and male domestic dominance are occasionally reversed in circumstances tightly defined in time, place and content, and operating through the context of dance. Two unprecedented threats now confront the community: the arrival of a rival religion carrying the potential for the establishment of a competing form of social authority, and a reversal in physical terms of the atoll's mythological rising from the ocean.

The Coral Atoll Community: Takū

From sea level only 15 km away, Takū's tallest coconut trees are still invisible over the horizon, and the highest point of land on any of the atoll's small islets is less than a metre above high tide mark. Its low outline caused several European ships to miss it altogether between the sixteenth and nineteenth centuries, and its small-ness prompted most vessels sighting it to steer clear, fearful of its encircling reef and channel currents. Somewhat ironically, its inhabitants were renowned sailors until the late nineteenth century, regularly travelling in pairs of ocean-going canoes to other atolls several thousand kilometres to the south-east for purposes of trade. Situated some 200 kilometres east of Bougainville, Takū lies within Papua New Guinea's North Solomons province, although its cultural affiliations are with a loose string of atolls running roughly north-west to south east through Melanesia: Takū is a Polynesian Outlier, most likely colonized from Samoa or Tūvalu in a reverse migration that, on linguistic evidence, may have occurred as much as 2,000 years ago (Green and Kirch, 2001: 292, note 7).

Almost circular in shape, the atoll consists largely of an encircling reef up to 100 m wide and completely covered only at high tide, when canoes can safely travel over it *en route* to ocean fishing grounds. Three reef channels also allow canoe access to the ocean but only one of these is deep and wide enough to allow the entry of larger vessels and, even then, a tightly twisting course must be followed immediately on entering the lagoon in order to avoid the several shallows and coral heads. Along the south-eastern edge of the atoll is a series of islets, and one further island lies at the northwest corner. Takū's climate experiences seasonal variation. The south-east trade winds blow from around June to October, and from December to May the prevailing wind is the north-west trade wind. By contrast, there appears to be little seasonality in agriculture, and households plant and harvest their taro crops on an as-needs basis throughout the year. The sole commu-nity is currently located on Nukutoa island where most of the 140 houses are of the traditional type, with thatched roof, woven mat walls and a doorway at each end, and arranged in ten lines paralleling the beach front, the larger distance between the second and third row constituting the 'main road'. This wider strip of land is necessary to accommodate groups of dancers as they process from the southern end to the *marae*, an unbounded ritual area adjacent to the house of the chief, the *Ariki*. At each tip of the roughly triangular island are yards where more than seventy canoes are stored and a further dozen or so are under construction at any given time. Men attend daily to their canoes, bailing them out after rain and checking their leaf or mat coverings on sunny days.

On Takū Island, which lies some 600 m to the south of Nukutoa, are the commu-nity's gardens, some 8 hectares excavated to ground water level (Moir 1989: 43) which are visited by most families several times each week. Being the location of the island's prehistoric settlement over many centuries, Takū Island is also rich in mythological, historical and religious associations. The other islands in the atoll are very small and are visited principally for their supplies of coconut and pandanus materials. Takū is a part-foraging, part-farming community, dependent in the first instance on the reliable availability and abundance of fish, and in a secondary sense on garden produce.

Because of the community's small size, all the residents are well known to one another and most are connected by kinship ties. The primary kinship unit is the patrilineal clan, of which there are five, identified in terms of the name of the house in which its elder resides. Each elder is responsible for the spiritual leadership of his clan and, until 1974, also oversaw communication with recently deceased clan members via a medium. The *Ariki*, lying in direct though distant descent from the first founding ancestors of the island and thus being the senior direct descendant, is considered to have the best credentials to contact both deceased clan members and intermediary spirits and to request appropriate assistance from them in time of need on behalf of the community as a whole. His role is complemented by a secular counterpart, the *Pure*.

With locally derived annual family income averaging less than £50, the island does not represent a viable taxable income source to central government. Indeed, the opposite is the case for the provincial government, which funds a medical worker, the island council and 'magistrates' who preside over minor cases, as well as the sole ship servicing Takū and its neighbouring atolls. Even on the larger islands within the Province, Takū has a low profile, and its European name, Mortlock Island, has become a generalized term for the three Polynesian outliers at the extreme north-east corner of Papua New Guinea's political territory.[1]

In some respects, Takū itself represents an anomaly: its community has chosen to augment geographical remoteness by a policy of discouraging visitors, formalizing this by a permit system, but on the other hand its inhabitants have an rapacious appetite for artistic novelty, actively seeking out foreign performance material while travelling off-island and enthusiastically teaching and dancing it to an appreciative audience. The fact that this situation has endured throughout the historical period, and as far back as the mythological era according to oral tradition, suggests the existence of a system whereby social stability is maintained by a complementary accommodation of contrasting elements: a balance. In this chapter I explore forms of balancing which have been incorporated into the island's survival formula, and the role of the performing arts in some of these.

Performance as Reaffirmation of Community

Takū has succeeded in coping with multiple vulnerabilities in the natural world by the creation and maintenance of strengths in the world of interpersonal relationships, matching force with counterforce. The principal means of proclaiming such relationships was – and is – singing. I use the verb form deliberately here, because 'music' suggests an abstraction whereas for Takū's residents, 'music' is performance and all performances are vocal. For a community of some 160 adults, the more than 1,000 songs in the active repertoire is impressive, but to ask 'why so many?' is perhaps to miss the point. The more relevant question is 'why is there so much singing on Takū?' and to begin to answer that question, we must try to identify the functions of singing. What the people sing about represents their idealized world – ideal sets of inter-personal relationships, ideal catch levels for fishing expeditions and gardening productivity, and even ideal conditions for the dead to continue doing the activities they held dear in life, of which dancing figures most prominently. In a small, isolated community perpetually living within a few weeks of famine – if weather conditions turn bad and fishing is impossible – there is a constant need for reassurance that the sets of relationships binding a group of people into functioning networks still exist in the here and now. People need to know that they are still recognized, accepted and functioning individuals in that community, and singing about those relationships is one way they, as a corporate group, can affirm what amounts to a secular creed; not in any prescriptive sense but rather by detailing the domestic action consequences of a set of principles underpinning the society as a whole. Each day there are challenges to the unity of this community because of the potential dangers that fishermen face each time they paddle out onto the open ocean in small canoes, so it is not surprising that one principal theme of song poetry (by which I refer to the song lyrics) is successful and safe ocean fishing, along with the support of family members back on shore. These kinds of constant potential dangers to social unity are matched and neutralized by constant singing about secure and effective social relationships. Such relationships extend beyond the living to encompass ancestor spirits, whose accessibility and powers of assistance constitute an integral part of activities whose successful outcomes are believed to lie beyond purely human endeavour, such as the capture of prestige fish and successful gardening.

To put performance practice into clearer perspective: the free and potentially unlimited supply of coconut toddy, an alcoholic drink of deceptive potency, allows most of the adult population to become sociably intoxicated at least once a week, through carefully controlled drinking either at private gatherings beside domestic houses or at the large drinking houses – one each for men and women – at each end of Nukutoa Island, the location of the community. At these gatherings, each man is expected to contribute a 5 to 20 litre container of toddy, some of which is taken to the adjacent women's house for distribution, and singing starts soon after the shared cup has made a few rounds. Dancing follows, and normally continues for as long as the toddy lasts, which may be eight hours or even longer. Although their drinking houses are only a few metres apart, up to 80 men and women sing and dance simultaneously but independently in joyful cacophony, so that more than a hundred items in total may be performed on a single day.

General musical competence is an assumed attribute of adulthood, and willing participation in musical performance is one of many social responsibilities that one accepts on attaining adulthood. It is at such large-scale gatherings that universality of musical competence is plainly revealed. The general expectation that 'everyone' will participate, by singing as a minimal level of contribution and also by dancing, is largely borne out. Even those who have been escorted from the mourning houses and initially sit silently with head bowed are eventually induced to stand and dance, solemn-faced and silent at first but progressively thawing under the influence of the general air of excitement and the toddy to become vigorous and audible participants, before being escorted back to isolation, heads again bowed in resumed grief.

In contrast to these secular gatherings in various places within the village, ritual singing and dancing occur in a single, designated location, the *marae*. It is expected that the 'whole' adult population will gather on this open arena of some 200 m² situated next to the *Ariki's* house, and its status changes from mundane to sacred by the presence there of the *Ariki* himself wearing the emblems of ancestral spirits and flanked by the similarly clad elders of the other four clans. New vocal material presented there requires formal teaching at rehearsals spread over many days or weeks. Takū residents are enthusiastic presenters of foreign material at commemorative rituals (*tukumai*) not so much because of its foreignness as its novelty, for which there appears an inexhaustible desire. The stated function of the *tukumai*, to relieve sorrow (*ki pesi te aroha*), is also served by the audience's absence of solemnity while watching such material, possibly fuelled by a corresponding absence of understanding of the dance songs. For similar reasons, the number of new local compositions produced each year may be as many as seventy. In both secular and ritual performance contexts, however, the principle of egalitarianism (*hakataupēlā*) is applied, in audible and visible form, and in order to contextualize this particular application I provide a brief overview of the overarching principle itself.

Egalitarianism and Performance

In technical terms, Takū's social system represents a compound structure with periodic complex features, individual households catering for their own small-scale subsistence needs but dependent on labour from other households for certain large-scale activities. Of the situations whose successful enactment in terms of activities or use of materials necessitates co-ordinated action, fishing is the most common, both within the reef and on the open ocean. The men of all households who participate in group fishing immediately receive an equal share of the catch, regardless of the extent of their individual contributions. The highly perishable nature of any fishing catch renders useless any attempt to accumulate surplus food on any long-term basis, and individual ownership of a large number of serviceable and fully equipped canoes minimizes any status difference based on unequal possession of material goods. Similarly, the practice of payment of bride wealth ensures the movement of luxuries among families. By sharing what is at hand, the community achieves its social levelling and through application of the parallel principle of reciprocity assures its rights in turn to share in others' windfalls.

The equal apportionment of the results of group fishing is based on idealized equality of participation, just as on land, mere attendance at a house-building or canoe launching also qualifies a man to receive acknowledgment in food form on a scale equal to that of those contributing labour to the project. For most men, however, attendance implies participation, and even the oldest can find themselves a job commensurate with their physical ability. Only the *Ariki* and the *Pure* refrain from contributing labour on other than their own property, on account of the sanctity of their persons, although both men routinely dignify the occasions with their presence. House building involves much of the community's adult population because the necessary labour to complete the task in one day cannot be supplied from within a single family. The operational principle here is egalitarianism: the skills for the job are held as being possessed by 'all' the men and can therefore be applied to any and all individual instances. Even one's presence constitutes confirmation of social identity and therefore legitimate incorporation into the community.

Other devices also contribute to the levelling of social responsibilities. The widespread practice of infant adoption by families having no children of their own allows a cultural refinement of normal child-rearing conditions, whereby more children are able to receive direct parental attention, instruction and care. Moreover, the custom of sponsorship, whereby throughout life each individual can call on the material assistance of two unrelated persons to assist with such things as food, clothing, sleeping mats, school fees and uniforms, and items for bride wealth. This practice has the effect of increasing the probability of an individual's healthy childhood, through gaining access to more than one source of food and, for males, sponsorship also improves the chances of being able to provide a satisfactory quantity of bride wealth. Although publicly visible only at crucial moments in the life cycle, sponsorship spreads a continual overarching mantle of support over the entire community. It seems no coincidence that these and other devices feature in fables (*kkai*), where the adverse effects of non-compliance can be illustrated, in detailed yet risk-free manner.

As an operating principle, then, egalitarianism appears to offer the greatest survival opportunities to the greatest number of people at the level of secular activity. Group economic activities having a common goal beyond the reach of an individual acting alone apportion equally the fruits of labour to all participants, producing a gender-based dichotomy of men as providers and women as distributors and processors. And in a small society in which the economic contribution of individuals can be crucial to the physical well being of an entire family, adoption and sponsorship spread responsibility and thus reduce the potential for economic difficulties at family level.

In the area of the performing arts, the principle of egalitarianism crystallizes cooperation through temporal simultaneity, creating pre-arranged sets of actions that participants choose to perform together, whether as song or dance. All songs are group songs except the short songs embodied in spoken fables. But there are no predetermined song leaders and in theory anybody may start the singing of a song of his/her own choice from the repertoire of a category appropriate to the performance occasion itself. The very structure of each song exemplifies what might be considered as the ultimate in egalitarianism, because all singing is in unison, with the sole exception of the second or two of solo singing as an item starts. Dancing exhibits parallel features. With the exception of three dances, all of acknowledged foreign origin, there are no leaders and all movements are performed in unison by all dancers. For a few dances, sent back from the dead via a medium, spatial positioning within a group is determined on the twin bases of seniority and membership of the deceased's own clan, but elsewhere, anyone present is free to get to their feet and move onto any part of the dancing area.

The distinction between producer and consumer of artistic enterprise is blurred, most evident during dancing. Virtually all those who are not dancing are singing, the only exceptions normally being principal mourners (who sit silently with heads bowed for much of the time) and pairs of people in spontaneous private conversation, for musicking is a time for social contact as well as artistic expression.[2]

But, at the same time, not all those present maintain a single status – dancer, singer, spectator – for the duration of each song. Singers as a group commonly take 20 seconds or more to get to their feet and dance in all but the formal presentations on the *marae*. Older dancers who tire easily may regain their seats before the items have finished, and those seated around the dancing area may alternate between singing and conversing. It is not, however, the case that dancers stand in relation to singers as producers to consumers, because the plateau of emotional stimulation characterized by one's body hair standing erect is capable of achievement by both groups. Because performance represents a closed loop with participants free to move between categories – now a singer, now a dancer – but always drawing their numbers from the same population pool, executant ability is shared, with only a few individuals achieving distinction by the quality of their dancing.

For all the significance attached to egalitarianism, differences in individual levels of executant ability are recognized. A few of Takū's dancers, men and women, are identified by the complementary term *tīhana*, 'lithe', as evidenced when all of a dancer's body is totally involved in the movements, and interpreted as evidence of the kind of intense mental concentration which eliminates all else from the mind. The notion of *tīhana* literally embodies a personal identification equivalent to empathy with the poetry. As one man worded it, 'If a man is pleased with his canoe, then he will achieve *tīhana* when dancing to a song about it.' The overall concept of unison movements (*auna hakapā*) thus accommodates degrees of acceptability.

Defining the value of cultural intangibles in terms of absolutes is a process fraught with potential difficulties of philosophy and terminology, a largely artificial process of unestablished academic merit. Suffice it to say that the Takū consider the cultural value of both ongoing creativity and accurate preservation within the performing arts to be such as to establish the institution of another kind of outstanding practitioner, a specialist (*purotu*) in song and dance whose twin duties are to compose and teach new material on request, and to memorize, teach and lead performance of material already in the active repertoire. This term, or a cognate form, is found in several parts of Polynesia (see McLean, 1999: 384). The formal mechanism of patrilineal inheritance ensured its perpetuation within each clan, at least on Takū Island itself until the 1890s. Each of the *purotu* in the five clans was also a ritual assistant (*tautua*) in his own right, and exercised a blend of privileges and responsibilities both on and off the ritual arena. Through natural attrition and the absence of any trained successor, the five officeholders were reduced to two by the 1960s: Sāre Amani (for Hare Ata clan) and Willie Tekapu (for Hare Mania clan). Willie died around 1975, without nominating a successor. Sāre died in 1973 and was succeeded by Tave Atimu who assumed the new role of *purotu* for the entire community, leading the performance of existing items, as well as taking responsibility for the composition, teaching and performance of new additions to the repertoire. Tave himself continued in this capacity until 1994 when a sudden illness killed him and ended an entire cultural institution on the island; having been in good health prior to 1994, he had not trained any successor. Since the time of Tave's death, Nūnua Posongat has assumed the *de facto* role of *purotu* but is not formally recognized as such because he was not trained for the position nor appointed to it by his clan head, nor is he a ritual assistant for that clan. Much of the island's music education is entrusted to him, but on a private basis because breathing difficulties now prevent him from leading group singing for more than short periods of time. Nūnua is frequently joined at the drum by Terupo, a son of Sāre, but his voice also is not loud, and there is a widespread view that performance standards, particularly the drumming which accompanies several types of dance, have declined since Tave's death. As one man worded the present situation, *Tātou e samu vare saita nei* ('We beat the drum in ignorance now').[3]

As a model for social order, the principle of egalitarianism is consistent with the existence of differing levels of skill in activities shared by all those of sound body and mind, and with public acknowledgment of those differences, because both relate to operational levels within action categories rather than the categories themselves. In parallel vein, the entrustment to specific individuals of whole clan repertoires of performance-related information for later use on behalf of the clan for clan benefit is but a semi-secular manifestation of the institution of clan elders, who hold ritual information for parallel purposes; 'semi-secular' in that *purotu* were also ritual assistants in their own right, each officiating at the behest of his clan elder. Both are forms of outstanding practitioners and both co-exist in conceptual comfort and practical productivity. Through the institution of performance specialists, each clan's existing song and dance repertoire is curated and new items created and taught. Headed by the *Ariki*, clan elders ensure the continuation of an environment of spiritual safety for such activities to occur.

As a model for group activity, egalitarianism is occasionally replaced by its opposite value – competition – in formal events having tight controls but designed to allow individuals to act briefly for their own betterment. Of these events, men's fishing competitions are the most common, and they are also characterized by the temporary reversal of another cultural attribute, that of male domestic dominance, for it is women who organize and control the associated onshore events to the extent of giving sanctioned verbal and physical abuse and humiliation to under-performing male participants, and also requiring them to display their dancing abilities. And it is also women on other formal occasions who temporarily suspend the normal brother-sister avoidance relationship and submit men – even the *Ariki* himself – to the double humiliation of dancing inside the women's drinking houses and together with female relatives whose company is normally shunned. By the sanctioned violation of the image of danced singing as an essentially segregated activity, perceived social imbalances are afforded a measure of redress, and both types of event constitute managed and voluntary violations of normal social behaviour functioning to release social tensions. In quite another sense, competition has the effect of defining short-term, small-scale egalitarianism insofar that is demarcates clearly those with whom one is *not* co-operating. Canoe races, fishing competitions, the Independence Day sports events, the group dancing at the annual school concert – all cast the principle of egalitarianism into sharp relief by the temporary presentation of its opposite quality.

Whether led by a clan *purotu* or a first-time composer, the learning process is aided by the existence of poetic and musical stereotypes, but in that same respect poets and composers alike walk a fine line between apparently opposing forces. The process is clearest for *tuki* fishing songs, of which three to five are composed on the death of a local resident, but each year, traditionalists both inside and outside the deceased's family express disappointment bordering on disgust at the high incidence of poetic (and to a lesser extent, musical) redundancy in new compositions. My analysis of *tuki* composed for commemorative rituals held in

1995, 1997 and 1998, for example, indicates that more than 80 per cent of the melodies were based on existing compositions. Established composers may provide as many as four (or even more) new items each time the ritual is performed, but additional songs must be sought elsewhere. For their part, lesser composers and family members reluctantly agreeing to requests for several *tuki* acknowledge the reduced effort required to produce a song based merely on an assemblage of stereotyped poetic and melodic phrases, a view endorsed, predictably, by singers at the many rehearsals. Takū is grappling with the dilemma of 'an ideology that wants to encourage freedom of expression while preserving social harmony' (see McClary 1987: 41).[4]

The significance of singing and dancing is highlighted in a further and somewhat unusual manner by the presence in the community of Apava Pūō. Apava, the second-oldest man, is a recluse by choice and rarely attends social gatherings; when he does so, he usually sits and does not join in the singing, although it is well known that even he can occasionally be persuaded to stand and dance two or three specific *tuki,* which praise his own fishing ability as a younger man. The criticisms privately directed at Apava, repeated and sometimes intense, focus on his refusal to engage in the acts of egalitarianism and reciprocity that define social maturity. Involuntary social isolation resulting from infirmity of mind or body is excusable, but the voluntary severance of social obligations is considered as violating the very principles of communal existence. Apava's presence at singing parties is tolerated only because his social invisibility permits his physical presence to be ignored.

Poetics of Song

The creation of a new *tuki* song/dance to satisfy musical, linguistic and aesthetic standards can therefore be reduced to a balance between boredom (excessive repetition) and destabilization (excessive innovation). The one maintains interest, the other maintains overall performance unity and unison, on the reasonable assumption that poets and composers do not intentionally set out to create either of these two extremes. Most contemporary *tuki* represent disposable commodities that are used once in public and then discarded. They do not normally re-emerge at parties, although a small number may be heard at a *hāunu* grief-diversion ritual, where the poetic focus for at least part of the event is narrowed to songs closely associated with, or composed about, the person for whose death the principal mourners grieve. On the level of pure theory it would be possible to deduce a formula for minimal originality (thus ensuring instant oblivion after the initial performance):

- melodic content – a copy of an existing melody, or having extended level movement;

- rhythmic content – few durational values;
- poetic content – conventional structure, stereotyped phrases.

A composition embodying the opposite attributes is more difficult to categorize in detail, because a 'good' song is usually identified simply as being *tonu* 'correct' (in the sense of reflecting historical reality) and having poetry and melody that 'fit'. The *tuki* songs composed by the *purotu* Sāre and Willie are frequently identified as exemplary, allowing a certain amount of deduction of their superior features. The extrapolated features of Sāre's and Willie's composition which may constitute their superior status are:

- melodic content – distinctive, new;
- rhythmic content – several durational values, clapped accompanying pulse or rhythmic ostinato;
- poetic content – conventional structure, innovative wordings, preservation of real-life sequence of events.

Musicking does not construct island identity so much as it identifies and sustains interpersonal relationships, and it achieves these goals in several ways, the most prominent of which are contained within poetry.[5]

Song poetry, particularly that of *tuki* songs, expresses the loss of a loved one. Typically, poetic references use the first person singular perspective and speak in a half-verse of 'my sympathy goes to' one or more people standing in a specified relationship to the deceased, the reference amplified in the following half-verse by inclusion of the personal name(s). The results of a survey of more than 300 *tuki* poems are revealing.

The statistical occurrences of relationship terms in *tuki* song poetry were as follows:

aku tama (my children)	20	*aku tinana* (my mothers)	1
taku tama (my child)	5	*aku tipuna* (my grandparents)	1
taku kave (my sister)	5	*hai taina* (pair of same-sex sibs)	1
[a named individual]	5	*hai tipuna* (grandparent and	1
taku soa (my special friend)	4	grandchild pair)	
hai tinana (mother and child pair)	4	*mātou hānau* (we brothers)	1
te hānau (the brothers)	3	*ia anau* (myself)	1
aku kave (my sisters)	2	*te atu hata* (large-scale social group)	1
aku mokopuna (my grandchildren)	2	*te vaka aku tama* (my children's canoe)	1
taku taina (my brother/sister)	1	[a named location]	1
taku hina (my sweetheart)	1		
taku tamana (my father)	1		

The comparatively large number of references to children reflects more than recognition of the loss of a parent figure; they frequently acknowledge and bewail the fracture of a functioning family unit caused by residence off-island of one or more members: *aku tama e noho mmao* – 'my children living far away'. Children also figure poetically through a unique referencing system. When first identified simply by personal status in song poetry, individual adults stand alone, as it were, and only later in the poetry is their relationship to other named individuals specified, but generic references to children invariably establish the relationship to the singer even before specific names are provided. Thus, in the recorded collection there are no references simply to *te tama*, 'the child'. The initial reference is *taku tama*, 'my child', or *aku tama* 'my children', as adult poets, composers and singers alike reaffirm the ongoing nature of the bonds and responsibilities of parents and older family members in a public statement of relationship and duty.

Like all Polynesian languages, that of Takū includes both inclusive and exclusive forms of its first-person dual and plural pronouns – 'we', 'us'. In this respect, the act of singing may proclaim a conceptual position either within or outside the group assembled at the time when the song is sung. *Lani* and *hula* songs frequently used *mātou* meaning 'we [plural, exclusive]' as they highlighted the psychic as well as physical separation of gangs of labourers working off-island in the 1960s and 1970s and those who stayed behind. By this same means the poetry of *sau* and other dance songs brought from the dead adds a linguistic level of separation of the human and spiritual worlds. In the entrance songs each performs while entering the arena for festive dancing, the village divisions of Tāloki and Sialeva not only proclaim their separateness in *rue* dance songs but boast of their corporate individuality (see Example 1.1).

Tā mai tā mai, tā mai nā rue, nā anu atu	Sing, sing those *rue* to us as we dance forward
Anuatu, anuatu, mātou e tapolo	Dance, dance, we're doubling [the speed]
Tapolo tapolo Tāloki e havela	'Double' the speed, double the speed: Tāloki is 'hot'
Hāvela, hāvela hāoti e.	Keep it 'hot' until the end.
E nau he tama e uru he tama te soa nei	I am the one, the one at my [drinking] place
E mata mai, e kila mai mātou	We look, we gaze at it
E nau he tama, e nau he tama Sialeva.	I am the one, I am the man from Sialeva.

Example 1.1 The two songs which self-identify the village divisions of Tāloki and Sialeva

By contrast, *tuki* songs honouring the dead by praising successful fishermen in the deceased's family or clan personalize their poetry. In my recorded collection of *tuki* performed between 1994 and 2000, the word 'we' appears only twice, but 'I' occurs in virtually all such songs, providing each individual singer with the poignancy of personal identification.

The overall recorded sample of more than a thousand songs allows a further generalization about poetic style. Singing about a past event *ipso facto* brings that event into the present, especially as the poetry normally uses the present tense. Performance generates a whole spectrum of emotional responses among singers, from muffled weeping to shouts of delight, responses that sometimes parallel those of the original event and that may be detailed in the poetry itself. Some song poems use the past tense, others use the present and still other songs contain a mix of both. But not one song out of a thousand recorded refers to the future. For reasons we can only guess at this stage, singing is a means of celebrating what was and is, but whatever *will* be is evidently not part of the poet's repertoire of topics, an enduring area of vernacular silence.

By convention, the language of song poetry is that of understatement. In a small community whose houses are so close together that even domestic conversations are audible from neighbouring dwellings, few events of consequence are known by only a few people, and well-developed skills of memorization ensure that details can be recalled and discussed for many years. No practical purpose is served, therefore, by detailing in song poetry what is already common knowledge. Consider the *rue* men's dance song in Example 1.2.

Tere mai taku rono, tere mai te rono Arehu.	News of me spread, news of Arehu spread.
Ku sopo i te aumi, huri sara i te murivaka.	It leapt in my wake, turning away from the stern.
Taku aitu ni hano ma nau ku tō i te o rua te laku.	Together, my spirit and I caught it by the bill with a double hook.

Example 1.2 The poetry of a *rue* song using generalized language to refer to a specific incident

The most literal of translations identifies the subject as the catch of a fish, and one may infer even without prior cultural familiarity that it is of significant type or size, but it takes local knowledge to move understanding to the level of appreciation of significance. The fish was a marlin; foul-hooked around its bill, it leapt clear of the water alongside the outrigger canoe as Arehu struggled to retain a grip on his handline. He eventually succeeded in subduing the catch in what was only the second time in living memory that such a fish had been caught. Singers are not the passive and obedient instruments of a composer, but react on individual levels of emotion as a song is performed and sometimes on a level of intensity disproportionate to that of the emotive content of the poetry itself. Because of the poetic custom of understatement, the triggering sentiments are not merely expressed in the words, but arise from them as they are uttered, generating memories and associations whose upwelling emotive content produces spontaneous reactions on a continuum from grief to delight, according to context. Many years after the event, Arehu's exploit continues to afford delight to male singers and dancers alike as they vicariously celebrate the achievement of the fisherman's dream.

As a balance to the widespread desire for sung and danced novelty, there exist two dance songs that have maintained the status of favourites for more than a generation, and both have been in the repertoire for more than a century, on the evidence of their poetic content. They are sung, often at the very end, during all-night commemorative rituals, and also by men and women independently at virtually every large-scale drinking party. One focuses on the timeless satisfaction of comeuppance: a young man defies parental advice not to go night-fishing because of impending bad weather, but returns empty handed and suffers the shame of having to eat cold taro rather than part of his own freshly cooked catch. The other song evidently relates to the 1843 visit to the island by an American *beche de mer* collector who landed first at the small island of Nukurēkia within the atoll, ignored demands to leave, killed two local residents and bombarded the village. Adopting the perspective of the *Ariki* himself, the poem assigns to the singing stabilizer the reference to the ever-changing direction of the wind, an omen of danger, and the sole reference to the disaster. The *Ariki* dons his ritual pair of pandanus belts and with supernatural assistance repels an impending invasion (see Example 1.3).

Through devices of understatement, indirect referencing and linguistic compression, the poetry acts as a mnemonic to all islanders familiar with the story's details, which is virtually the entire adult population. The song's enduring popularity focuses on the *Ariki's* successful intervention as a truly memorable example of the power at his disposal.

Because song poetry focuses on an idealized representation of the culture, it also constitutes a useful indicator of dependency, because either generalized or specific references to non-local institutions and concepts, or to introduced items in the material culture, identify the level of attraction of, if not reliance on, foreign worlds. The composition dates of songs in Takū's active repertoire is linked to specific events or people and therefore can be calculated. The overall period spans more than a century, providing the time depth of several generations to any dependency survey. On the evidence of my own recorded collection, the results are consistent through time. The only songs that identify or allude to foreign lands – and they are few in number – are those composed by Takū sailors crewing on either the ocean-going canoes in the pre-Contact period or coastal vessels during the period of Australian administration (1921–75). In those of the first category, the references are intended as a chronicle of the journey and in those of the second, the dominant theme is that of homesickness. For the most part, the idealized image of island life is one of self-reliance. This generalization needs one important qual-

Se vaka ni ā? Se vaka ni aro mai ki taku henua.	What did the boat do? The boat rowed ashore at my island.

hakamau hua Nimo ake, takai ake, e
noho ka tohitohia ko taku henua nei
hati Uāiē, se vaka ni ā?
Se vaka ni aro mai ki Nukurēkia.

stabilizer The wind shifted and went right
around as my island was shattered.
refrain Oh, what did the boat do? The
boat rowed ashore at Nukurēkia Island

Uāiē, hakatautau ake i taku ahana,
nau e noho i taku ahana, nau e
tara ki te maro pure, nau e huna ki
te kie tahi,

Oh, it came ashore at my beachfront.
I was there at my beachfront, I donned
my inner belt and wrapped around my
outer belt.

Uāiē hakasurasura i ana matahenua,
tokatoka iho ki taku henua,
Uāiē noho iho se tanata i tua tana
henua, e noho iho ma tana avana;
Uāiē, Hakaepārua i tua Te Marumaru,
e noho ma Te Lanikivakiva.

Oh, I walked to the headlands, gazing
at my island.
Oh, there was someone there at the
back of his land, living with his wife;
Oh, Hakaepārua was there behind Te
Marumaru, living with Te Lanikivakiva.

Example 1.3 The *tuki* dance song composed in 1843 and still popular 160 years on.

ification, because self-reliance does not imply total reliance on the human self but, rather, on an informed and methodical partnership with the spirits of one's ancestors. The elders of the five clans are not only the human repositories of their own clan's mythologies and ritual protocols, but also have responsibility for the overall wellbeing of clan members. On an individual basis, wellbeing is maintained through the application of traditional cures for a variety of illnesses. But group welfare is achieved through direct appeal to the realm of the supernatural, and occurs at the location where spirits are known to be attracted to in times of singing and dancing, the *marae*.

The centrality of the performing arts to Takū concepts of idealized life is such that the human, spirit, freed from time constraints of domestic activities after death, devotes its time to endless singing and dancing. Takū's community believes strongly in this on the evidence of the many songs sent back from the dead which detail the performances; the one in Example 1.4.

I spoke earlier of singing as a survival strategy, not just as the embodiment of collectivity and egalitarianism, but also as a means of countering potential threats with poetic assertions of positive forms of resolution. The socially integrating function of song performance as an activity is enhanced by the content of the such poetry which, as a rule, avoids reference to the negative, in particular to the limitations and potential hazards inherent in atoll life, real and recognized though they

Ē ko aku tamana i tai Te One	My fathers are at the sea at the Afterworld
hati Nau e noho i loto Te One	*refrain* I am living inside there.
Tū te aitu i loto Te One	There is a spirit living inside there.
Tū Pūkena i loto Te One	Pūkena himself lives inside there.
Sopokia mātou te mārama	We are caught out by the rising moon [as we dance]
Ē ni momoe ake tana urutono.	The spirit slept at its own patch of mangroves.

Example 1.4 Song poetry typical of descriptions of life in the Afterworld

are. Rather, the poetry focuses on the kinds of skills and positive achievements necessary to counter such threats to social order and the society itself (see Example 1.5).

Threat	Poetic counter-theme
garden failure or famine	success of crops
failure at fishing	successful fishing
inadequacy of fish stocks	bountiful supply of fish
ineffectual water craft	skilful canoe building
personal loss at death	perpetual union with ancestors after death

Example 1.5 Themes of real threats and counter-themes of song poetry

Songs from the spirits of the dead add a further dimension of social stability of particular consolation to the survivors because such songs relate to the individual identity of a person close to them. As with the statements of positive achievement found in *tuki* songs, so with the compositions from the dead – generally there are no direct references to the soul's potential or actual problems, but rather these are identified only by inference (see Example 1.6).

Inferred adverse condition	Thematic counter-measure
loneliness	the continual company of members of parental generation
lack of leadership	the company of the Chief or clan elder or primary spirit
lack of social structure	maintenance of the elder's position after death
insecurity/social disincorporation	legitimate incorporation within the appropriate Afterworld

Example 1.6 Themes of individual and group adversity and counter-themes of song poetry

Post-death social structure of a sort is implied by the presence in the Afterworld of the spirits of those who were once human community leaders and the adducement of their maintained status as contributing to the spirit's well-being within existing social units. By such means, song poetry presents members of the community with images of what they can achieve if traditional values and practices are honoured during their lifetime, and what will happen to individuals in the Afterworld after death. The notion of social security deriving from social stability as detailed in such poetry foregrounds the enduring presence of positive cultural elements together with the means of effectively countering the existence of negative cultural features.

It is probably fair comment that even the most innocent tourist now accepts that much of the Polynesian world presented on stage in travel brochures and floor shows for the benefit of non-local consumption no longer exists and indeed may never have existed at all, as commercial idealism triumphs over cultural reality. Explorers, colonizers, missionaries and traders in turn spread their blend of influences over local cultures, and what was once distinctive and organic became mosaics of potpourri. Arguably the most enduringly visible influence has been that of Christianity, whose mantle spread over both sacred and secular life, replacing indigenous religious life with its own practices, symbols, ideologies and structures with remarkable success. One now speaks of Polynesian religion in the past tense. But not everywhere. In the 1960s, the Takū Council decided to institute a ban on missionaries and churches on the island, having viewed with concern the effect on the culture of neighbouring islands of the proselytizing activities of fundamentalist Christian churches. Takū's desire to separate itself from encroaching European religion was a function of its ability to live according to the principles and values that for many centuries had cemented a group of people into a functional community.

The *Ariki* inherited the authority to voice a decisive view on virtually every matter affecting the community. This authority, together with his ability to invoke the atoll's most potent spirits for the continuation or restoration of physical well-being and social order created in his institutionalized person what Lieber (1994: 11) calls the 'tangible manifestation of the community's integrity'. From this, it follows that any perceived weakening of the *Ariki's* authority or effectiveness will impact negatively on communal integrity; the most likely context for such a situation appears to be the establishment on the atoll of the rival religion. Takū traditional practice made few allowances for group activities for the young, who were left largely to their own resources until puberty. Christian churches have exploited this absence of existing structures to introduce their own programmes, backed up with the machinery of international organizations which, in a sense, they represent. Off-island training, admission to church-owned schools, eligibility for scholarships, promotional literature, song sheets and prerecorded cassettes of inspirational singing, and the visual attraction of uniforms and proliferation of executive titles – all these attributes combine to offer to Takū's children a powerful instrument of ideological persuasion. Traditional values and practices can offer little effective defence. For the young, evangelical Christianity appears to afford a degree of compensation for a subordinated social position by offering individual recognition and a well-defined infrastructure allowing for progression through formalized ranks to provide a balance of responsibility and authority unparalleled in secular community life. Similar attractions appeal to some of the adult female population, particularly those whose husbands are absent for long periods, for example, crewing on coastal vessels. For men, however, Christianity is considered more a form of threat to their own authority within both the family and clan. Although friction erupts infrequently and on an individual basis, the growing influence of the Church seems poised to progress to more assertive forms of social presence that will without doubt impact on singing and dancing judged to be 'heathen' on the simple grounds that it is not Christian. Already, converts apply the same means of group expression and unity as their unconverted older generation, singing in public locally composed songs calling for the island to be saved and for Christ to return quickly, and boycotting some rituals.

An even more significant threat to the island is now the fact that it is sinking at the rate of several inches per year as the result of tectonic plate movement. The possibility of the permanent and total abandonment of a familiar environment and relocation in a foreign environment looms large, to universal dismay and disbelief.

Takū is a community founded on a set of balances. Balance between long-term co-operation and short-term competition, human endeavour and supernatural intervention, the practice of small-scale initiative but submission to the broad authority of the *Ariki* and *Pure*, and between acknowledgment of environmental fragility and group statements of social solidarity. With this balance operating within a gender-based division of labour, Takū residents have achieved an enduring formula for self-sufficiency in economic, social, artistic and religious activities, accommodating new relationships through birth, adoption and marriage, and coping with the severance of relationships through death. However, these balances are relational. There has been a recent shift towards imported foods and Western material goods and a determined effort by a minority towards an imported, rival religious system. These shifts have produced organizational changes which seem close to taking structural effect on the society as a whole, rocking the boat and bringing about changes that will surely impact comprehensively on its unique island music.

Notes

1. More specifically, the term is applied in an undifferentiated sense to any fair-skinned inhabitant of these atolls. A 1994 national radio announcement during

nearby Rabaul's volcanic eruptions that a 'Mortlock Islander' had been killed caused initial concern on Takū until an identification of the body confirmed a non-Takū origin.

2. I use Small's (1998) term here to refer in a comprehensive manner to all types of contribution to a musical performance.
3. Nūnua died in late 2002.
4. McClarey identifies a comparable situation within the structure and perform-ance of J. S. Bach's Brandenburg Concerto No. 5, a parallel that fits neatly with Small's (1998) universal theory of musicking.
5. In many cultures one important function of singing is the construction of local identity, but the issue does not arise on Takū because of its geographic isola-tion and the absence of any single 'other'; song poetry exists from and for local residents and indeed, only two poems are known to include the island name.

References

Kirch, P. V. and Green, R. C. (2001), *Hawaiki, Ancestral Polynesia: An Essay in Historical Anthropology,* Cambridge, Cambridge University Press.
Lieber, M. D. (1994), *More Than a Living: Fishing and the Social Order on a Polynesian Atoll,* Boulder: Westview Press.
McClary, S. (1987), 'The Blasphemy of Talking Politics During Bach Year', in Leppert, R. and McClary, S. (eds), *Music and Society: The Politics of Composition, Performance and Reception,* Cambridge: Cambridge University Press, pp. 63–104.
McLean, M. (1999), *Weavers of Song. Polynesian Music and Dance,* Auckland: Auckland University Press.
Moir, B. G. (1989*), Mariculture and Material Culture of Takuu Atoll: Indigenous Cultivation of* Tridacna Gigas (Mollusca: Bivalvia) *and its Implications for Pre-Europrean technology: Resource Management and Social Relations on a Polyneian Outlier.* PhD thesis, University of Hawaii.
Robson, R. W. (1994) [1965], *Queen Emma: The Samoan-American Girl who Founded an Empire in 19th Century New Guinea,* fifth edition, Brisbane: Robert Brown & Associates.
Small, C. (1998) *Musicking: The Meanings of Performing and Listenin,* Hanover and London: Wesleyan University Press.

Recommended Listening

The original field recordings are lodged in the Archive of Maori and Pacific Music, University of Auckland.
Moyle, Richard M. (1998), 'Tuki song from Takuu, Papua New Guinea', in

Klangfarben der Kulturen: Musik aus 17 Ländern der Erde. CD and booklet (especially pp. 73–4 and track 13). Berlin: Staatliche Museen zu Berlin.

–2–

Spitting into the Wind: Multi-edged Environmentalism in Malagasy Song

Ron Emoff

Mba tsy tovana ho avy itsika é
ka 'zaho mandrora mantsilagny é

We won't last long
if I spit into the wind.

Mily Clément,
Mandrora Mantsilany

Globally mediated news about Madagascar often hinges upon the immediacy of environmental problems on the island. Decimation of forested areas through slash-and-burn rice agriculture and large-scale soil erosion, for example, recur as topics of attention, even as justification for appropriation and control of Malagasy land by organizations from outside the island. One of the early internationally accessible commercial recordings of Malagasy musics, *A World Out of Time* (Shanachie, 1992), also plays upon Madagascar's ecological susceptibility. This title, staged by American musicians David Lindley and Henry Kaiser, suggests not only that Madagascar runs on its own sense of time, at the very edge of 'our' time, but that the island has run out of time with which to resolve its vast environmental problems.

The Spring 2002 turmoil over control of the presidency in Madagascar was a prominent global media topic. This political conflict itself rests in part upon a bifurcation of geographies in Madagascar. Marc Ravalomanana, sworn in as president in May 2002, has had popular support in the capital region of Madagascar, though previous president Didier Ratsiraka refused to cede the presidency to Ravalomanana officially. Ratsiraka, half-Betsimisaraka, a Malagasy group from the

East Coast, has the support of many people in Betsimisaraka territory, where he has purportedly installed his own cabinet. Ratsiraka's factionalism and recalcitrance threaten to split the country upon economic among other lines, a divisiveness that could bring about disastrous consequences (Didier Ratsiraka has since ceded presidency to Mark Ravalomanana). Disastrous, that is, for *côtiers* (Malagasy people inhabiting the coastal areas of the island) who could become further distanced from a national government historically centralized in the capital, and for those in the capital who could be deprived of supplies arriving through Tamatave, the main east coast port in Madagascar.

Local Malagasy themselves strikingly are often erased from political/environmental discourse that prioritizes instead land and fauna in Madagascar. The environment becomes a supra-human domain from which Malagasy people are defaced and dislocated – they even become implicated as a primary threat to their own environment. Rarely have ecological concerns – usually voiced by international aid and development agencies, both governmental and NGO (non-governmental organizations) – been expressed in popular songs performed by Malagasy musicians. The texts of such songs more likely extol the difficulties of daily life, sentiments for other people and toward ancestors, or proverbial advice about proper behaviour and belief. In an admonitory capacity, Mily Clément's 1993 song, *Mandrora Mantsilany* (literally, 'spitting on oneself' or 'spitting into the wind') thus bears some textual similarity to a number of other Malagasy songs. Clément's message, though, conveys a multiplicity of experience in and of Madagascar that commonly pits environment – the land and its zoological extensions, such as lemurs – against Malagasy people themselves. While *Mandrora Mantsilany* is sung by a Malagasy voice (in the Malagasy language), its text bespeaks an environmentalist message that is specifically global. Clément voices an international environmentalist cause that might even subvert local Malagasy concerns and points of view.

Internationally audible Malagasy musicians Rossy and Tarika have also released songs in which they engage with environmental issues. Rossy in particular has sometimes taken a very direct stance in voicing political/environmental problems. In one song Rossy asks pointedly (in Malagasy), 'Who owns this land? The people who have money own it.' Implicit in this criticism is the fact that many of those who have money in Madagascar are foreigners. One afternoon at Rossy's home in an Antananarivo neighbourhood, we were watching a news broadcast on French television that was featuring a story about an eagle in South Africa that had been wounded, captured by members of an international wildlife organization, and had been undergoing massive medical attention. This was in 1993, with apartheid's demise only nascent. Rossy expressed extreme agitation and alarm that so much attention – specifically international environmentalist attention – was given to an animal while so many local people were starving and dying, both in South Africa and in Madagascar. Rossy exclaimed with frustration, *Ankizy gasy marary sy mangataka sakafo amin'ilay arabe eto Antananarivo fa ilay vorona manana dokotera maro!* ('Malagasy children are sick and begging for food in the street in Antananarivo while a bird has its own team of doctors!'). Similar contradictions are sometimes woven into Rossy's song texts. Among global Malagasy pop stars, Rossy is perhaps the most openly cognizant and expressive of, if often metaphorical about, the necessarily political complexity of environmentalism in Madagascar.

International ecological concern as song text topic notably escapes much music that is performed exclusively within Madagascar's boundaries. This chapter attempts to examine some of the underlying significance of the unique appearance of ecology-oriented song texts – their poetics and politics, which are both globally attuned and locally impacting – within Madagascar, as well as without.

A clarification needs to be made when attempting to envision an expressive/ commercial category called 'the popular' in Madagascar. Much musical perform-ance throughout Madagascar, of any genre or category, can embody in Malagasy people deeply felt connections to other people, places, the past, and to revered ancestral personalities. Such evocations of Otherness arise not only from textual references or allusions but often from musical form, structure, style, gesture, and process themselves. Various popular musicians in Madagascar, Jaojoby for one, a very well-liked musician from Diégo in the north,[1] have said to me that they have seen audience members at their concerts become possessed by ancestral *tromba* spirits (see Emoff, 2002a) because their music is so reminiscent of that used for *tromba* possession ceremonies. Jaojoby told me that his popular *salegy* dance music, a dance distinctive to the Diégo region in the northeast of the island, is connected – rhythmically, modally, harmonically, in terms of tempo, and spiritually – directly to the *salegy* played on accordion for *tromba* spirit possession ceremonies (see Emoff, 2000, 2001, 2002a, 2002b, 2002c). He even coined a term for his own amplified professional music, *vakondrazana électronique* ('electrified ancestor's music'). Popular expressive culture in Madagascar – that which, for example, is widely distributed and received, and is somewhat profitable to the performing musi-cian (though usually not enough on which to subsist)[2] – often contains spiritual, historical, and other extra-commercial potency. Simultaneously, the sacred commonly is not contained as a distinct or insular realm, entered only on ritual or ceremonial occasions throughout Madagascar. Sentiments of and feelings for, as well as texts about the sacred or ancestral emerge commonly in Malagasy popular/commercial genres. Among *tromba-istes*, music for spirit possession cere-monies commonly is also the most popular musical form even outside of *tromba* performance.

Often 'popular' is determined in Madagascar by what is available for airplay over the Radio Nationale from Antananarivo, or from the very few privately run stations on the island.[3] Here popular means transmitted with sometimes alarming frequency, and very well liked among most Malagasy people. Thus, songs by Michael Bolton, Stevie Wonder, Bryan Adams, or Ace of Base might be much more familiar and popular to many Malagasy than songs by Rossy or Tarika. Several of the songs from Mily Clément's *Mandrora Mantsilany* cassette tape (the only format on which it was then available in Madagascar) received regular airplay over the Radio Nationale. Malagasy people were often as familiar phonetically with the song text (in English) of Bryan Adam's *Everything I Do, I Do for You* as with Mily Clément's *Mandrora Mantsilany*.

Backing the Cause

Environmentalism, as international passion, often has a public countenance among people from outside of Madagascar, as a *cause* to take up, implement, support, a cause born of an urgency to protect disappearing land and wildlife. This urgency is typically borne of non-Malagasy peoples' perceptions, sometimes exoticized,[4] of endangered wildlife and land 'out there' somewhere in an environmentalist imaginary. The ecology of Madagascar is endangered, but the perception of the cause is often backed up by limited insight into the variety and dynamics of ecotypes (particular habitats with distinct fauna/flora) that exist within Madagascar. Certainly 'save the rainforest' organizations, for instance, have done much to protect forested areas. Yet the very slogan of such an environmentalist cause might conspicuously sidestep, subvert or silence a crucial *local* plan of action, one for saving or protecting the rainforest *people*. One would hope that implicit in 'save the rainforest' is embedded an extension of concern that also means save these people.[5] In Malagasy environmentalist actualities, this hope commonly is not realized in the development and implementation of plans of action for an alternative means of survival for Malagasy, once the forest itself is protected (which often means that this land becomes prohibited territory *to* Malagasy). While there *are* songs sung in Madagascar that evoke in varied ways the environment – Jaojoby's *Omeo Rano, (Give Us Water)*, for instance – the texts of such songs do not align with international environmentalist causes which tend to draw upon elision of such human needs.

Furthermore, inherent in environmentalist reasoning is often a paternalist, even colonial-like inference that Malagasy are incapable of properly taking care of themselves in a modern, ecologically sensitive world, and thus require international intervention. Environmentalism as international cause can efface a particular daily 'cause' among Malagasy themselves, to survive. Global causes commonly stop short of implementation of a plan of action, once the rainforest is protected, for the survival of Malagasy people who have been depending on these lands for generations.[6]

Tavy

Throughout the forested areas of the East Coast of Madagascar, slash-and-burn rice agriculture is the predominant method of subsistence. This method of farming, called *tavy* among Malagasy of the area, quickly leaches nutrients from the soil, making it useless for sustaining crops after only one growing season. Terracing rice fields is a technology that most Malagasy in this area have not been taught, nor do they have the technology to implement, although it for one would prolong the potential of the soil over numerous growing seasons. Malagasy though do not maliciously or self-indulgently slash-and-burn their own forested-land. Rather, they farm rice the only way they know how to do so, to feed their families, to subsist. In fact, many village *chefs* throughout the east coast forested region of Madagascar told me that they would gladly alter their method of rice agriculture if they knew of some other less environmentally rapacious way to farm. They are quite aware of, and worried about, disappearing land on which to grow life-sustaining rice, and commonly lament that people from different villages are now meeting unexpectedly in the middle of slashed away forest. Rasoamandry, a woman who was *chef* of the village of Betampona northwest of Fénérive-Est, was quite worried that *efa lasa ilay tanitska* ('our own village's land is all gone').

Development organization statistics commonly emphasize that 80 per cent or more of the Malagasy rainforest once extant has now disappeared. Such decimation of forested land is almost always attributed, solely, to Malagasy slash-and-burn rice agriculture. One researcher however states that 'deforestation in Madagascar is directly related to the [French colonial] introduction of coffee cash cropping. As the most fertile areas were devoted to export crop production, [Malagasy] cultivators cleared forested slopes for subsistence' (Hagan, 1996). Furthermore, roughly 70 per cent of Madagascar's primary forest was destroyed between 1895 and 1925, a period throughout which Madagascar was under French colonial control (Hornac, 1943, cited in Hagan, 1996).[7] Malagasy on the East Coast and their farming practices are clearly de-historicised in development organization discourse that indicts Malagasy, even if implicitly, for wilful destruction of their own lands. International organizations commonly create a historical snapshot, a still image, of one type of deforestation that elides previous and more large-scale destruction of Malagasy land, by foreign interests.

In another de-historicizing moment, current sapphire mining and logging projects, commonly initiated and implemented by foreigners to Madagascar, escape indictment for ecological devastation in much global discourse. Huge mining towns of tens of thousands of people have sprung up in regions previously very sparsely inhabited. In the *Ilakaka* mining operation in the south-west of the island (approximately 210 km from Toliara), a staggering 300,000 hand miners are searching voraciously for gems. These mining towns have brought with them much violence (often involving firearms, not previously a common possession in Madagascar), prostitution, and alcohol abuse. In addition the mines have wrought devastation of the land as runoff of pollutants and soil erosion are resultant by-products of mining procedures (in addition to the personal pollutants left by individual miners). Sapphire mining epitomizes current environmental, as well as moral devastation in Madagascar. Yet such foreign mining often eludes indictment or emphasis in the voicing of international environmentalist causes.

Singing for the Cause

Frequently broadcast over the national radio station in 1993, Mily Clément's *Mandrora Mantsilany* had become quite popular throughout Madagascar especially among younger Malagasy. A video of the song was also broadcast over the national television station.[8] In the video Clément was seen singing in front of forested scenes of Malagasy countryside or views of Indri lemurs (ones not in the wild, but in captivity).[9] These two images, of a 'natural' environment, provide the central visual focus of the video, engulfing the smaller fore-grounded image of Clément.

Clément admonishes Malagasy in the text of *Mandrora Mantsilany* that it is their responsibility to protect the environment, just as it is God's *(Zanahary)* to protect humans. Interestingly, he attributes human characteristics to the forest itself, singing that 'beasts in the forest are our friends' *(biby namantsika)*. He also relates forest animals to *olombelona* (literally, 'living people'). Throughout Madagascar, elders especially are highly respected, in part for being closer in lifespan to entering the realm of ancestral spirits. These spirits themselves are sometimes addressed with kinship names, such as grandfather. Anthropomorphosis of the environment in Madagascar has its own history. There are forest spirits, *angatr'ala,* that sometimes take human form. Certain animals in the forest have been signs of or mediums for spirit presence and power. For example, the Parson's chameleon (the model chameleon for those featured in the Budweiser ads) is capable of rotating each of its bulbous eyes, independently, in a near-180° plane. One legend attributes this capacity to look behind and ahead simultaneously to the potency of ancestral spirits, who can move through the past, the present, and into the future, even to bring about a confluence of varied temporal realms (see Emoff, 2002a). Some varieties of lemur have also been attributed throughout the past with having spirit power, even with being spirit mediums. Clément's song voices a strange biological subversion, a trading places in which animals become elevated to human status while humans are portrayed as almost subhuman threats, literally, to themselves. In addition, an alternative to spitting upon oneself, a metaphor itself that suggests ignorance, recalcitrance, even arrogance, is never proposed by Clément. If Malagasy people were to immediately do as Clément suggests in this song, it would bring about their own immediate self-destruction. It is unlikely that people anywhere might transcend their own hunger so as to protect an environment, presented in this song text as an imaginary and timeless domain (even though it is running out of timelessness).

Clément goes on to lament the human putrefaction of the forest (*ala tsy fotsifotsifo,* literally, 'forest not white') and of the water *(rano maloto).* Clément juxtaposes 'unclean water', which makes people ill, with the healing capacities of the forest. *Ala fagnafody* admonishes Clément, by which he means that the forest contains medicine, or herbs, roots, tree barks, and flowers used in Malagasy healing practices, as well as in others' healing practices.[10] Malagasy have long been aware of the healing potential of the land and the flora contained there, and they are quite cognizant that their well being beyond just rice agriculture depends upon the forest. This provides another cause for anxiety among Malagasy, who literally must choose between cultivating rice and having available the flora that is one of their main resources in medicinal practices. Malagasy people realize more than anyone how far their backs are from the wall. They are offered no choice but to spit upon themselves.

Just before a 1993 concert performance in Tamatave, on the East Coast of Madagascar, I had my first conversation with Mily Clément outside the Palais de Jeunes, the hall in which he would perform that evening. We discussed, among other things, the effects of musical performance used in *tromba* spirit possession on his own 'popular' *salegy* (*tromba* music in the Diégo region on the northeast coast of Madagascar, Clément's homeland, is also called *salegy).* As quite a surprise to me, Clément proclaimed fervently that there is *no* connection between his own mode of popular *salegy* and that performed in *tromba* ceremony (contrary to Jaojoby's contention and that of many other popular Malagasy performers). Clément expressed recalcitrance toward spirit possession practices, which are commonly performed in his homeland in Diégo as well as throughout the east coast. His reaction against *tromba* may echo his call for Malagasy people to modernize, to act conscientiously with respect to the global cause, to protect the land, in other words, to give up older practices of subsistence (spiritual or other).

Clément's message *Mba tsy tovana ho avy itsika é, ka 'zaho mandrora mantsilagny é* ('*We* won't last long, if *I* spit into the wind') implies that responsibility for the collective is in the hands of the individual. This suggests another sort of global ideal – Western emphasis on individuality. In east coast villages in Madagascar, it is much more typical that people work in co-ordination with one another, favouring the village or extended family over personal or individual desires and needs. Clément's inference that protecting the forest begins as the responsibility of the individual is unrealistic on the east coast of Madagascar, where individuals commonly do not feel themselves individually empowered or entitled, agriculturally, spiritually, or aesthetically to put into effect such ecological transformations.

When I discussed the text of *Mandrora Mantsilany* with teenagers throughout Madagascar, the majority of them indicated that they liked the song because it was *salegy*, good to dance to, not because of its message. In fact, most of them did not know what to make of the message. 'How do we stop growing rice?' was a common response to the question *Inona ny dikany ilay teny Mily Clément aminao?* ('What do Mily Clément's words mean to you?'). To heed Clément's message immediately, to stop slash-and-burn agriculture, translates to many east-coast Malagasy as starvation, thus as ludicrous. In *Mandrora Mantsilany*, Clément attempts to convey to local Malagasy an environmentalist cause, the virtue of which becomes muddled to many of them.

Panoramic Ecology

Tarika is a Malagasy musical group that has become quite popular, almost exclusively outside of Madagascar. Singer and instrumentalist Hanitra Rasoanaivo spends a great deal of time in London. Tarika has become known as a pan-Malagasy ensemble – its members celebrate their practice of mixing musical and other performative influences from throughout the island (see Emoff, 2002a). In Tarika's song *Hainteny*[11] (Drought) the singer laments a generalized ecological state of 'making sad' *(mampalahelo)* throughout Madagascar. References are made to *tavy* fires in the forest *(afo)*, drought-stricken land *(maina ny tany fa tsy misy rano)*, and the death of children from starvation *(maty zaza é fa tsy ampy sakafo)*. This song evokes a panorama of environmental sadness in Madagascar, from the drought that so commonly effects southern Malagasy in the desert-like environments there, to the *tavy* fires of the northeast coast, to a more broad image of death by starvation, something possibly familiar most anywhere in Madagascar. The drought of the song's title is almost antithetically juxtaposed with rainforest fires (not at all affected by drought, of course). It is critical to recognize that this song is sung in Malagasy, though most often to an audience outside of Madagascar largely unfamiliar with the Malagasy language. Thus, the audience generally understands only what Hanitra explains in English as introduction to the song, about a generalized environmental hazard in Madagascar. No distinction is made between Antandroy for instance plagued by drought in the south or Betsimisaraka grappling with disappearing forest in the northeast.[12] These are two very culturally distinct groups of Malagasy people with quite different modes of daily life, belief system, music, and more. In this instance, the notion of ecological devastation combines with the sound (most often without semantic comprehension) of the Malagasy language itself, to create a sound-image of sadness in Madagascar for primarily non-Malagasy audiences. The actual text poetics of Tarika's as well as of Clément's songs, then, in themselves clearly cannot resound effectively among global audiences, nor do they voice realistic actualities of or among the lives of real, varied peoples in Madagascar. The instrumental accompaniment for *Hainteny* is produced on a *valiha* (a tube zither, a stringed instrument popular in varying form throughout the island), standard guitar, electric bass, and electric slide guitar. The glissandi of the slide guitar presumably accentuate a feeling of sadness or loss, as might the slide guitar in blues or the pedal steel in country music. One might argue that the capacity of a slide guitar sound to convey sadness or loss might be specific to certain cultural situations on the mainland of the US. Certainly, much slide guitar performance in Hawaii, for instance, seems to denote a cheerfulness (one only has to listen to the guitarist Sol Hoopi, for one). In *Hainteny*, the *valiha* and slide guitar engage in call and response interplay. In voicing a global musical dialogue between British slide guitar player and Malagasy *valiha* player, might the choice of including this extra musician, not typically a performer with Tarika, imply aurally a sympathy from outside of Madagascar for ecological concerns within the island? In playing in part upon *tavy* destruction of rainforest land, the text of *Hainteny* conflates varied reasons for ecological sadness in Madagascar in part by incorporating a 'Western' glissando mode of sounding itself often iconic of sadness. While this song might be perceived as a statement of a global cause, it blurs several particularities of both sound iconicity and ecological referent in Madagascar.

Saving Madagascar

Conservation International (CI), an organization with a prominent presence in Madagascar,[13] states:

> CI has worked in Madagascar for most of the organization's history. Protecting the island nations' (sic) endangered species and instituting better park and forest management techniques are CI's main priorities in this region. CI also works with members of the private sector, such as the mining industry, to establish biodiversity sensitive practices (2002, www.conservationinternational.org).

This CI promotion continues to enunciate a hierarchy of priorities:

1. Ensure the protection of priority parks and reserves.
2. Create new protected areas in the regions of high biodiversity.
3. Focus on key endangered species to prevent their extinction.
4. Develop conservation policies and best practices that protect natural resources.
5. Facilitate the development of locally owned enterprises and environmental education programs.

Finally, Conservation International's website promotion on Madagascar concludes:

> Along Madagascar's eastern stretch of forest is the Mantadia-Zahamena region or corridor. It spans over more than 1,200 km and contains some of the last remaining lowland rain forests in the country, as well as a large tract of intact primary forest. This region is under intense threat from slash-and-burn agriculture and logging. CI is working to set conservation priorities that will involve local communities, protect parks, address threats, and raise awareness about its rich biodiversity on local and national levels.

'Rich biodiversity' stops strikingly short in this literature of including humanity – this statement elides over *human* biology and diversity. The 'intense threat' identified above refers unequivocally to Malagasy people themselves. I recall numerous conversations with American Conservation International authorities in Madagascar between 1993–5 in which Malagasy people indeed were discussed with some repugnance, as mindless ravagers of their own territory. Such sentiment is pronounced, alarmingly, in the following excerpt from a scholarly text on Madagascar: 'In truth, this wonderful wilderness lacks status in the unromantic Malagasy imagination' (Allen, 1995: 174). More accurately and truthfully, environmentalist concerns with protecting the land constitute a cause that most Malagasy do not have the luxury of taking upon themselves.

There is no agenda in CI's literature above for teaching less land-consumptive methods of rice agriculture to Malagasy on the east coast. Rather, Malagasy are commonly set, not so implicitly, as villainous enemies of the land and its rich biodiversity. Inevitably, Malagasy are prohibited from their own lands in developmental deals with the national government so that 'biodiversity' can flourish. These lands commonly become reservations for lemurs, foreign researchers, and ecotourism.

My own interactions with and observations of numerous Conservation International workers (including the head of the Madagascar project at the time) reinforce that at a local level, these workers were unequipped for, even unconcerned with, addressing the needs of Malagasy in the countryside. Indeed, they commonly projected a colonial-like image and presence that was disdainful to many Malagasy in the region, for example, by occupying the largest colonial-style houses in the east coast Tamatave region (and hiring *local* Malagasy as house servants), driving large 4×4 vehicles throughout the area (something virtually no Malagasy own), and dating wealthier Malagasy women. To intensify such matters among local Malagasy, Conservation International employees commonly brought Merina (the predominant group of Malagasy in the capital, Antananarivo) girlfriends, as well as hired help from the capital, with them to Tamatave. They did not engage with or employ Malagasy from the East Coast other than as servants – in other words, east coast Malagasy were not employed for the more 'mindful' work carried out by CI representatives themselves. These CI choices of action commonly evoked anxiousness and disdain among East Coast Betsimisaraka, who have a long history of being oppressed or mistreated by Merina from the capital. Indeed, several East Coast Malagasy friends commonly told me that the presence of CI replayed for them a new wave of Merina hegemony, supported this time by Americans, a presence that recollected among Malagasy *côtiers* the early nineteenth century invasion by the Merina monarchy into Betsimisaraka territory.

Many Betsimisaraka on the East Coast of Madagascar thus saw CI employees, both American and Merina, as strangers, unwanted to varying degrees, in their territory. For supposedly being on the receiving end of international aid, Betsimisaraka often experienced CI activities to be peripheral, irrelevant, and sometimes self-indulgent.[14]

Conclusions

In Madagascar there are clear divisions between local senses of environmental priority and those introduced into the island by an international environmentalist imaginary, a cause that seeks sometimes myopically to save 'nature', and against which Malagasy are commonly portrayed as a threat. While Mily Clément and Tarika express international environmentalist causes, they, in an unfortunately common environmentalist fashion, do so as they silence or at least glance over Malagasy actualities of daily life. Tarika's own imaging of the sadness pervasive in the drought experienced by Antandroy in the south of the island neglects the sort of environmental hazards that Antandroy face when they leave their beloved homeland to search for wage labour in other parts of the island. For example, in Tamatave, Antandroy often take up residence in the soiled streets of town in their capacity as guardians for wealthy business owners. Tarika thus somewhat romanticizes Antandroy suffering in the south for a certain musical effect, while overlooking another sort of environmental poverty they experience once they leave the south. This experience is most often accompanied by a severe sadness among Antandroy people who are separated from beloved ancestral homeland in the south.

At the time I was interacting with him, Mily Clément was involved in no particular environmental efforts at the local level. In fact, he had even left his homeland in the North East, an area heavily affected by ecological devastation, to live in Antananarivo, far from the actual daily problems of smouldering forest hillsides and widespread soil erosion (though Antananarivo of course is not without its own desperate environmental problems). Hanitra Rasoanaiva, of Tarika, spends the better part of her time outside of Madagascar and thus rests disconnected to some degree from human realities there.

In Madagascar 'environmentalism', an internationalized cause, is quite often disjunct from 'environment' itself and what actually fills in the environment as a lived in, politicized, peopled place. Popular Malagasy songs available for consumption outside of Madagascar have favoured, self-consciously or not, environmentalist-like themes, often expressed with a concomitant erasure of local people from their own environment.

Notes

1. Jaojoby's music can be heard on the CDs: *Salegy!* (1996), Danbury, CT: Xenophile 4040; and *E Tiako* (1997), Paris: Indigo Label Bleu LBLC 2533.
2. In one of Clément's songs, *Tsy moramora mitady vola,* on this same album, he laments the difficulties of finding money and of obtaining daily essentials.
3. Between 1993 and 1995 there was one such station in Tamatave on the east coast, called Radio Voanio (coconut). This station attempted to programme more internationally popular songs than did Radio Nationale, which featured Malagasy artists. Radio Voanio's capacity to succeed in its mission again was limited by its very small holding of recordings of foreign artists.
4. For instance, fluffy toy stuffed lemurs or lemur-like characters on TV shows that in part anthropomorphize this lower primate outside of Madagascar; or creatures resembling the Malagasy Parson's chameleon that are featured in beer commercials. Such commercial mediation of the Malagasy landscape denudes, ignores, and reifies this landscape's actual qualities and conditions of being.
5. That Malagasy people might need to be 'saved' itself echoes an earlier missionizing statement.
6. For example, the land and fauna protection strategies of the World Wildlife Federation (WWF).
7. One American researcher I met while I was in Madagascar had been searching in the Arisivim-Pirenena, the Malagasy National Archives in Antananarivo, for documentation of French logging practices in Madagascar. She told me that she had found evidence that over 60 per cent of the original forested areas in Madagascar had already become deforested by 1960, the year of Malagasy independence from France, due largely to French commercial logging on the east coast of Madagascar.
8. Tamatave, an East Coast provincial capital (*faritany,* in Malagasy, designates the six geographic regions of Madagascar) had a transmitter for the national television station. Only very few Malagasy in Tamatave owned a television set or had access to one.
9. Duke University was heavily involved at the time with funding and implementing the renovation of the zoological park in Antananarivo, the capital, in which one could view lemurs in captivity. Most Malagasy could not afford the admission fee to come and regard remnants of their own disappearing environment.

10. For example, the Malagasy periwinkle, *Catharanthus roseus,* contains the alkaloids vincristine and vinblastine effective in treating certain forms of cancer. *Catharanthus roseus,* initially from Madagascar, has long been cultivated in other warm climates throughout the world. In addition to comprising alkaloids effective in some cancer treatment, other alkaloids found in this plant (there are at least seventy different alkaloids in *Catharanthus roseus*) have been used to treat diabetes (in lowering blood sugar levels), high blood pressure, and inflammation, among other afflictions. Two other alkaloids found in the plant, reserpine and serpentine, can be powerful tranquilisers (Snyder, 1996).
11. *Bibiango.* Green Linnet CD 4028.
12. I have heard Tarika perform this song numerous times outside of Madagascar, and thus have also heard Hanitra's introduction. Tarika did not perform in Madagascar in the two years I was there.
13. I refer specifically here to the period between 1993–5 during which I was in Madagascar in the east coast region of Tamatave performing ethnographic research on the confluence of musical practice, spirit possession, remembering, and colonization. I focus upon Conservation International because I was in regular contact with several of its members and its Malagasy operations head while I was in Madagascar.
14. Crewe and Harrison (2000) expound upon this phenomenon in sub-Saharan Africa. They also discuss similarities between aid organizations and colonialism, as both made assumptions that local people need to be helped with problems they cannot solve independently.

References

Allen, P. M. (1995), *Madagascar: Conflicts of Authority in the Great Island,* Boulder CO: Westview Press.

Crewe, E. and Harrison, E. (2000), *Whose Development? An Ethnography of Aid,* London and New York: Zed Books.

Emoff, R. (2000), 'Clinton, Bush, and Hussein in Madagascar', *The World of Music,* 42(2): 51–73.

—— (2002a), *Recollecting from the Past: Musical Practice and Spirit Possession on the East Coast of Madagascar,* Middletown CT: Wesleyan University Press, Music and Culture Series.

—— (2002b), 'Phantom Nostalgia and Recollecting (from) the Colonial Past in Tamatave, Madagascar', *Ethnomusicology* 46(2): 265–83.

Hagan, K. L. (1996), 'Deforestation in Madagascar', at http://www.american.edu/ted/madagas.htm.

Hornac, J. (1943), 'Le déboisement et la politique forestière à Madagascar', in

Mémoire de Stage. Mémoires de l'Ecole Coloniale ENFOM. Archives d'Outre Mer, Aix-en Provence. Archives Nationales de France.

Snyder, L.A. (1996), 'Description and Natural History of the Periwinkle', at http://biotech.icmb.utexas.edu/botany/perhist.html.

Recommended Listening

Clément, Mily (1993), *Mandrora Mantsilany* (cassette tape). Antananarivo, Madagascar: Mars Recording.

Emoff, Ron (2001), *Accordions and Ancestral Sprits*. Compact disc sound recording of my field tapes; includes booklet of notes and photographs. VDE Gallo, Genève, Switzerland.

Emoff, Ron (2002c), *Spirit Musics from the East Coast of Madagascar*, Paris: UNESCO/Naive. Compact disc sound recording of my field tapes; includes booklet of notes and photographs.

Jaojoby, Eusèbe (1996), *Salegy!* (CD), Danbury, CT: Xenophile 4040.

Jaojoby, Eusèbe (1997), *E Tiako* (CD), Paris: Indigo Label Bleu LBLC 2533.

Kaiser, H. and Lindley, D. (1992), *A World Out of Time: Henry Kaiser and David Lindley in Madagascar*, Newton NJ: Shanachie 64041 (product of a thirteen-day long recording session made by Kaiser and Lindley in Antananarivo, Madagascar's capital.)

Rossy (1993), *One Eye on the Past, One Eye on the Future*, Newton NJ: Shanachie 64046.

Tarika (1994), *Bibiango*, Green Linnet CD 4028.

–3–

Island Musicians:
Making a Living from Music in Crete

Kevin Dawe

One of my first lines of inquiry when researching this chapter was to type 'Island musicians' into an Internet search engine. This revealed a host of personal, co-operative, and corporate Web pages featuring working musicians on islands around the globe. From Prince Edward Island, Canada to Ascension Island to Vanuatu to Hawaii, from wedding musicians to tourist party-bands, from Irish harpists to hotel combos and day cruise brochures from Fiji featuring an all singing, all guitar-playing crew. Many of the Web sites were informative, easy to use and included details of bands or individuals, with varying notions of repertoire given, and an e-mail contact but not usually fees. These pages were usually engaging and colourfully presented, well illustrated with pictures of 'the island', linked to island Web sites (some to archives, heritage centres or tour operators), or in the case of recording artists, record companies. In this chapter, I am not inter-ested in island music 'superstars'. My focus is upon local, professional musicians who may or may not make the occasional locally produced record – those musi-cians based most of the time in their island home.

One might deduce from my introduction that musicians are becoming as good at promoting themselves in cyberspace as they are at playing live gigs, and that the musicians' grapevine therein is yielding a bumper harvest. Some of them are well and truly connected and can be booked online. Presumably Web site maintenance increases not only musicians' dependence on those with the skills to maintain/ construct them (if they cannot do it themselves) but also their financial outlay? However, in terms of what is achieved through these sites as promotional culture, it is clear that island musicians are not only aware of the potential of the Internet but all too aware of their 'islander-ness' and how this might be interpreted, presented, sold and marketed. After all, there might not be much else for islanders to make a living from at home and so it is understandable that they should put what musical talent they have to work. Island musicians usually have the added attraction and selling point of being from 'exotic' places with quite unique musical traditions. There might be few of them left. There might be quite a few of them playing the same music and so they need to promote themselves carefully. Certainly, the knowledge and skills of musicianship (aesthetics, application, concentration, dedication, ability to hone and develop technique, business sense, rapport with an audience) are crucial in an increasingly competitive market and are enabling of work in new and ever diverse contexts. At least, they may add to the musician's potential to take up an increasingly broad range of opportunities.

The chapters in this book reveal much about the role of musicians in various island cultures. Whether Torres Strait islander songwriters, British composers, DJs in Ibiza, *calypso* musicians in Trinidad, women singers of Cuban *timba*, or musicians from Chindo island regarded as national treasures and funded by the government. These accounts and ethnographies enable us to carefully consider what is meant in each case by the catch all term 'musician'.[1] Throughout this book, what we mean by 'island musician' will hopefully become clearer in relation to the cultural contexts in which we find musicians.

I have met a range of island musicians in my work as an ethnomusicologist. I have had contact with village and club bands in Papua New Guinea, resort bands in Mauritius, a Holiday Inn jazz combo in Fiji, folklore troupes in Madeira and Malta, wedding and club musicians in Crete, and worked the county band circuit back home in England. Despite an apparently other-worldly attitude in some cases, I have learnt that the average professional musician is very much a man or woman of the world. If they want to stay in the circuit, on the books, develop their niche, get talked about, become known and be remembered musicians must not only be aware of and monitor the local musical world but must be proactive in making their mark by fully engaging with it. However many rewards (financial and other) the musician accrues this is a tightrope to walk. Endless residencies in clubs and hotel bars can demotivate musicians who go through 'the routine' every night. Drink and drugs do indeed take their toll as the very idea of making music turns stale.

Musicians' activities become embroiled in many different kinds of power relations that come into play between themselves and their patrons and audience. These set ups depend on more than contractual obligations. Issues of class, gender, race, ethnicity, identity and 'other-ness' feed into notions and definitions of 'the musician' in the contexts in which he or she tries to make a living and shape how that living will be made. For the musician, the intimate relation between musical structure and social structure can be empowering and 'being a musician' is to take on a role that usually embodies a range of extra-musical values, duties and obligations. Each culture has established roles for musicians to play and will value them accordingly. To a great extent, musicians' performances are a reaffirmation of these values in society and, accordingly, a recreation and legitimization of their role. Most professional musicians I have met are devoted to their art; but whether gifted or not, survivors have one thing in common: the tenacity to keep on going against all odds. Technique is not everything but it helps; however, foresight, planning and the ability to make the right connections and moves are skills and talents that also have to be honed and developed as part of 'the business' and as obligatory career moves. After all, a four-nightly club or hotel gig that supports the musician and his or her family might not be there for ever as the size, tastes and demands of audiences change along with fluctuations in the local economy. The club or hotel management can also change overnight. The work might be seasonal.

I have found the problems of professional musicians to be particularly acute in island contexts. Here competition is often far greater. Opportunities exist but within a smaller area and within a limited number of venues. Specialization may be required. Less able musicians may also try to muscle in (for example, playing for tourists). Well-established musicians fill the securer niches, and the musical economy is often controlled by a limited number of powerful musicians, producers, clients, patrons, families, or officials. It can be difficult for young musicians to break into the scene. The available niches provide precious sources of income and they often depend on family and kinship ties and connections, systems of reciprocity, reputation and perhaps a one-hit record or television appearance. All of these keep the musician in place where the proprietors of a particular venue, their clientele and the musician develop a symbiotic relationship. If musicians manage to break into the international market there might also be the added and sometimes lucrative injection of capital back into the local community and the possibility of local celebrity status.[2]

The values and standards of performance practice are often thrown into question as tourism and the tour operators offer new and/or extra work and start to dictate the ways in which performances should be organised for the consumption of tourists and others (for example, businessmen and businesswomen). Traditional repertoires are played alongside an international set and, in my experience of Greek-island '*bouzouki* nights' neither type of music seems to benefit. Amidst the plate smashing and the innuendo of some club reps and others one hears an age-old melody that can reduce a local audience to tears, but here its meaning is irrevocably lost. How do professional musicians cope with their often 'between worlds' existence? Do they always try to accommodate the demands of local and non-local audiences? Rather, how do they manage to keep in tune with the demands of home audiences as well as those of visitors? In many cases they do not. Some musicians turn their back on 'tourist music'. Musicians specialize in different sectors of the available market. Some of their activities overlap but nevertheless specialists develop within a niche market. I will explore these other questions in relation to the work of professional musicians in Crete.

Musicians in Crete

What makes the Cretan musician? Performers of *lyra* music[3] in the Greek island
of Crete might be seen as 'keepers of a tradition' in a rapidly changing music
industry. There is a squeeze on employment in an island economy that makes
increasing and particular demands upon them as it intersects with international
market forces. *Lyra* music is what is meant by most Cretans when they talk about
'Cretan music'. *It is unique to the island*, lies at the very heart of a well-established
local recording industry, and is performed live at celebrations and in clubs all over
Crete. The music is said to run through 'the arteries and veins of the island' and
there is no doubt that it is omnipresent and in high profile. Yet over the years, the
musical community has had to develop and mobilize a set of finely tuned strategies for dealing with its increasingly 'between worlds' state of existence. Veteran
musicians have honed their musical and business skills, reworking local notions of
value and exchange into an effective and upgraded modus operandi. This has
enabled them to maintain a niche in the local musical economy and use it to move
into national and international networks. Some of the virtuosi are well travelled.
They have played for Greek and other audiences in the US, Canada, and/or
Australia for many years. They are plugged into a network that gains them work in
a remote mountain village one week and then, via a flight to Brisbane, work in the
Cretan diaspora the next. This does not happen all the time but occasionally it does
for the better known or well-connected members of the musical community.
Musicians in Crete are no strangers to making a living in an island context and
exploiting their island connections to the full in a world market. In Crete and in
places (as one local put it) 'more Cretan than Crete' the Cretan musician epitomizes the island, its people, and all they stand for.

Cretan musicians' two main sources of work are the summertime village
wedding celebrations and residencies at *kendra* (clubs with live music and food)
throughout Crete. A small number of professionals either teach as much as they
perform, usually in music schools, or supplement their livelihood by informal
teaching. Other occasional sources of income include royalties from record sales,
work at festivals throughout Greece requiring Cretan representatives, and so-called
'world music' festivals in places such as Paris and Amsterdam requiring a Cretan
contingent. Professional musicians in Crete work long and awkward hours and
diversify their activities to make ends meet. He (nearly all professional and semi-
professional Cretan musicians are men) embodies the strength, authority and
virtue of the Cretan people most of the time, linking the past with the present and
pulling it all into the future. This is an ideal role for the musician and one that is
often contested by those who employ him (as musicians are often seen as philan-
derers and drunkards, outside of mainstream society, constantly on 'the move') or
rib him at performances. Another ideal is that through musical performance, dance

and celebration, Cretans everywhere remain connected to the home island. Cretan musicians are gregarious actors on the stage of social life, not necessarily extrovert but certainly confident and stoical. Embroiled in myth and legend (ancient and modern) in Greece, the Cretan musician is often seen as the epitome of the 'traditional' musician in that country. Greeks openly talk about and recognize the importance of the musician in their own regional and island communities. After several years fieldwork on the island I believe that social activity and musical performance can be seen to coalesce as the musician 'takes the lead', 'goes solo', negotiates melodies and contracts and provides the 'driving force' behind dances and deals. He also sets the tempo of events and exchanges, and navigates a route through an ocean of sound and not-so-sound musical possibilities. My research has focused on individual musicians and their families, as much as the local music industry and how it works, noting how musicians keep their heads above the water, working alongside producers and club owners to keep the island's music industry afloat. I am interested in what Douglas and Isherwood (1996: 100) call the 'scale of the operation', not just the nature of the Cretan market place but the role of individual operators within an island music scene.

Island Business

Where does the money come from to finance a music industry and regular musical performances in Crete? Crete is one of Greece's leading regions in the production of olives and olive oil, grapes and citrus fruits, and much of its produce is shipped to Greece through Iraklion airport or the ferry port. Hundreds of villages all over the island supply the city and several towns with home grown, home made produce: from meat to honey, from lace to leather. The main port and airport in Crete, Iraklion, acts as a thoroughfare for tourists and other visitors *en route* for elsewhere on the island, coming on or off numerous package flights or ferries. Its main attraction is the archaeological museum of mostly Minoan treasures and the nearby ancient city of Knossos. Major tour companies and hotel chains have offices in Iraklion. All the major banks, finance and insurance companies in Greece are represented in Iraklion. There are several dedicated television and radio stations based in the city. There are hundreds of shops selling designer clothes in the early 1990s and all the other mod cons of modern life. Iraklion is Greece's fifth largest city and in the early 1990s was, per capita, the wealthiest city in Greece. The hub of the music industry (record companies, record shops, instrument makers, musical virtuosi) in Crete is located in the island's capital city, Iraklion.

The city is a cosmopolitan thoroughfare locked into national and international political and economic networks and appears to embody the 'classic' symptoms of cultural heterogeneity as discussed by Redfield and Singer (1954). However, recent changes building on earlier developments have updated Iraklion's facilities

70 • *Dawe*

as a major political and economic base in the Aegean (see Dawe, 2000). The Cretan music industry has sprung up within this changing scene but over the decades has grown and worked with new developments and the influence of outside forces coming in, establishing a context in which musicians consider making their living from music alone, even turning professional. Iraklion still has its poorer quarters that stand in marked contrast to the luxury hotels and penthouse flats located in the more scenic areas with sea views. But it is nothing like the place of contrasts that I visited first in 1980 and where I returned for eighteen months of fieldwork in 1990. Tour operators and professional musicians are still among those living in luxury, whilst many fishermen, tinsmiths and others still live in areas once made up almost exclusively of hovels. In 2003 the city was more than ever a confluence of cultural forms with Virgin Records, McDonalds and dance clubs vying for business alongside long established local music stores, record companies, Cretan music clubs, and shops selling a variety of local products (see Dawe, 1998, 2000).

Throughout the 1970s and 1980s, the ferry port, airport, international flights and package holidays facilitated the rise of a well-organized and well co-ordinated tourist industry on the island administered locally but largely overseen and owned by the giant tour operator companies based in Athens, Piraeus and elsewhere. There has been considerable government and local capital investment in Crete. Many hotels and resorts have excellent facilities and the city and other coastal towns, in particular, have most early twenty-first century amenities. Iraklion has grown, however, into the place of the 'hard sell', where many tourist souvenir shops sell almost exactly the same items and jostle and hustle for business during the usually crowded summer season. Musicians move to Iraklion from the villages. They earn a living as opportunities arise – a club residency perhaps, a wedding, a recording session and even some casual work for the tour operators or local television and radio stations. Musicians look for ways into the local music industry and develop strategies to stay afloat and employed. Sometimes established musicians and producers can extend a generous helping hand and help recommend promising young musicians. But in general, the old hands in the local music business have a rather mixed reputation amongst Cretan people who were bold enough and interested enough to comment. The less able musicians tend to eke out a living playing tourist clubs and bars in places like Elounda. They play on an *ad hoc* to semi-professional basis. I can say quite categorically that this gives visitors to Crete a less-than-impressive introduction to Cretan music as it is mostly played by rank amateurs in this context. Performances can be staged, disjointed and irreverent. This is a far cry from the virtuosic work of such musicians as the late Thanasis Skordalós and Kostas Moundákis. Ironically, tourists and other visitors to the island can pick up the complete works of Skordalos or Moundákis, for example, in any of the Cretan or international record shops that line the thoroughfares. When Cretans speak of Cretan music, they have a very high standard of performance in mind. It is taken for granted that the *lyra* player, in particular, but also his accompanists, will be highly advanced players with great technical ability and vast knowledge of Cretan melodies, rhythms and poetry – such is the level of expectation of the professional musician in Crete. A few musicians break this mould and go for a more intuitive, less elitist and less business-like interpretation of 'the tradition', such as Psarandonis. It would be wrong though to suggest that any one of these musicians is less interested in the financial rewards his talent and prowess in the field can bring.

Most professional musicians eventually turn their back on the tourist market. That is, despite the deceptive but relatively slight overlap between the music industry and the tourist sectors of the local economy (seen most obviously in the presence of *lyra* players at Cretan nights and the more gaudy cassette racks selling package tour versions of Cretan 'favourites'). The leading lights of *lyra* music play primarily for the home audience and Cretans everywhere. *Lyra* music is dependent on the local economy as it interfaces with international monetary systems (as subsidized by tourism) but also has to 'speak' and sell itself to locals who define themselves and 'the music tradition' in opposition to tourists and the non-Cretan world. There are those people who make a living exclusively or largely from music. And those who use musicians and music as part of their wider entrepreneurial strategies (recording studios, radio stations, and owners of music shops and clubs). I will focus on the former here.

The Work of the Bandleader

How does a musician make a living on an island like Crete? In an attempt to answer this question, I will focus on the work of the lead musician in the Cretan *lyra-laouto* ensemble, the *lyra* player who is usually the bandleader. I worked closely with the Iraklion-based bandleader, Dimitris Pasparákis throughout my time in Crete and it his activities that I will discuss here. Born in the plains-village of Armanoyiá he also has family in the renowned musical mountain village of Anoyiá. Both villages lie more-or-less in the centre of Crete. His case is unique in some ways but in most respects provides a good example of how most *lyra* musicians eke out a living on the island. In his band work, in his role as head of a family unit (with a wife and two sons), and as one of four brothers in a large but close extended family, for Dimitris bonds of kinship and trust had their own attendant and unspoken rules. There were crucial obligations to be fulfilled to the family and to the community and, if that was not enough to do, these pressures were added to by his reputation all over Crete as 'the teacher of Cretan music' (and a regular teaching schedule at a music school in Iraklion).

Dimitris Pasparákis's role as leader of an ensemble was multifarious. He exploited his considerable organizational skills in many ways throughout the course of a performance. These skills were expressed not only in his playing and his poetry but also through his management of the whole event. As lead musician and thus the prime mover in the evening's celebrations he was (next to his employer for the night) ultimately responsible for the success or failure of the occasion. As bandleader and *lyra* player, Dimitris's picture alone appeared on the poster advertisements in the town or village in which his band was due to perform. He arranged the engagements, owned the PA (which he maintained), drove and maintained the transport, oversaw and helped with the setting up of the equipment and sound check all whilst socializing with clients and passers by. Moreover, he was responsible for the collection and collecting up, and counting and division of earnings (set fees and tips). On top of all this he had to perform every engagement to the best of his ability mustering up enough imaginative improvisation whilst displaying sensitivity to acoustic space, flow of events and the mood of perform-ance which he aimed to control in order to hold the event together. Cretan cele-brations are fast and furious events that are intensely challenging and gruelling for even the most experienced musicians. I have written elsewhere about the ways in which musicians work musical and verbal structures (musical themes and rhyming couplets) up into extended improvisations to facilitate and accompany dance (see Dawe 1996).

Musical skills are pushed to the limits with increasing intensity as the speed and rhythms of the dances are alternated in rapid succession; the virtuoso improvisa-tions of the *lyra* player feed off the acrobatics of the dancers and the verbal inter-jections of guests. There is a movement away from known melodic material accompanied by an intensification of melodic and rhythmic invention whose 'highs' are punctuated with cries of encouragement, whistles, and gunfire. The musical strategies of the musicians, their manipulation of musical themes, tempos, improvisations, and poetry occurs in a way that takes into account and manages the moods and sounds of the total environment in their attempts to orchestrate a successful performance – a performance that is convivial for participants (dancers, guests who want to intone poetry, those listening) and profitable for musicians. The essential interplay between all these elements can be seen to create a community of *machismo* at the celebration.

A further part of the bandleader's responsibility was the teaching of old and new musical materials to the band. In effect, the younger musicians serve their appren-ticeship with him. Dimitris ran a tight ship; he had close friends and family members who he could trust and rely upon in his band. The importance of kinship and family bonds also found expression in a band setting. The regular members of his band were his long time teaching assistant and his nephew; both of these musi-cians would play *laouto* for him and were also highly proficient on other instru-ments (*lyra*, mandolin, *bouzouki*). But the band has to be a flexible unit; the style of music allowing for additions and subtractions. This depended on the demands of each performance (a village celebration which can last up to sixteen hours perhaps requiring three *laouto* players and someone to take over *lyra* for a short time) and whether the regular members were available at any one time. Deputy musicians had been tried out before and were trusted friends.

Musicians travel throughout the island whenever it seems practically and economically viable to do so. But they usually work the patches in which they live. Dimitris taught regularly not only in Iraklion but also in several towns in Iraklion province. This would also be the main area in which he would work the wedding circuit in the summer although he did travel further afield sometimes. Patrons usually request a local musician to play for them. They will know of Dimitris through his teaching, his recordings but also from his reputation as someone who is a regular player on the live music circuit. For a number of reasons weddings take place in the summer, from June to early September. At this time of year in Crete the weather is reliable and usually very hot (so most of the festivity takes place from late afternoon onwards). There is more disposable income at this time of year from the harvest of agricultural produce, the tourist trade and from expatriates returning home (see Dawe, 1998). Indeed, some of the better known Cretan virtuosi return to Crete to play the wedding circuit in the summer.

Conclusions

The stock sounds, metaphors, and images involved in the presentation, production, promotion and teaching of the *lyra* music of Crete make powerful statements about Cretan-ness, roots, authenticity and difference within the Cretan world at large and also about the island as a distinct and unique place. Even though one can draw a line around Crete on the map (as generations of Cretans have done so before), the 'inside' and 'outside' of the island are negotiated in Cretan terms. The boundaries of the Cretan world can be expansive enough to incorporate Cretans around the world but still not let anyone else *in* – so far. As an island there is no doubt that Crete stands out not only as the largest island in the Aegean Sea but as a staging post between and a meeting place of worlds (Europe and the Middle East, Europe and Asia, Europe and Africa, Cretans and others, Cretans and tourists). It is impor-tant among the possessions of the Greek state as a territory and as an expression of the *ethnos*. It is at once central and peripheral in Greek terms. Yet Cretans see themselves as more Cretan than Greek. They see Crete as an island nation. The uniqueness of the island's *lyra* music reinforces this ideal. Crete might be seen as a confluence of Mediterranean cultures, proudly acknowledging its place in antiq-uity and the formation of Western *civilization* yet it denies its connection to other places and cultures in the Mediterranean (whose influence can be seen in its music, for example). These negotiations of space, place, ethnicity and identity are clearly played out in the work of musicians from *the inside looking out* in the face of a range of *outsiders looking in.*[4]

At the heart of the matter is the crucial relationship between music and masculinity, most clearly played out and negotiated in, through and as *lyra* music. Ultimately, this is a contested performance, where power and control are sought within the labyrinthine corridors of the music industry (in sound and image), in studios, at celebrations, in coffee houses, and in talk and gossip about music and musicians. Cretan musical phenomena are located not only within local and broader definitions of performance (music, poetry and drama are inextricably linked) but conflated with an omnipresent, all pervasive and largely village-based moral geography. The mapping of this moral geography onto everyday life (in rhetoric and hyperbole, sound and image) sets Cretan music and most importantly Cretan men's music apart from the rest of the world in thought, word, gesture, action, and deed. The images on record, cassette and CD covers locate Cretan music in a very local island world but takes into account both village and city life. Some musicians don shepherd's clothing, others open-necked shirts and leather jackets, whilst a few of the older virtuosi wear business suits. They appear prepared. Most seasoned Cretan musicians appear very efficient at dealing with all that life can throw at them. To the best of my knowledge Cretan *lyra* musicians do not yet have Web sites but they do have mobile telephones.

Notes

1. See, for example, Becker (1976, 1982), Blum (1975, 1978), Lees (1988), Waterman (1990), Cohen (1991), Shank (1994), and Lortat-Jacob (1995).
2. See Guilbault (1993) for a Caribbean perspective and Hayward (1998) for perspectives from the Pacific region.
3. Performed by the *lyra-laouto* ensemble. The *lyra* (lira) (plural = *lyres* (lires)) is a three-stringed, upright, bowed lute; the *laouto* (lauto) (plural = *laouta* (lauta)) is a four-course (eight strings grouped in pairs), plucked, long-necked lute. This ensemble is often augmented by a second *laouto* or mandolin. The *lyra* player is usually but not always the lead singer within the group.
4. For further discussion of all these themes see the work of Michael Herzfeld (1985) and (1991).

References

Becker, H. (1976), 'Art Worlds and Social Types', *American Behavioural Scientist* 19: 703–18.
—— (1982), *Art Worlds*. Berkeley and Los Angeles: University of California Press.

Blum, S. (1975) 'Towards a Social History of Musicological Technique', *Ethnomusicology* 19(2): 207–31.

—— (1978) 'Changing Roles of Performers in Meshed and Bojnurd, Iran', in Nettl, B. (ed.), *Eight Urban Musical Cultures*, Urbana: Illinois University Press, pp. 17–32.

Cohen, S. (1991), *Rock Culture in Liverpool: Popular Music in the Making*, Oxford: Clarendon Press.

Dawe, K. (1996), 'The Engendered *Lyra*: Music, poetry and manhood in Crete', in *The British Journal of Ethnomusicology*, 5: 93–112.

—— (1998) 'Bandleaders in Crete: Musicians and Entrepreneurs in a Greek Island Economy', *The British Journal of Ethnomusicology*, 7: 23–44.

—— (2000), 'Roots Music in the Global Village: Cretan ways of Dealing with the World at Large', *World of Music*, 42(3): 47–66.

Douglas, M. and Isherwood, B. (1996) [1979], *The World of Goods: Towards an Anthropology of Consumption*, New York & London: Routledge.

Guilbault, J. with Averill, G., Benoit, E. and Rabess, G. (1993), *Zouk: World Music in the West Indies*, Chicago and London: University of Chicago Press.

Hayward, P. (ed.) (1998), *Sound Alliances: Indigenous Peoples, Cultural Politics and Popular Music in the Pacific*, London and New York: Cassell.

Herzfeld, M. (1985), *The Poetics of Manhood: Contest and Identity in a Cretan Mountain Village*, Princeton NJ: Princeton University Press.

—— (1991), *A Place in History: Social and Monumental Time in a Cretan Town*, New Jersey and Oxford: Princeton University Press.

Lees, G. (1988), *Meet Me at Jim and Andy's: Jazz Musicians and their World*, New York and Oxford: Oxford University Press.

Lortat-Jacob, B. (1995), *Sardinian Chronicles*, Chicago and London: Chicago University Press.

Redfield, R. and M. Singer (1980) [1954], 'The Cultural Role of Cities', in Press, I. and Smith, M. (eds), *Urban Place and Process: Readings in the Anthropology of Cities*, London: Macmillan.

Shank, B. (1994), *Dissonant Identities: The Rock'n'Roll Scene in Austin, Texas*, Hanover: Wesleyan University Press.

Waterman, C. (1990), *Jùjú: A Social History and Ethnography of an African Popular Music*. Chicago: Chicago University Press.

Recommended Listening

CDs of Cretan music can be obtained from www.trehantiri.com and www.Cretashop.gr

–4–

'Ay Díos, Ampárame' (O God, Protect Me): Music in Cuba during the 1990s, the 'Special Period'

Jan Fairley

Cuando Robinson abrío los ojos,	When Robinson opened his eyes
Y vío que estaba solo en una isla,	And he saw he was alone on an island,
Soló en una isla,	Alone on an island,
Como tú, Y yo. Como tú, Y yo.	Like you, And me, Like you, and me.

Carlos Varela, Robinson

On 24 April 1999, Carlos Varela sang *Robinson* to a massive Cuban public on the Malecón Promenade outside the key cultural institution, Casa de las Americas. *Casa Viva!* was a free concert to celebrate the fortieth anniversary of this intellectual powerhouse (1959–99) involving musicians from Spain, Latin America and Cuba. Organized by Cuban *nueva trova* singer Silvio Rodríguez it implicitly referenced a pivotal international event organized by Casa's back in 1967, the Festival de la Canción Protesta.[1] While protest song as such is not the subject of this chapter, I have written elsewhere about why the denomination of 'protest song' has been rejected and continues to be rejected by all those concerned. Considerations of how people in Cuba publicly voice opinions which may not concur with those of the government controlled status quo, have been, I would argue, particularly relevant in the 1990s in Cuba, this very special island.

Cuba is special for a multitude of reasons but for the purposes of this chapter I will pinpoint just three. Firstly, it is home to arguably the world's most influential musical traditions, feeding to and from Spain, Africa and the Americas, as well as into many other countries and cultures (including Japan and Scandinavia). Secondly, this music has thrived in a country that is the only place in the world to have a revolutionary government for more than forty years during which North America has maintained an economic embargo. Paradoxically, Cuba has strong ties to the US through its diaspora and cultural proximity. Thirdly, economically Cuba is outside the direct sphere of influence of the World Bank (through which many countries are tied to North American policies in the late twentieth to early twenty-first century). The Cuban music business is in the control of the government and since the 1990s foreign companies (but not directly North American).

The singer-songwriter genre known as *nueva trova*, the one post-revolutionary musical tradition perceived by some cultural bureaucrats as challenging the state, was effectively accepted (though it was thought by some to have been co-opted by the state in the 1970s and 1980s). During this time to oppose or express views contrary to those officially recognized was to risk some form of censorship or be driven into exile. A characteristic of *nueva trova* since its inception has been a tendency to express itself through metaphor, allowing for ambiguous polysemic interpretations. Indeed, while such multi-interpretation is arguably and inextricably part of most cultural forms, much Cuban art could be interpreted as having coped with the stringencies of state control in this way. Epitomized by the work of Silvio Rodríguez and Pablo Milanés, the uniqueness of *nueva trova* is that it is a music that has fought for and gained the space to express the inner worlds of feeling and lived experience within the revolution.

At the beginning of the 1990s Carlos Varela, a member of the next generation and more a *trova*-rocker than a *nueva trova* singer, picked up the mantle of Rodríguez and Milanés. Songs like *Robinson* and *Guillermo Tell* (William Tell) in which he asks his 'father' to consider reversing the William Tell story and to let him have a go with the bow and arrow to shoot the apple off his head instead, were the public voice of a new generation seeking trust, power, responsibility, critical of prevailing paternalistic attitudes and the government's inability to allow more freedom for initiatives on the island.

In songs like *Fotos de Familia* (Family Photos) Varela articulated the pain and grief felt by many Cubans families and friends who had for one reason or another fled the island in various exoduses. This included the occupation of the Peruvian Embassy in 1980 that led to the Mariel boatlift; and the *balseros* of 1994. The shift suggested by these and similar songs was to see such people as entering the 'diaspora', a 1990s re-definition of those once defined officially as a *gusano* (worm) for leaving and therefore 'betraying' the revolution and its aims. Until the 1990s anyone else wishing to leave Cuba or function outside the control of the state system inevitably had to play the system (the US awards 20,000 visas a year to Cuban applicants distributed by ballot) or defect, as for example, leading musicians Paco de Rivera and Arturo Sandoval did in the early 1990s.

In this chapter, I argue that in the 1990s a 'new' compelling, polyrhythmic dance music called *timba*, directly associated with the culture of Cuba's black, urban population came to prominence, challenging the status quo at a time when the Cuban system itself was changing politically, economically and ideologically. I argue that the *timba* (inextricably music, song and dance) monitored the impact of such changes on Cuban society. This music was not conventional 'protest' and had nothing to do with *nueva trova*. Indeed, many Cubans would argue that it is simply an extension of a modernized form of Cuba's national music, *son*. *Son* was a development of the early twentieth-century synthesis of music that enabled African slaves to survive the desperately harsh life on the sugar plantations with the musical heritage of poor Spanish immigrants who came to grow tobacco as small tenant farmers.

Before a discussion of *timba* it is important to consider the dramatic changes that happened in Cuban society in this period and that led to subsequent radical changes in the Cuban music business.

Economic, Political and Ideological Change of the 1990s, the 'Special Period'

Significantly, the period that saw the emergence of *timba* saw a total sea change not only in Cuban economic and political life but in its state ideology too. These are worth considering in detail.

Economic change

The year 1990 saw the demise of communism in the Soviet Union and the dis-integration of the USSR upon which the Cuban economy was dependent. Cuba found itself in a 'period of crisis' which forced the Cuban economy to make a dramatic shift and it begin to introduce a mixed dollar-based economy based on tourism. This completely changed the conditions for music making and the music business on the island.

I would argue that Cuban music has always been inextricably tied up with the economy of the island. Historically Cuban music has come from the cultures of Afro-Cubans brought as enslaved peoples and Spanish colonialists and immigrants whose lives produced Cuba's two essential products, sugar (cane/rum) and tobacco (cigars). Music itself has, as Cuban ethnographer Fernando Ortíz persuasively argued throughout the early twentieth century, emerged from this *contrapunto Cubano*.

Religious change.

The visit of the Roman Catholic Pope to Cuba in 1989 was the visible expression of a more open acceptance and recognition of religious belief within the Revolution, allowing Cubans to be less inhibited to publicly embrace Catholic, Christian and other faiths (given that previously the Revolution had openly discouraged religious adherence). Significantly the Afro-Cuban religion of Santería, which emerged and developed in earlier centuries out of the beliefs of enslaved peoples, thrived in the 1990s. Its followers include enormous numbers of people in Cuba, most but not all of them poorer, rural and urban black Cubans.

At the Fourth Congress of the Cuban Communist Party, held in October 1991, the Congress took the landmark decision to open the Communist Party to religious believers. There was also a symbolic return to indigenous roots of Cuba's own brands of nationalism and socialism through the open embrace by the Congress of Cuba's Afro-Cuban heritage.[2]

Ideological change.
In December 1991 Cuba's National Assembly of People's Power voted to drop the philosophy of Marxist-Leninism from the Cuban constitution as the official state ideology, and in its place embrace the thinking of Cuban intellectual and national poet José Martí, who had been extremely active in Cuba's independence struggle against colonial Spain.

Musicians the New Elite

The important point is that musicians came to form one of Cuba's most influential elites, one that the government worked hard to keep in control during the mid-1990s. During the late 1980s and early 1990s, as more and more Cuban groups travelled abroad to earn hard currency, they became some of the prime movers of the economy bringing in money or sending it home. They also importantly serviced and were the focus of the renascent tourist industry. This made some Cuban musicians not only top earners but publicly visible symbols of a new materialism and hedonism fuelled by tourist culture, particularly evident through the wearing of gold jewellery and designer clothes of obvious foreign origin and the ownership of the latest models of foreign cars. Musicians could and did earn substantial amounts of money at venues frequented by tourists in top hotels and clubs, taking a good percentage officially and unofficially from the door.

Key Changes in the Music Business

Cuba's main economy has revolved around the growing of sugar and tobacco, nickel mining and the export of a number of other goods. Cuban music is at the heart of its culture and one of its most important cultural exports, constantly feeding to and from Africa and Spain where its roots lie, into world wide jazz, Latin and salsa sounds. Until the early 1990s, all recordings were habitually made at the state-run and owned Egrem studios and label whose broad eclectic regional policy towards Cuban music was inhibited by scarce resources. Few ordinary

Cubans owned hardware to play records or cassettes, making radio, live performance and TV the main outlets for music.

The State Musician turns Self-employed Professional

Fidel Castro has said on various occasions in recent years that culture is one of
Cuba's main assets. Music is part of the domain of the Cuban Centre for the Export
Promotion of Cuba called CEPEC, an export item alongside visual arts and hand-
icrafts. Today the state receives its moneys from every aspect of the business:

- it charges Cuban musicians for visas to travel abroad;
- it taxes their earnings;
- it taxes Cubans resident abroad if they wish to retain their citizenship and passport, whatever their income;
- it takes a percentage of all money taken in Cuban venues;
- it has licensed the Egrem archive to record companies all over the world (viz
  the plethora of Cuban music compilations available worldwide).

This new system which puts Cuban musicians in line with their peers in the
rest of the world was a huge change. Until the 'special period' Cuban musicians
were state employees working for an *empresa de espectaculos,* receiving a
monthly salary from a tiered system dependent on their classification grade as a
musician. Within the agency they were assigned a 'representative' to organize
their work on their behalf, with certain obligations known in Cuba as a work
norma. They were expected to rehearse (which most did diligently and the
present quality of practically every Cuban musician shows this), create new
music, and perform a required number of times per month or year to a cross-
section of the island's social communities. This meant that while new styles
developed and new groups appeared, largely traditional repertoires, styles and
indeed whole groups and orchestras (by embracing changing personnel) were
also heavily preserved. Those given permission to tour abroad (trusted not to
defect) were allowed to keep a percentage of foreign currency earned in dollars
to spend in an allotted time in Cuban state dollar shops. In the mid-late 1980s,
some groups gained permissions to buy technology and equipment available
only outside Cuba while on tour.

While one popular term to describe Cuba's new mixed economy has been
capisol (a play on the name of a Cuban soft-drink), a tropical hybrid of capitalism and socialism, José Luís Cortés, the leader of pivotal *timba* group N.G.
La Banda, described Cuba's 1990s economy as 'neo-socialist'. As a successful
artist living mostly from performances, royalties and recording contracts he told
me:

Before, we had financial guarantees whether we were working or not and we had money to support ourselves with while we were creating. Today, we have to go out and look for support for our work and any projects. We can make a lot of money but we have to work out how to do so ourselves.

On this theme his 1999/2000 song, *Tirando piedras por todos lados* (Throwing Stones To All Sides) pays tribute to innovative Cuban groups over the years, within a contemporary context of having to create initiatives.[3]

End of State Monopoly: Cubartista becomes Artex

Until 1989 all foreign tours were organized by Cubartista, the state booking agency, whose people-heavy bureaucracy oversaw contracts and finances. At the start of the 'Special Period' Cubartista was supplanted by Artex. Run on an independent model within a state system of companies, it provides an infrastructure inside and outside the country, from organizing main music venues throughout Havana and the rest of the island, to record and merchandising sales in Artex shops. State-owned companies have had to become self-financing and balance their own budgets. The impact on the music industry has been huge with musicians allowed to opt out and negotiate their own lives from recording contracts to concert tours, bringing Cuban musicians more into line with the rest of the world.

The monopoly of recording exercised by the state recording company Egrem ended, allowing foreign individuals and companies to rent studios, using their own or local technicians, contract Cuban musicians on their own terms, effectively make and market their product with no recourse to the Cuban government. Egrem has reorganized and is expanding, and a number of new recording companies like Bis music have appeared. Despite the blockade a Bis Rumba record won a 2002 US Grammy.

At the same time new recordings studios have been built, notably those on the initiative of *nueva trova* singer Silvio Rodríguez. Following his desire to invest a great percentage of his high foreign earnings in modernizing the island's music infrastructure, Rodríguez built the small compact Ojala! recording studios in a house in an uptown side street, and was directly involved in planning, building and raising the capital for the state-of-the art Abdala recording studios used today by many international artists. Pablo Milanés' also built studios in a large house he converted into the premises for the Fundación Pablo Milanés. While Milanes soon closed down the Foundation proper, due to overwhelming 'red tape', today the *in situ* studios are used by many young artists.[4] Other existing studios on the island have been updated with new technology, notably the studio at the ICAIC Film Institute and the smaller state-owned Egrem studios in Vedado. Paradoxically, the older down-town Egrem studios, treasured for their ambience (where Ry Cooder and Nick Gold of World Circuit music record the Afro-Cuban All Stars and the Buena Vista Social Club records) remain picturesquely dilapidated with older equipment.

New Copyright Law

The revolution of 1959 and the resulting North American blockade resulted in the breaking or suspension of most copyright payments. The opening up of the music industry resulted in new agreements concerning author's rights and music copyright. Many musicians signed to European companies have found it beneficial to collect their monies through Spain through the SGAE (La Sociedad General de Autores y Editors – The Society for Authors and Publishers). As a result money has been filtering back into Cuba, most of it not directly to the state but to individual musicians.

Two Musics: *Timba* and the *Buena Vista* Phenomenon (the Revival of Pre-1959 Classic *son*)

Buena Vista Social Club

One outcome of change and transformation has been the emergence of two kinds of music: one for people on the island itself; and one for tourists and a foreign market abroad who know little about everyday Cuba. The latter is epitomized by the international best-selling evergreen sounds of the records of the loose collective that records as *The Buena Vista Social Club* on the UK-based World Circuit label. This music has been marketed internationally through revivalist rhetoric and self-created 'authentic' mythologies spun by its producer maverick North American guitarist Ry Cooder and by the eponymous film of the project made two years after the original recording by German director Wim Wenders. Indeed, these recordings are of old musicians whose music was esteemed and still heard from time to time but with little direct relevance to Cuban cultural life in the 1990s. It was the first example of the clear divide between music produced on the island for the consumption of Cubans which also searches for international outlets and audiences, and that recorded on the island by foreign producers and companies as a commercial product for non-Cuban consumption.

Timba

Timba has long circulated in Afro-Cuban parlance used in the discourse of musicians to positively denote music having 'heart', 'feeling' 'profundity', 'weight' associated with the moment when a piece of music, notably *son,* holds all the potential for a transforming climax. It is a word that can be used for a piece of music, the playing of it or a dancer. Among many possibly etymological derivations and associations the ones most relevant here relate to the Afro-Cuban words 'tumba' and 'timba' both denoting drums, the latter also used for 'the belly' (heavily implicated in *timba* dance).

It is also worth considering the closeness of *timba* to *rumba*, a generic term also derived from dance terminology. They are both similar to *mambo*, a particular innovation within orchestras of the 1930s–50s. Another argument concerns the use of *timba* as a Cuban alternative to terms used in North America, notably *salsa* and *salsa dura* (hard salsa). The usage of these terms has been affected by Cuba's relationship with the outside world: once avoided they are now largely accepted but have effectively if temporarily been eclipsed by *timba*. While *salsa* is based on Cuban music notably *son*, significantly it does not embrace the specific musical innovations of *timba*.

Timba notably exhibits differences and developments to *son* in both traditional and modernized forms. The emergence of *timba* was heralded by the music of Los Van Van who developed *songo* out of *son*, modernizing through the big band format by introducing electric instrumentation and rock and other perceived non-Cuban musical influences, without losing the identifiable *son* structure. This was a clever innovation as it could be argued that a totally new dance music or imitation of Western rock might have lost the support of both the authorities and the public (indeed the few Cuban rock groups like Los Kent did stay outside the system until the 1990s).

As a driving dance music associated with a vital black Cuban dancing public, four features of *timba* must be mentioned here. Firstly, *timba* takes *son*'s bi-partite structure, often but not always foreshortening its first part organized around several 'story telling' verses, and extends the second part, the classic '*montuno*' section. This second section of *son* has always been the improvised part of the music, responding directly to the dance has in *timba* been given even more emphatic importance. It became an extendable heavily improvised section involving a dynamic between lead singer(s), chorus, singers and public. Lyrics respond not merely as usual to the sung verses of the first part, but laterally, so as to reference current events and concerns of the audience (referencing the inter-textuality of Cuban everyday popular culture).

In terms of the rhythm, *timba* music usually shifts the root time-line of Cuban music, called the 'clave', from a *son* clave to a 'rumba' one. The difference may seem small as it means shifting a beat, but it affects rhythmic accentuation making the music more compulsively propelling, the *rumba* clave having more insistent drive than the *son* clave.

Secondly, the creation of *timba* music has been fed by the cream of the Cuban music system. According to Cortés, the impulse that led to the development of *timba* came not only out of dance and its social economic environment but also out of the very particular musical climate at the beginning of the 1990s. Then, a generation of career musicians graduating with the highest qualifications in classical music, grew up playing popular music and jazz. Engaged in experimentation, constantly pushing each other on, they began to create a new music. Cortés himself studied at the ISA (Instituo Superior de Arte) in Havana, the top place to study fine arts; and then won a scholarship to the Tchaikowsky Institute/Conservatory in Moscow.[5]

Typically for *timba*, a big band plays densely orchestrated instrumental layers of interactive rhythms in virtuosic style. Elaborate arrangements challenge the musicians talents. In terms of arrangement, instrumentation and voicings, much impact has come from investing the music with jazz structures, values, practices and sensibilities. And just as the music is working on many interconnected levels, so are the lyrics. What may seem to be a fun dance-song telling gossipy stories and including street slang is actually using age-old poetic traditions, full of structural complexity, subtlety and imbued with multiple levels of interpretation.

Thirdly, the lyrics of *timba* monitor social change in Cuba during a time of Cuban history officially designated as 'the Special Period'. The lyrics of *timba* music of the 1990s map radical social change of the times and implicitly challenge revolutionary cultural values. This is what I define as the 'oral newspaper' function of *timba* song: *timba* lyrics wittily chart the impact of the newly invented tourist economy, the arrival of dollar rich foreigners and their lifestyles and essential aspects of personal relationships arising between Cubans, and between Cubans and foreigners. They have dealt with a host of daily changes and new conditions of everyday life (such as soya rations instead of fish and meat). Most significantly they have been the essential expression for the public emergence of the Afro-Cuban religion, Santería, as a sustaining belief system during a period when many ordinary Cubans felt the Revolution had failed them.

Fourthly, there is an inextricable relationship between the development of *timba* and the dance scene in Cuba. This has to be understood within the larger cultural context of what in Cuba is known as *jineterism* (the procurement of services, goods and/or dollars through association/'friendship' with non-Cuban visitors to the island). While the behaviour associated with *jineterism* may have historic antecedents, in dance terms it specifically focused on the bodies of women and saw a gender shift in Cuban dancing styles.

Song as a Newspaper and Barometer of Cuban Everyday Life

Cuban culture is orally based with a limited state-controlled press and a number of monthly or irregular journals each with limited print runs. Although many people in the country do read newspapers, they are not the essential source for finding out what is happening in the country. Cubans might also monitor official government and Communist Party news, views and events. Cuba has no 'free press' as such, or any known oppositional or underground press. Many Cubans watch the TV news, listen to the radio but most of all they continually discuss news, views and gossip with each other in public and private spaces. Talking, chatting and discussing are key Cuban activities. The grapevine is rapid. There is as yet no mobile phone culture, indeed 'phones themselves were conspicuous by their absence until 2000/1 when a new externally funded public system of public street phones was introduced.

In such a climate I would argue that song texts function in Cuba as newspaper articles and columns do in the cultures of many other countries. Song lyrics can be read as a barometer of Cuban life and music as the major cultural marker of radical and historic change on the island. When I discussed this with Cesar 'Pupy' Pedroso, one of the founders and main songwriters of Los Van Van, one of Cuba's top groups for over thirty years, he told me he and the groups' leader Juan Formell 'compose around an anecdote we have heard ... writing things about contemporary issues like a newspaper ...'[6]

Such songs take a pragmatic and often witty approach to describing changes in Cuban everyday life. The themes of songs (like Cuban jokes) can be taken as an indication of the preoccupations of Cubans on the street, what they are thinking and what is happening. Pupy's response to where he got themes for hit songs from was typical of other Cuban *timba* musicians I have spoken to:

> The majority of the time my songs are products of stories, of real life events that I hear about through conversations in my neighbourhood, with my neighbours. In every area, every building people talk and gossip, that's the way they reflect on the way of life of the place they live in and Cuba in general ...

Asked about hit songs on the 2000 Grammy winning Los Van Van album *Llegó Los Van Van*, such as *Mi Chocolate se Fue* (My Chocolate Girl has Gone) he explained:

> It's a story I have heard over and over again ... [a Cuban girl abandoning her boyfriend for an Italian and going to live in Italy with him. Apocryphal stories talk of this as a real story and of the girl being held in a cage by her Italian lover] ... And things like *El negro esta cocinando* (The Black Guy Is Cooking) [about a divorced black guy who has various women calling round at different times of the day, cooking and sharing different courses for each of them] came out my own life ... I wanted to write it full of double meaning because Cubans are very picaresque and I love that humour.7

Groups like Los Van Van and N.G. La Banda maintain their position as top groups in terms of continued popularity with the Cuban public by continually creating new 'hit' songs and trying them out in live performance, in particular the Salon Rosada Beny Moré to a majority black working class audience. According to Pedroso, Van Van have remained at the top for thirty years because: 'The Cuban public are very demanding and they give you a lot of oxygen: they demand a new hit every 5–6 months and if you don't produce one then you go out of fashion fast. You've got to be constantly creating with the dancer in mind.'

La Charanga Habanera Incident

A watershed moment of the 1990s Cuban *timba* music scene which took place in 1997 when the boom was at its height shows the tension that existed for the government benefiting from *timba* music but no longer in control of it. At an evening concert to mark one of the high points of the country's hosting of the Fourteenth World International Festival of Youth and Students, leading group La Charanga Habanera, officially invited by the organizing Union of Young Communists. They made their arrival at La Piragua open-air stage on the famous Malecón promenade super-star style by dis-embarking from a helicopter 'borrowed' from the Cuban military. Going out live on Cuban TV and filmed simultaneously by several foreign TV crews, Charanga Habanera performed a selection of their outspoken dance songs. These featured witty ironic lyrics, a hedonistic celebration of street concerns of the times, involving among other things, 'safe' sex (*Usa condom*), money and tourism (*La Bola*), choreographing their performance with their famously outrageous pelvic routines complete with suggestive hand gestures.[8]

Publicly challenging more than a few taboos, one song boasted about marijuana smoking, while another made ironic allusion to Fidel Castro ('the big green mango who refuses to fall from the tree'); and one of the band dropped his trousers. They also encouraged the Cuban people unofficially enjoying the concert from behind barriers, to leap over them to take the opportunity of fostering personal acquaintance with Youth Festival delegates.

The state's response was to ground the group for six months, to allow the band to 'evaluate their artistic projection and image'. During this period Charanga Habanera leader David Calzado appeared on television to offer what amounted to a public apology and the group split. The freedom of Charanga Habanera and others celebrating materialist and individualist values over any revolutionary ones that spoke to a new generation of mostly black Cubans, was over. They could no longer easily make the music they wanted and perform it as they saw fit.[9]

The state's official response to the event made it obvious that Fidel Castro's original cultural dictum of the early 1960s, 'within the revolution everything, outside the revolution nothing', still holds. Had the concert not gone out live on television and the incident not been reported in the international press, Charanga Habanera might have got away with it.

I would argue that Charanga Habanera and the *timba* music of the 1990s might have been perceived as subversive to the status quo at a far earlier date. However, during the early 1990s economic crisis, music and the tours of many musicians became a potent source of foreign income for the regime. This put musicians in a very strong position as one of the island's few elites. Events such as the Charanga Habanera one suggest that for a time musicians were outside the control of the cultural bureaucrats, until the economy started to swing back beginning in 1997 when this incident took place.

Timba Dance Music

In Havana in 1999, 2000 and 2001 I found myself dancing to much music whose subject matter made direct reference to the Afro-Cuban popular religion Santería religion, notably N.G. La Banda's *Papa Changó*; Los Van Van's, *Ay Díos*, *ampárame*; and Orquesta Revé's *Papa Eleggua*. Talking to Cuban colleagues and friends about the theme I was soon directed to Adalberto y Su Son's, *Y que tu quieres que te den?* (What Do You Want From Them?); Charanga Habanera's, *Estano ateos* and Dan Den's, *Viejo Lazaro*.[10]

While the subject of the present popularity of Santería among both black and even white Cubans is not possible within this chapter, it is important to recognize that it is a syncretic religion whereby the *orishas* of Santería are twinned with Catholic Saints. Most significantly formal and informal worship of the gods of Santería is primarily through music, percussion, song and dance and is therefore musician driven. In the 1990s many musicians showed themselves openly to be followers of Santería, wearing their Saint's colours on stage, emblematic beads and often a gold amulets.

Santería practices first openly entered Cuban popular music through usage of non-sacred sets of sacred *batá* drums. Everyday Santería worship needs no church, nor even a *babaloa* priest of the religion. People can talk to their own *orisha* wherever they want to, in their own home, before their own shrine or simply anywhere at any time. According to J. L. Cortés:

> The ideology of the songs comes from the neighbourhoods where over fifty-per-cent of the day everyday has something to do with religion and that present cannot be separated from the music one makes and if the people believe in that then of course they bring the force of that belief into the music. You can't make dance music without it having something to do with religion, that's for sure ...[11]

A revealing scene concerning Santería occurs in the Wim Wenders documentary, *Buena Vista Social Club*, when singer Ibrahím Ferrer welcomes the camera into his then home in Old Havana. A sunflower (*girasol*, in Santería the symbol of Oludummare, creator of the world) is first seen on the kitchen table. Ferrer then points to a small shelf in the corner of the room, which bears a sculptural effigy to

Saint Lazarus, known as the *orisha* Babalu-Ayé, his wounds covered up by tradition by a lace and material cape. Ferrer, who carries an African staff associated with Lazarus given to him by his mother, explains his relationship with the African gods:

> I believe strongly in my Lazarus ... He's the one who opens the paths, he helps the disempowered ... I place flowers for him ... light a candle ... give him honey ... perfume ... rum. We Cubans can maybe give thanks maybe to Him up there that we are like this because if we'd followed the way of possessions we'd have disappeared a long time ago.[12]

There is a high percentage of Santería practitioners among musicians. Many have shrines in their studios and homes. Indeed, Los Van Van often joke in improvised parts of a song that they number three *babaloa* priests in their ranks. Within a long history of songs for the *orishas*, the 1990s saw a notable increase in songs to the gods, reflecting a shift in Santería worship into the public domain. I would argue it is today as much lifesaver as its antecedents had been for slaves and descendents prior to the revolution. Many Cubans felt their lives were falling apart in the early 1990s and embraced beliefs of one kind or another to nurture their everyday strength and hope. According to José Luís Cortés:

> It has become much stronger because the Cuban people have had a lot of problems with the actual Cuban system because of the position of Cuba in the world with the blockade and everything: the lack of money, of medicines, of food. Human beings have to take refuge in something to calm their anxieties ... since the Pope came it's all got much easier because before that you could not be in the party [i.e. Communist Party] or take a [government] position and also be religious ... All popular music is linked to religion because the force of Cuban music is in its rhythms and the rhythms have everything to do with Afro-Cuban religious music ... you are playing dance music and even salsa with those rhythms and the people begin to dance as if they are dancing to the Saints.

Papa Changó

While the lyrics of each song about Santería merits detailed discussion, I will mention only two songs here: N.G. La Banda's *Papa Changó* and Los Van Van's *Soy todo: Ay Díos, Ampárame*. The lyrics of *Papa Changó* are written in the first person with someone addressing Changó (the *orisha* of drums, virility, music), thanking him for good luck and asking for protection against any bad luck that may befall them. The chorus asks Changó to send a ray of light as a sign he is there, appealing for light and strength. During the transition into the *montuno* section belief and love are expressed. The second section itself is a symbolic enactment (with gestures when danced) of the cleansing ritual Santería adherents follow. The outcome is *tremenda salvación* (huge consolation).[13] This text contrasts with everyday Cuba where since 1959 people have had to trust the leadership and government Fidel Castro. In some Cuban popular street mythology Castro himself is spoken of as a Changó figure.

The lyrics of Los Van Van's *Soy Todo* (I Am Everything) also referred to by the key *montuno* chorus phrase, 'Ay Díos, Amparame' ('Oh God Protect Me'), are by Cuban contemporary poet Eloy Machado.[14] Sung in the first person it is a poetic evocation of Santeria and Cuba through detailed naming of Gods and Cuban musical genre. Individual concerns are eventually sublimated into those of the group, Los Van Van and then all Cuba. In the passionate liturgy-like *montuno* section the performance involves Santeria ritual actions as part of the dance. There is a dramatic moment when to show faith involving the lead singer sinks down into a kneeling Santería pose as blessings are asked for and the call is given: 'Oh God, protect me'.

Jineterism

The other major *timba* theme concerns the impact of tourism and shifting social relationships, notably the emergence of *jinetera* culture. Cubans need to acquire dollars to obtain material goods unavailable for the local *peso*. In the words of Manolín (El medico de la salsa), 'You've got to keep *arriba de la bola'* (You've got to keep on top of the dollar) (*bola* being slang for dollar, also 'the game', meaning life).[15] Unless receiving dollars through the overseas diaspora, one of the only ways for Cubans to acquire dollars is through official or unofficial, formal or informal contact with tourists. In the early 1990s Cubans experienced strict rationing of even the most basic foodstuffs. Today although basic rations are guaranteed but the most honest Cuban has to somehow get hold of dollars to buy shoes never mind luxuries.

The term *jineterism* comes from the etymology of horse racing, the common understanding of the term, which embraces a gamut of Cuban cultural attitudes, activities and beliefs, is of someone 'riding' tourists to make dollars fall from their pockets. Many translate *jineterism* as prostitution and indeed there are many selling their bodies in one way or another for money or gifts in kind. However it is a much more complex and insidious culture, an attitude born out of desperation in many cases. It's a term that not only pinpoints Cubans who have direct contact with tourists but more generally an attitude fostered by the fact that Cuba's two-tier financial system has effectively created an apartheid in the country (those with/without access to dollars/tourists) driving Cubans to improvise ways of using their talents to obtain the money they need. *Jineterism* as the 'charging' for services of one kind or another, has filtered down to permeate much Cuban thinking. The 'jinetera' culture of the 1990s was essentially pre-figured by the money coming in from 3 million Miami-Cuban families, which produces distortions to the internal economy.

Noted Cuban folklorist and writer Rogelio Furé believes *jineterism* dates right back to the sixteenth century when Havana serviced the Flota de la Indias and major shipping between Europe and the Americas. Provisions and water and time ashore, with Havana inhabitants providing the *fiesta* was the Havana economy way before sugar or tobacco.[16]

Songs on Themes of Tourism and *Jineterism*

Of the various songs that have dealt with the impact of foreign tourism and ensuing sexual liaisons on the relationships between Cubans themselves, I can briefly mention only two contentious examples here: N. G. La Banda's *La Bruja* and Charanga Habanera's *El temba*.[17]

La Bruja brought down the wrath of the Cuban Women's Federation (FMC) on the head of its composer Cortés – apparently the organization's first ever complaint about a misogynistic song's lyrics, following formal public debate by the FMC on sex and tourism beginning in 1995. From a 'macho' viewpoint, it tells of a man leaving home alone looking for his partner, who has gone out in a tourist taxi to Buena Vista area of Havana leaving him to his own devices. The language use (turi-taxi) and the location intimates that she has gone off to service a tourist. Foregoing any critique of what might drive a woman make such a decision, the song apportions blame: 'you think you're an artist ... you exchanged my love / for cheap amusements / the price of the spirit / cannot be auctioned ...' Depicting women as unfeeling and predatory, the *montuno* improvisation leaves little to the imagination, 'That's why I compare you to a witch / with no feelings / a crazy woman / (sexually) frenzied ...', heaping insults, albeit playfully, on the woman, telling her to get on a broomstick.[18]

By the time the song was challenged it was already extremely popular. Cortés raised the polemic by defending, insisting it was based on genuine personal experience and its intention to reassure Cuban women of their value. The irony is that the bodies of the women addressed in the song are the very same bodies that attracted tourists into the clubs where *timba* bands like N. G. La Banda were playing and making their money. *Jineterism* culture was and is directly linked to tourism and *timba*. In the 1990s, tourists saw the popularity of downtown venues where they could meet Cubans through dancing. But such venues closed down after tourism gained a bad name in 1997 when far too many articles in the foreign press focused on Cuba as a sex-tourism destination and the city was effectively 'cleaned up' to safeguard the reputation of 'new' Cuban tourism. The important point here is the fact that *La Bruja* voiced the deep and complex contradictions of the moment for all concerned.

There can be no doubt that the feelings expressed (the frustrations of the Cuban male at his economic powerlessness to stop his own women looking to foreigners for their future rather than to him) are genuine enough. However, it follows the pattern of nineteenth- and twentieth-century traditions of romantic song and *son* lyrics, including *bolero*, in Cuba and throughout the Spanish speaking world, by which the blame, failure and betrayal for love and relationships is always laid squarely at the feet of capricious women. The underpinning ideology of such songs is almost always phallocentric – women simultaneously objects of desire and derided for their sexual availability.

The classic *El cuarto de Tula* (revived in the 1990s by the Buena Vista Social Club) depicts women who 'service' men as having insatiable sexual appetites. The difference with *timba* is that while *Tula* was an evergreen classic of veteran musicians performing abroad, *La bruja* was/is being performed while the situation it depicts was/is happening as an everyday occurrence. It mirrors a new and complex set of gender relations in Cuba: at once a misogynistic male lament, an account of jineterism, and a celebration of women and their newly found 'powers'.

El temba by La Charanga Habanera (1996) is a song on the same theme which controversially challenged revolutionary values, as a timely parody of *Tengo* (I Have) a famous poem by Cuba's national black poet Nicolas Guillén. Initially written as a tribute to revolutionary achievements and celebrate how the revolution had banished the 'apartheid' of the 1940s and 1950s when North American cultural values and tourism meant an effective colour bar. The chorus advises girls to look for sugar daddies to maintain them (implicitly the revolution cannot fulfil this function). The song's subversiveness stems from the implicit inference that in the 1990s with the dollar and tourist enclaves, the gains Guillén celebrated have been eroded.

Music Driven by Women Dancers:
The Body as Convertible Currency

All of these songs were performed in venues for a dancing public where the lyrics were danced out in the musics shifting polyrhythms and structures which themselves form and mirror coital narratives. The most obvious essential connection between *timba* dance and tourism is the focus on the sexual body of the woman. I would argue that firstly the dancing 'drives' both music and musicians; and secondly that this dancing maps the complexities and contradictions of the new 'tourist' dollar economy.

The most significant development was the movement centre stage of the body of the solo female dancer. In contrast to previous styles, (including *son*, *casino*, *salsa* and *rueda*), the *despelote* and *tembleque* movements for *timba* dancing shifted away from couple dancing with the man leading, to the woman's dancing body driving the whole show the man effectively an accessory to her movements, even if simultaneously the objective. In the 1980s this was first visibly symbolized by the prominence of *despelote* dancing – women gyrating their pelvis and bottom often with their man standing behind so as to be sexually stimulated in the process. In the 1990s this developed into the *tembleque* which sees the female dancer simulate moves showing the sensual pleasures of the female body with intense rotation and swirling of the pelvic area with shuddering movements. The implicit suggestion is self-pleasuring. According to Cortés:

> Cuban dancing has always been sexual and exaggerated from rumba through, the movements are very sensual and can be quite astonishing … but I think it is getting a bit confused … the women dance and get the attention of the macho and it is exaggerated … you see them move so fast and some with their mouths open and tongues hanging out [from rumba and folklore movements] … there's a humour there … but sometimes it's incredible and you see women dancing and it's as if they were making love …[19]

I would argue that many performances of *timba* during this period represented a symbolic exchange of Cuban women by Cuban society, represented by the Cuban musicians on stage and dancers in the audience, with non-Cubans, represented by the foreigners in the dancing audience. Cuban women dancing in between the two groups of men (and women) in front of the stage become the symbolically transacted body, the tourist trophy. Indeed, in the mid 1990s there were several reported cases of evenings when in a spirit of playfulness Cuban groups like N. G. La Banda invited Cuban women up on stage. In competitive fashion they offered a prize to the one chosen by the audience as the 'best' dancer, a symbolic 'auction' of a woman and her 'wares' to the highest bidder. While on the one hand this was seen by all those involved as a bit of irresistible fun, it was heavily discouraged when it resulted in adverse publicity. This and other incidents reported in the foreign press resulted in the closing of various key venues in 1997 during a general clamp down.

Gender Contradictions

This focus on the solo female body is full of contradictory gender messages for all concerned. On one level the female body becomes a 'convertible currency'. At the same time there are interpretations, that due to pragmatics, paradoxically see this as representing 'new' choices for Cuban women. While equal in terms of educational and economic opportunities, in reality most Cuban women are bound to classic gender roles by both public and private practices. The fact that in the 1990s Cuban women could 'sell' or 'exchange' their friendship and their bodies if they liked to foreigners who might reward them with attention, material goods and dollars, paradoxically gave them new status and independence. In many Havana neighbourhoods, it is admired rather than frowned upon if a woman or man is seen to be working within *jinetera* culture. Their initiative is often celebrated as such a liason can only benefit families strapped for any cash never mind access to foreign currency. The deep ambiguities of such opinion cannot be explored here but it is not clear if this is empowerment, that is, proud Cuban women making their own choice; complete alienation; or a confusion of both. It seems the experience is as confusing for men. Various songs express how it is the Cuban male who is now left lamenting waiting for his woman to come home. The lyrics are playful but their subject matter is totally new and relevant particularly as this is happening within a society imbued with patriarchal values. It seems unlikely that without a shift in gender ideology, economic and social liberation the position of women in Cuban society will change. I have so far not yet come across any women singing songs about the experiences of *jineterism* from their perspective.[20]

Conclusions

In this chapter, I have argued that themes of *timba* music in 1990s Cuba voice the impact of dramatic changes in Cuban society as a result of the transformed mixed economy and socially divisive dollar tourism. I chart the impact of such change directly to aspects of Afro-Cuban culture. Dance music and the performances of high profile groups, hitherto regarded as 'entertainment' challenged the status quo. The lyrics of dance songs referencing religion and social behaviour within a popular culture context act as chronicles of social change, serving as an important barometer of everyday Cuban life on an island with a fully controlled media.

Musical changes are driven by both musicians and dancers with the sexualized solo female body (as opposed to that of the couple) becoming the central 'object' focus of dance music. The female body becomes the site of symbolic exchange between Cuba(n) and foreign men. I suggest that *jinetera* culture as expressed through music has implications for traditional gender roles.

Notes

1. I am grateful to The British Academy 2001 for a small-research grant to support research in Cuba. Self-funded research was undertaken 1978/9, 1989, 1999, 2000, 2001, 2002. Research in Cuba includes interviews and conversations with numerous musicians and numerous people in the music business (not all mentioned here), including as cited: Cesar 'Pupy' Pedroso, Havana (November 2000; February 2001); José Luís Cortés, Havana (November 2000; February 2001). Also, Silvio Rodríguez; Pablo Milanés; Juan de Marcos González, Ibrahím Ferrer, Cachaíto López, Pablo Menéndez, and

Omara Portuondo. I would like to thank those who enabled me to present preliminary findings as papers at the ESEM conference in memory of John Blacking, Queens University, Belfast, September 2000; in Havana at the Casa de las Americas Conference of September 2000; at ILAS London in November 2000; the Latin American Seminar, ILAS, University of London, November 2001; in teaching seminars at the University of Durham (March 2002), Glasgow RAMAD (April 2002), IPM Liverpool University (2000, 2001, 2002), the Department of Anthropology at the University of Manchester (October 2002), and in public lectures as part of Glasgow Si Cuba! Festival (2000 and 2001). I would also like to thank John Street, Simon Frith and Martin Cloonan for reading a first draft and making pithy comments.

2. Sarduy, *Introduction to AfroCuba*, LAB 1993.
3. *Scotsman*, 19 July 2000, S2, p. 14
4. Interview Pablo Milanés. See also 'The dark side of the island', Jan Fairley, *Guardian*, Thursday 20 May, 1999, S2, p. 12/13.
5. Interview Cortés, November 2001, studio, Havana.
6. Interview Pedroso, November 2000, rehearsal, Havana.
7. Interview Pedroso, February 2001, rehearsal, Havana.
8. Fairley, *Scotsman*, 2 November 2001, S2, p. 4).
9. In 2001, after playing a concert in XXXX, which was ill-advised given Cuban foreign policy, the XXXX, led by XXXX (who brought together the Buena Vista Social Club for Ry Cooder and Nick Gold of World Circuit) were officially 'grounded' for six months to a year. This meant that they were not granted visas as a group (although they could travel abroad as individuals). XXXX joined the original members of the *Buena Vista Social Club* for Buena Vista Real concerts in Mexico in May 2002. PARAGRAPH CENSORED.
10. I would argue that the habit of Cuba's top groups writing songs on the same theme, and responding to each others new songs through constant inter-referencing in both music and lyrics of each others work, can be seen as another form of the popular Cuban competitive tradition rooted in the old Spanish tradition of *desafío* (verse challenge). This inter-textual referencing is the heart the competitive performing practices of Cuba's top bands.
11. Interview with Cortés, Havana, 11 February 2001.
12. See the film *Buena Vista Social Club* directed by Wim Wenders, a Road Movies production in association with Kintop Pictures and ARTE, 1999.
13. Interview with Cortés, Havana, 11 February 2002. *Papa Changó* see N.G. La Banda CD, recommended listening.
14. See *Van Van 30 aniversario*, recommended listening.
15. See Manolín, el Médico de la Salsa, *Para mi gente*.
16. Personal conversation, Havana, 24 May 2002. See also p. 37 *Tambor*, Rogelio

Martínez Furé, in *Essays on Cuban Music: North American and Cuban Perspectives*, ed. Peter Manuel (1991), University Press of America. For the *jinetera* theme in contemporary Cuban literature see Luís Manuel Garcia, *Habanecer, Cuento* (1990), de las Americas Premio; Daniel Chavarría (2002) *Adios Muchachos* (Editorial Letras Cubanas). See also the film *Tropicola* made by US independent film maker Steve Fagin, with US-Cuban production.

17. See N. G. La Banda, *The Best of N. G. La Banda*, Hemisphere 7243 5 21391 2 5, 1999; for *El temba* I have only a pirate cassette but it came out in Havana around 1995.

18. Textual analysis is extremely illuminating, particularly for performance recordings. One song that sums up the subject more playfully and with complex inter-textuality with Cuban popular culture is Los Van Van's *Temba, Tumba Timba* from their Grammy award winning album *Llegó Los Van Van*, Havana Caliente Atlantic, 83227–2, 1999 (see also Fairley, forthcoming).

19. Cortés, interview Havana 11 February 2001.

20. *Jineterism* as a culture is taken as a necessity by most Cubans who spend their lives bartering and exchanging things to get everything they need, from screws to cement to food (see Fairley forthcoming).

References

Fairley, J. (1985), 'Annotated Bibliography of Latin American Popular Music with Particular Reference to Chile and to Nueva Canción', in Middleton, R. and Horn, D. (eds), *Popular Music 5: Continuity and Change*, Cambridge : Cambridge University Press, pp 305–56.

—— (1999), 'Ibrahím Ferrer: Rejuvenating Cuba at 72', *Classic CD*, June, pp. 78–82.

—— (1999), 'Cuba Roots', *Scotsman*, 23 October, S2, pp. 18–19.

—— (1999), 'The Dark Side of the Island', *Guardian*, Thursday 20 May, S2, pp. 12–13.

—— (1999), 'All-Singing but Unsung', *Sunday Herald*, 21 November, S2, p. 4.

—— (2001), 'Just Havana Wonderful Time', *The Herald*, Monday April 16, p. 11.

—— (2001), 'The Salsa House Rules', *Scotsman*, 2 November, S2, p. 4.

—— (2001), 'Cuban Polish', *Sunday Herald*, 4 November, S2, p. 8. (forthcoming), 'Dancing to Cuban *Timba* Music in the 1990s', in *Popular Music and Dance*, Special Issue of *Popular Music*.

Recommended Listening

Calzado, David y La Charanga Habanera (n.d.), *Tremendo delirio*, Universal Magic Music FMD 76087.

Cooder, Ry (1987), *Buena Vista Social Club*, World Circuit.

Los Van Van (1999), *Van Van 30 aniversario*, Caribe Productions 9555.

Los Van Van, *Llegó Los Van Van* (1999), Havana Caliente Atlantic, 83227–2.

Manolín, el Médico de la Salsa (1995), *Para mi gente*, Caribe Productions, CD9472.

Mazurre, Ileana and Aaron Vega, (nd), *Van Van empiezó la fiesta!* Video ICAIC, Cuba.

N. G. La Banda (1999), *The Best of N. G. La Banda*, Hemisphere 7243 5 21391 2 5.

Varela, Carlos (1993), *Monedas al aire*, Qbadisc QB 9010.

Varela, Carlos (nd), *En Vivo*, Discomedi Blau DM 227 02.

–5–

Chindo Music:
Creating a Korean Cultural Paradise

Keith Howard

January 1984, 7.30am: I woke to the whispers of children. They were poking holes in the new paper covering the wooden lattice frame of the door, trying to see in. This was the first time in living memory that a European had visited Sop'o village, and I was staying as a guest in the old people's meeting house, the *noin tang*, built in a traditional style with doors that doubled as windows. The children crouched on the wooden veranda outside; I had been sleeping under a quilt on the heated floor. I had struck a mutually beneficial deal: in the mornings I was to teach village children English, and in the evenings members of the local percussion band would teach me their music. Before meeting the children for the first time, I collected water from the communal well three hundred meters away. Breakfast was prepared in the mud-floor kitchen.

Sop'o[1] is located in Chindo, an island county at the south-western tip of the Korean peninsula stretching from 125°37′ west to 126°23′ east, and from 34°07′ south to 34°34′ north.[2] This was where I conducted fieldwork between 1982 and 1984.[3] Within Korea, Chindo is a place well known for its arts, and particularly for music. Indeed, Chindo has more musical Intangible Cultural Assets – a designation made by government agencies to preserve and promote performance arts and crafts – than any other Korean county. This, then, is a story of how music has become the lynchpin in the reinvention of Chindo as a cultural paradise. Chindo has become a national repository for Korea's heritage, and is now promoted to both national and international audiences.

Thirty years ago, 105,195 people lived in the county; by the time I first visited, this had dropped to around 80,000. Most of the population struggled to make a living tending small agricultural plots, although several thousand worked as casual fishermen. Farming, as elsewhere in Korea, valued rice production most highly, but green (spring) onions grown in dry fields (*pat*) were a cash crop, with a few orchards to the east and small tobacco plantations in the centre. Around Sop'o there were extensive salt flats, and laver (*kim*; porphyra sp.) and kelp (*miyŏk*; undaria pinnatifida) production was, as in most other coastal villages, a supplementary source of income.[4] In 1982, Chindo remained isolated, reached by a ferry at the end of a 50 km unmetalled road from the nearest mainland town, Haenam, or by larger boats plying between the port of Mokp'o and outlying southern islands. I had initially stayed to the west of the island in Inji village, an hour by bus from the four contiguous villages that together form the central township of Chindo-ŭp. Sop'o was twenty-five minutes further along the dusty track.

Back in the 1980s, my research, on music and shamanism, concerned the interface between the old and the new. Chindo proved an ideal location. Few foreigners had visited this corner of Korea, and the outside world was still perceived as very distant. The journey from Korea's capital, Seoul, still took a whole day, although old people remembered the route taking four days before mainland roads were tarred. Some old people, in a legacy of the colonial period that ended 40 years earlier, assumed I must speak Japanese.[5] Today, though, things are very different. After a rural exodus repeated throughout Korea, the population has shrunk to around 40,000.[6] A cantilever bridge joins the island to the mainland (built by a British company jointly with the Korean conglomerate Hyundai), and new roads mean that both Inji and Sop'o are less than 10 minutes from the township. Buses run all the way to the capital, Seoul. Chindo has become a tourist destination. Circular routes are marked out on the island, and tourist buses are a familiar sight. Each Saturday, the local government runs its own tours. Hotels and nightclubs vie for customers in both Chindo-ŭp and in Nokchin, the village at the island end of the bridge to the mainland.

A brief history

In Korea, the pace of rural change has been incredible. At the end of the Korean War in 1953, the Republic of Korea (South Korea) was a virtual economic disaster. Corruption was rife, and average per capita GNP was below that of the then East Pakistan (now Bangladesh). By the mid-1990s, after 30 years of economic growth averaging around 8 per cent annually, Korea was the eleventh largest global economy. Development involved new industry, and rural communities stagnated, although a government-sponsored New Village Movement (the *Saemaŭl undong*) did much to improve matters in the 1970s and 1980s.

On Chindo, the island had been divided where saltwater estuaries met the mountains. Isolated Chisan district to the west – where both Inji and Sop'o are situated – was home to five gigantic horse ranches until 1906; until the mid-1980s, the only land link with the rest of the island was a single mud track that clung perilously to a mountainside. Imhoe and Kogun districts in the south and east were the main agricultural areas, but until the mid-1960s, the sea penetrated to the centre of the island, virtually cutting them off from the central island township of Chindo-ŭp. In the 1930s, during the Japanese colonial occupation of Korea, mud and stone roads began to be cut, and the prevalent ox carts began to be replaced with a few buses. In the 1960s, the saltwater estuaries began to be drained and reclaimed, creating large swathes of new paddy land. In 1973, building on a tradition of communal teams known as *pumashi* and *ture* that until the 1950s eased agricultural work, and replacing American-inspired '4–H' clubs, the New Village Movement offered free cement to villages prepared to build access roads. Many Chindo village communities complied, receiving further cement the next year to construct communal buildings, meeting halls, and shops and storehouses for agricultural co-operatives. Corrugated tin roofing was then offered at highly subsidized prices, to obliterate the thatch that was considered to harbour disease-ridden rats and insects. Undermining local autonomy, New Village leaders were trained in new agricultural practices. The state provided fertilisers, subsidized the purchase of farm equipment, and encouraged a switch to high yield versions of crops such as 'unification rice'.[7] The island was joined to the national electricity grid in 1979, and wind-up telephones were replaced with modern equipment in 1985.

My story, though, must begin in more distant times. A local book, *Okchu ŭi ŏl* (1982: 81) argues that aboriginal groups inhabited Chindo some 100,000 years ago. Neolithic remains found on the island include 168 dolmens and some menhirs (Kim and Im 1968: 73–116). Pottery shards and metal tools indicate Bronze Age settlement. *Okchu ŭi ŏl* (1982: 19), gives the date 537 as the founding date of Chindo as a county but the earliest credible text mentioning the main island, as Okchu, and its position south of the mainland county of Muan, dates to 757 AD, the sixteenth year of King Kyŏngdŏk's reign. Okchu has sometimes been interpreted as a reference to the high quality of the island's agricultural land (Mikyung Park, 1985: 88). We can surmise that Chindo was already of strategic importance, since the channel between island and mainland was an access route and place of refuge between the Yellow Sea, Korea's eastern seaboard, and Japan. Although Chindo is not mentioned in surviving documents from the time, a garrison in the neighbouring county to the east, Wando, is, when Chang Pogo (died 841) was appointed in 828 or 829 as Grand Envoy to protect the coastline from marauding Chinese slave traders (Eikemeier, 1980: 16–17).

Chindo rose to prominence in the thirteenth century. This was a time of military rule, when three units, known collectively as the Three Elite Patrols (*Sambyŏlch'o*), were formed to undertake police and combat functions. Maintained by the public purse, the Patrols were essentially a private army used to shore up the regimes of Ch'oe Chunghŏn and his son Ch'oe U. In 1232 the Mongols invaded Korea, using the pretext of the murder of an envoy who had been visiting the peninsula. Knowing the Mongols' reputed dislike of the sea, the

Korean court was moved to Kanghwa, an island to the west of Seoul. Although Ch'oe sued for peace, the third Elite Patrol, made up entirely of men who had escaped Mongol captivity, was charged with organizing guerrilla attacks on the foreign predators. Unrest continued over the next two decades. In 1254, the Mongols carried off more than 200,000 captives in an attempt to subdue the Koreans, and four years later, in 1258, the last of the Ch'oe dictators, Ch'oe Ŭi, was assassinated. A formal treaty with the Mongols was negotiated, and the crown prince (later King Wŏnjong) went to Beijing to meet the Mongol leader, Khubilai (later Khubilai Khan). A decade passed until in 1270, when finally feeling secure, the king ordered the assassination of the paramount military figure and the disso-lution of the remnants of the Elite Patrols. The Elite Patrols rebelled and, under General Pae Chungsŏn, set sail with Kanghwa residents in what legend says were '1,000 boats'. Moving south, they landed on Chindo and set up a putative state, using the sea once more as a defence against Mongol invasion, and imposing control on neighbouring islands and parts of the mainland. They built two island fortresses, Yongjang Sansŏng to the east and Namdo Sŏksŏng to the west to protect their flanks and, according to local accounts, set up their administrative headquarters in Hyanggyo, today's Tonji village. A combined Koryŏ and Mongol force laid siege for two years before some of the rebels escaped to Cheju Island further south, where they committed mass suicide in 1273 (Han, 1970: 168–70; Joe, 1972: 231–6). Adjacent to Hyanggyo, some captured rebels were, again according to local accounts, imprisoned in Oktae. A grave in Nonsudong marks where Wang On, a relative of Wŏnjong declared king by the rebels only to be murdered by the Mongols, is buried. A century later, Namdo Sŏksŏng was rebuilt to protect islanders from Japanese pirate raiders. The island administration was headquartered here between 1350 and 1437. Again, between 1488 and 1490 and under King Songjong, the fortress was rebuilt by the military.

Chindo famously came to prominence at the end of the sixteenth century; this, though, is the stuff of legends. In September 1597, the invading Japanese forces under Hideyoshi were supposedly outwitted in the strait between Chindo Island and the mainland (Han, 1970: 271–3; Eckert *et a.l.* 1990: 147–8). General Yi Sunshin (1545–98), recently reinstated as admiral to the depleted Korean fleet, marshalled a token dozen boats and retreated from some '300' Japanese vessels. He is said to have massed local women on top of Chindo's Manggŭm Mountain, and on two adjacent mainland mountains, Ongmae and Yudal. Another hill was covered in straw, as if large stocks of provisions had been laid in. It was the harvest full moon, and the women sang and danced through the night. The Japanese chased the Korean vessels but fearful that they had sailed into a trap, hurriedly tried to withdraw, only to be caught by an unfavourable current. Thirteen boats were sunk, and this began a rout that marked the end of six years' national struggle. At Pyŏkp'a, where ferries docked until the new bridge was opened, a stone tablet astride a turtle (signifying long life more than swimming ability) commemorates the battle. Recently, a more impressive memorial to Yi Sunshin has been erected at the mainland end of the bridge. The remains of mud fortification can still be detected on the three mountains.

During the Chosŏn dynasty (1392–1910), Chindo became a place of banishment for aristocracy who fell into disfavour. To what extent this reflects reality remains to be proved, but it is clear that many artists – people with high levels of education and an appreciation of literati culture – settled on the island. We know that is was commonplace for aristocrats banished from the court to find solace in the development of personal artistic talents, and this perhaps explains how, according to Chindo scholars, some 150 local artists have to date won national prizes. The most famous of these, Hŏ Yu (1809–93), used the pen name Soch'i ('Little Fool') and retired to a house known as *Ullim sanbang*, 'Forest of mist below the mountain'. The house is today preserved as a local monument (No. 51), beautifully situated between a lake and a wooded hillside. Aristocratic artists were influential in island governance, and Chun (1984: 13) sees an anti-government stance as a legacy of this history. However, until December 1997 almost everyone in the south-western Chŏlla province (of which Chindo is a part) consistently voted for the opposition, national political leadership residing in candidates from the south-eastern Kyŏngsang province. In the 1980s, there was a high-profile police and army presence on Chindo, ostensibly to protect islanders from North Korean infiltration.[8]

Preserving the Jewel Island

Okchu, the alternative name for Chindo, translates as 'Jewel Island' or, more precisely, as 'Jade Island'. If once this referred to agricultural land, today it is reinterpreted: Chindo is a place brimming with culture, a virtual heritage museum. This allows for contemporary nationalistic pride, and the downplaying of any reference to a territory formerly guarded as a virtual prison. The arts are matched to natural beauty – Britain's St Ives or Dartington transported to Asia – and in this, the isolation of Chindo, as an island separated from the mainstream of Korea, is paramount. Much of the county is today a government-designated coastal park and flowers, coastal features and plants are protected. Two trees are designated as National Natural Monuments (*Kukka chijŏng munhwajae kinyŏmmul*), a torreya nut tree (*pija namu*) in Sangman village, Imhoe district and a silver magnolia tree (*hubak namu*) on the outlying Kwanmae island. These are designated as numbers 111 and 212, and the former is over 100 years old but is said to still produce six bags of fruit each year. In 1980, the British Kennel Club was asked to help create a pedigree line for the prized Chindo dog, a kind of spitz with a curly tail designated Natural Monument No. 53 since 1962. For several years, no dog could be taken off the island, and breeding was confined to just eight local kennels until four generations of healthy stock had matured. A habitat frequented by swans in the island's northeast and an evergreen forest in the southeast are also designated, as numbers 101 and 107. Chindo also boasts one National Tangible Cultural Asset (*Kukka yuhyŏng munhwajae*),[9] a five-storey stone pagoda near Tunjŏn village, and two National Historic Sites, the fortresses mentioned above (Yongjang Sansŏng as No. 126 and Namdo Sŏksŏng as No. 127). In addition to Hŏ Yu's house, five buildings and stone sculptures are similarly designated by the provincial government (of South Chŏlla), chief amongst them a Buddhist temple, Ssanggyesa, at the edge of the evergreen forest. Founded 1200 years ago by the monk Tosŏn, the surviving main hall of the temple was last rebuilt in 1697.

None of this, of course, justifies the presence of this chapter in a book devoted to the music of islands. The Korean heritage industry, however, extends to performance arts, and here Chindo is particularly rich. There are four National Intangible Cultural Assets (*Kukkha muhyŏng munhwajae*):[10] *Kanggangsullae*, a women's song and dance associated with the legend of the invasion rout of 1597 (No. 8, appointed in 1965); *Namdo tŭl norae*, rice agriculture songs (No. 51, appointed in 1973); *Ssikkim kut*, a shaman ritual, more song and chant than anything else (No. 72, appointed in 1980); *Tashiraegi*, a song and drama entertainment associated with a second burial custom (No. 81, appointed in 1985). The 'intangible' designation does extend beyond performance arts to crafts, as is clear in one of the three Provincial Intangible Cultural Assets now appointed: *Chindo puk nori*, a dance with the barrel drum, distinguished from other Korean versions because two sticks are used to strike the drum (No. 18, appointed in 1987); *Man'ga*, funeral songs (No. 19, appointed in 1987); *Hongju*, a red herbal wine made from bracket fungus (No. 26, appointed in 1995). Six out of the seven appointments, then, have a lot to do with music. Note that the percussion band from Sop'o (and related bands from elsewhere on the island), has not been appointed; nonetheless, band musicians are key to *Namdo tŭl norae*, *Man'ga*, and *Chindo puk nori*, and continue to provide loud punctuation at any public performance event.

Let me rapidly discard the commonplace idea that preservation cannot possibly succeed with music (as argued by Nettl, 1985: 124–7; Blacking, 1987: particularly, 112). The Korean system has reached its fortieth anniversary, and music continues to be promoted alongside nature and man-made objects. Indeed, the system is mirrored by UNESCO's 'Living Human Treasures' policy, and has counterparts in Japan, Thailand, The Philippines, Romania, France, and Italy. UNESCO's policy was announced in 1993 at the 142nd session of the executive board (as 142 EX/18 and 142 EX/48), following extensive debates;[11] Korea has played a leading role in promoting the policy, convening and participating in seven training workshops between 1998–2001. In March 2001 UNESCO announced the appointment of nineteen representative 'Masterpieces of Oral and Intangible Heritage of Humanity', many with music at their core.[12]

In Korea, the preservation system was initiated in 1962 by the incoming government of the former military general, Park Chung Hee, with the passing of Law 961, the Cultural Asset Preservation Law (*Munhwajae pohobŏp*). Fifteen amendments had been made to the basic law by the end of 1990, and a major revision occurred in 1999 setting up new legal and operational frameworks. Law 961 argued that conservation would strengthen Korean identity; it would 'contrive the cultural progress of the people and contribute to the development of the human culture'. It represented the culmination of debates held in the National Assembly during the 1950s, which, in turn, had echoed a loose nationalist grouping – often referred to as the *munhwa undong* – that in the 1920s called for the conservation of indigenous culture.[13] In fact, legislation goes back further. In 1911, the governor-general of Korea's occupying force, Japan, passed a Temple Act (*Jisatsurei*), which required an inventory to be made of all movable and immovable properties in Buddhist sites considered worthy of preservation. By 1923, 385 relics and buildings were listed for protection (Maliangkay, 1999). Much of the legislation was left intact after liberation – forty-four wooden and 104 stone structures were still listed in South Korea in 1959 – but Article Two of the 1962 law rescinded all previous legislation.

Revisions to the law have strengthened the intangible. Amendment 2333 (1970) enhanced the recognition of those nominated to conserve performance arts and crafts and established measures to record and collect products. Amendment 2468 (1973) established a licensing system for crafts. The 1982 revisions legally required appointees to teach students, but provided scholarships and established provision for nominating groups rather than just individuals. The 1962 law had instructed scholars to undertake research, both to discover what remained of the old and to suggest strategies for local and national preservation. Scholars produced reports; one series, the Cumulative Investigation Reports on Important Intangible Cultural Assets (*Chungyo muhyŏng munhwajae chosa pogosŏ*), reached volume 165 in 1985. All of these were reprinted between 1994 and 1996, but later reports have not been made publicly available. Reports were submitted to a committee of experts (the *Munhwajae wiwŏnhoe*), which made recommendations to the appropriate government minister about what should be appointed.

Expert performers and craftsmen are nominated as 'holders' (*poyuja*) of each Asset; from 1974 onwards, until revisions introduced in 1999 allowed administrators to consider personal need, these received a stipend equivalent to roughly 50 per cent of the average monthly wage. 'Holders' teach 'primary students' (*chŏnsusaeng*) who receive smaller stipends, and may be supported by 'assistants' (*chogyo*) and/or 'future holders' (*poyuja hubo*). From November 1986, funding has been available to support preservation associations. An Office for Cultural Asset

Management (*Munhwajae kwalliguk*) predates the 1962 legislation by a few months, but functioned until 1999 to co-ordinate publications, performances, exhibitions, and the system's day-to-day running. In 1999, this was replaced by a Culture Office (*Munhwajae ch'ŏng*). By 2000, 114 Intangible Cultural Assets had been appointed, covering (in the order given in Korean publications) music, dance, dramas, plays and rituals, manufactures, and three Assets concerned with food preparation and martial arts. Chindo has a greater proportion of these than any other Korean county.

Musical Assets

Preservation is an act of cultural intervention; it is political in nature. As national discourse, scholars, journalists and activists seek icons of identity, and plan strategies for documentation, dissemination, and promotion.[14] As local artistic production, though, ownership is locally manipulated,[15] as artists jockey for advantage, assessing and appropriating extra-local models, or rejecting change in favour of maintaining the 'authentic' and the 'traditional'. The debate is rarely fair, although space precludes a full consideration here of the financial rewards that may await those who comply with national directives, or the financial penalties that may befall those who refuse to adapt and retain local uniqueness while others create more stage-friendly versions. Today, we see the results of such activity, but the positioning of actors, policy makers and promoters tends to be hidden, if not lost. Accounts, recordings, and publications consider primarily and sometimes solely only standardized versions. And Chindo performers today only talk in terms of revival and restoration, and in so doing square the past with the present; any mention of Hobsbawm's accusative notion of 'invented tradition' would be summarily dismissed (see Hobsbawn and Ranger, 1983).

In Chindo, the shaman ritual *Ssikkim kut*, Asset No .72, illustrates this. *Ssikkim kut* is an all-night ritual most commonly given to cleanse – taking its name from the verb *ssikkida*, 'to cleanse (someone) else' – the recently deceased and to take their soul to the other world. It was once found throughout the south-western coastal area. Performed by shamans known as *tan'gol* who inherit their rights to perform, rather than by Eliadian ecstatic shaman,[16] spirits are coaxed into action by a mix of chanting, instrumental music, and dance. From this performative mix, the Chindo Asset team have condensed the ritual into concert-length amalgams suitable for urban stages at home and abroad. They have embraced international touring, as programme notes from London (1985), Berlin (1985, 1999), Hong Kong (1989), and America (for example, 1994) prove. In 1976, the first modern ethnography of *Ssikkim kut* (Son Sŏkchu, 1980) documented it around the south-western coast, but lamented its considerable and perhaps terminal decline. Two later reports for the Office for Cultural Asset Management focussed on Chindo

(Chŏng *et al.*, 1979, 1983). Since the ritual's appointment as an Asset, the music and dance of the Chindo team has become the most regularly studied of any Korean shaman tradition. Ten articles devoted to it were published between 1980 and 1995, twice the number written about the next most popular ritual,[17] and eight MA and PhD dissertations were submitted on it between 1983 and 1994.[18]

The team has recorded several 'highlight' albums such as *Korea: Shamanistic Ceremonies of Chindo* and *Chin-do Ssit-kim-kut*. They have featured on numerous TV documentaries, and in two feature films. Two of the three 'holders' of the Asset, Pak Pyŏngch'ŏn (b.1933) and Kim T'aerye (1935–2002)[19] began secular performing careers with the encouragement of the now-defunct Space Theatre (*Konggan sarang*) in Seoul, working with Korean and foreign musicians, and recording for Sound Space, the Korean-Japanese duo of Sohn Ah Sun and Ichiro Shimizu. Their recordings include *Unrestrained Sound (Kuŭm tasŭrŭm)*, *Salp'uri*, *West End*, *Dancing Winds*, *Ahn Sook Sun – Kim Dae Ryeh Live Concert* and *Ahn Sook Sun – Park Byung Chon: Ascend*. Pak Pyŏngwŏn and Yi T'aebaek, two former *ajaeng* (bowed zither) students of the third 'holder' of the Asset, Ch'ae Kyeman (b. 1916), also perform widely in secular ensembles.

Pak Pyŏngch'ŏn, a ninth generation member of a shaman family (see Pak Chuŏn and Chŏng Chŏngsu, 1988: 137–66; Howard, 1989a: 193–200), has for 20 years run his own studio in Seoul, where he makes his living as a musician and dancer. When I first met him, in 1982, he had just returned from a European tour for which he was billed not as a shaman but as a performer of *puk ch'um*, the drum dance. I first saw him perform as a guest in Seoul performances of Chindo *Tashiraegi*, several years before this genre was appointed as an Asset. Later, he was appointed director of the nightly Korean music and dance show for tourists at Korea House, and in the late 1980s he briefly became music director at the outdoor performance space, *Sŏul Nori Madang*. His second wife, Chŏng Sukcha (1939–2000), widely regarded in Chindo as having a poor voice but from 1993 to her death 'assistant' within the team, took dancing roles in Asset team performances. In *Chesŏk kŏri*, a ritual scene dedicated to the Buddhist thunder-god Sakra devanam Indra incarnate as a monk (So Taesŏk, 1980: 75; Covell, 1983: 44–7), she donned a long cloak, a pointed paper hat, and a red sash: she became a monk. So, although the core of the ritual is vocal chanting, Chŏng shifted the focus to dance, introducing elements common to many secular dances (Van Zile, 2001: 159). These elements became standard in Asset ritual performances. She would stand on one leg while rotating, and prostrate herself on the ground in front of the altar, actions imitative of contemporary Seoul-based forms of *Sŭngmu* and *Salp'uri* (these are both nominated separately as Assets: No. 27, appointed in 1969, and No. 97, appointed in 1990). Note that neither Chŏng nor Pak is mentioned in the account of the 1976 ethnographic documentation; Pak is given a prominent position in the 1979 report, and both are foregrounded in the 1983 report.[20]

Pak's success in Seoul means that Chindo shaman paraphernalia is now routinely used in contemporary secular dance choreography. For example, paper streamers, *chijŏn*, represent money in rituals, and are used in dance movements to instruct a visiting spirit to dance, to rest, or to leave (see Howard 1991–2: 70–4) – symbolism lost in secular dance. Again, a long white cloth is used in rituals to represent the 'path of life'. It is used to neutralize evil deeds done by the newly dead (knots in the cloth are pulled out as the shaman chants) and as the road along that the dead must be taken on the journey to the other world; little symbolism remains in secular dancing.

Pak has helped revive other Chindo music and dance genres. The barrel drum dance, *Chindo puk ch'um*, for which Pak is an expert teacher, has gone through a number of incarnations locally. First, it was used in the revived rice-planting song set, *Namdo tŭl norae*, adding dance interest from a putative leader – a role taken by Pak himself – throughout the 1970s. In the early 1980s, appropriating an idea from Miryang in Korea's southeastern Kyŏngsang Province, the solo performer was replaced by an ensemble of five men. At the same time, women were trained in a novel but short-lived larger ensemble in Sŏkkyo Village. In 1985, this became a dance for several dozen Chindo performers at the eighteenth Festival of Asset 'holders' in Seoul. In 1987, when *Chindo puk ch'um* was appointed a Provincial Asset, two solo performers were nominated as 'holders', Pak Kwanyong (b. 1921) and Yang T'aeok (b. 1919). In 1993, the five-man ensemble was revived when three 'assistants' were appointed.

Pak was also involved when the majority of *Man'ga*, the funeral song set, was lifted from the Asset shaman ritual, rather than choosing songs local to any particular village, although: '… informants say that the songs … seem different in each village over a hill or across a brook' (Kwon Oh-sung, 1983: 59). The variety that Kwon indicates is preserved to some extent in tape recordings made for the state broadcasting service, KBS, and by folklore scholars such as Sukjae Yim (1903–95) in the 1960s. But, justification for using *Ssikkim kut* was found in supposed activities of the shaman fraternity, who, it was said, were at unspecified times in the past hired as pallbearers.[21] Nonetheless, the singers chosen to revive the genre had no shaman connections. The song set was first performed in 1978, by Inji villagers at the nineteenth National Folk Arts Contest (*Chŏn'guk minsok yesul kyŏngyŏn taehoe*) in Ch'unch'ŏn. The first recording, issued on LP in 1989, featured two Inji villagers, the 'holder' of the rice planting song Asset, Cho Kongnye (1930–97), and her daughter, Pak Tongmae (b. 1960).[22] This recording had been made for a folksong collection issued five years earlier, but was held back by disagreement. In my own recording of *Man'ga* (VDE-Gallo CD-756), Cho and Pak are joined by Cho's brother-in-law, Kim Hyanggyu (b. 1925) who, again with no shaman connections, was appointed 'holder' in 1987. *Man'ga* are now taken as representative both of island and national repertories. They are the basis for one

PhD and two MA dissertations.[23] They were chosen to represent Korea for an international conference on Asian funeral songs held in September 2001 in Chindo hosted by the Korean Musicological Association and organised by the National Center for Korean Traditional Performing Arts. Yet, only one song from the *Man'ga* set is common to local repertories recorded elsewhere in Chindo and on adjacent mainland county, and no *Man'ga* song matches funeral songs recorded on the adjacent island of Chodo (Kim, 2001: 139–64).

Although *Man'ga* are taken from the *Ssikkim kut* ritual, they are now arranged as a set of songs that follows the sequence of a traditional funeral, beginning with the dead's sorrowful and slow departure from home, moving through a set of *andante* processionals, as the bier is taken across fields, and ending at the grave, where the assembled mourners conclude by stamping down earth on top of the body. The slow-medium-fast sequence is common to many Korean music genres, including *sanjo* ('scattered melodies' for instrument and drum) and the literati instrumental suite *Yŏngsan hoesang*. A similar sequence in the revived north-western vocal genre, *Sŏdo sori*, Asset No. 29, has been aptly characterized by Joshua Pilzer (2003) as contemplation (sorrow and loss), transcendence (overcoming), and celebration (rebirth).

A second sequence is played out in the rice agricultural song set, *Namdo tŭl norae*, Asset No. 51. This starts brightly, with two earthy and lively songs depicting the March removal of seedlings from their protected spring beds and two songs from the May or June transplanting. Two slow weeding songs continue the set, before a faster song from the final weeding period, and a concluding fast triple-metered processional. This sequence is more evocative of the symphonies, sonatas and concerti of European art music, or of anthropological rites of passage (for which, see Van Gennep, 1960: 20–1; Turner, 1969: 34; Small, 1987: 16). Pak was also involved here, helping to assemble the eight songs and linking them through percussion interludes into a continuous 25-minute set. The set was performed by a team almost entirely from Inji village at the 1971 National Folk Arts Contest. In 1972, Pak accompanied the scholar Chi Ch'unsang to Inji as the latter examined rice agriculture songs from five areas for Volume 98 of the Cumulative Research Reports on Important Intangible Cultural Assets. In 1973, *Namdo tŭl norae* was appointed Asset No. 51. Two 'holders' were appointed as masters of the genre: Sŏl Chaech'ŏn (1906–1986) and Cho Kongnye. Sŏl was a central informant for Chi's report; Cho replaced the equally important but recently deceased Pak P'aengyŏn. Sŏl, perhaps part because of his humour and aristocratic bearing, quickly became a favourite for journalists; Shin Kyŏngnim's *Minyo kihaeng*, for example, contains a long episode devoted to Sŏl, with the memorable quote: 'I only sing as in the old days. I wouldn't dare change anything' (Shin 1985: 210).

Cho, in contrast, became a favourite of students, and was the main informant for five graduate dissertations, by Chŏng Aeyŏn (1982), Chang Kwio (1982), Yi

Chŏngnan (1984), Chin Hoesuk (1985) and Na Sŭngman (1990). She became a teacher to many, including the Seoul-based vocalist Kim Yongu (formerly with the group *Seulgidoong*): 'I went [to Cho] in the university vacations; I went for my own personal holiday. And when the semester started I returned to Seoul. Teacher Cho influenced me very greatly' (interview; June 1999).[24] During my fieldwork between 1982–4, I worked closely with Cho, but I was also able to record *Namdo tŭl norae* on 16 occasions outside of Inji village. The Asset set was by then considered representative, as is clear from near-contemporary accounts of it by Ruriko Uchida (1980) and Han Manyŏng (1983). Most of the songs I recorded matched the set in terms of both melodies and texts, but to the east some texts differed (for which, see Yi Sora 1985; Hŏ Ogin 1986: 284–90; Paek Sŏnghyŏn 1988: 134). In Sop'o, old people – clearly embarrassed when I asked to hear 'old songs' (*yennal norae*) rather than the songs now known throughout the nation – sang distinct and different texts and melodies.

The standardized form was promoted through training. Sŏl and Cho had a number of named students, all of whom rehearsed between the fifth and seventh of each month at the Chindo Cultural Centre. From 1986, the Centre housed a preservation society funded by the Office for Cultural Asset Management, and this organized rehearsals and handled performance contracts. Texts had been fixed, and skeleton melodies were allowed only specific ornamentation. Costumes and props were uniform, 'a set of farming clothes unique to Chindo' (Paek, 1988: 135), brown *hanbok* trousers dyed with crushed persimmon for men and blue skirts for women. Crowns of arrowroot were incorporated after pictures for the 1982 Chindo folklore compendium, *Okchu ŭi ŏl*, had been taken (see 1982: 5), perhaps to reflect the final song's description of collecting mulberry leaves. Plastic rice shoots were bought with lead bases to imitate planting and transplanting for staged performances. An ox festooned with ribbons appeared for *Kilkkonaengi*, although a banner or a pantomime ox might suffice on some occasions, supposedly to represent a prize once given by the landowner to the most hard-working tenant (personal interviews, but also reported in Uchida, 1980: 112). Some islanders believed the ox was a prize given by the work team to the farmer with the most productive land (personal interviews, but also reported in *Okchu ŭi ŏl* 1982: 153–4).

The *Namdo tŭl norae* set is impressive, much more so than the single strophic farming songs later appointed as Asset No. 84 from the mainland districts of Kosŏng and Yech'ŏn, or those from Okku and Naju promoted as possible competitors in the early 1980s.[25] The set still takes centre stage in school textbooks on Korean folksong (for example, Yun Igŭn 1999). Chindo has also managed to exert a monopoly over *Kanggangsullae*, Asset No. 8. The legend now associated with the genre, based on the 1597 rout of the Japanese navy, links to an alternative title, *Kanggangsuwŏllae*, 'barbarian invaders from across the sea' favoured in some texts (such as Kim Yŏlgyu 1976: 7–8) but said to be a colonial era fabrication by others (such as O Changhyŏn 1976: 64; personal interview with Im Tonggwŏn 1992). Echoes of fertility cults and circle dances are evocative of potential roots several millennia earlier. In the mid-twentieth century, *Kanggangsullae* could be found along the south and west coast; one 1941 publication, *Chosŏn ŭi hyangt'o orak* (Korean Indigenous Games), listed seventeen locations where it was still performed (cited in Shim Usŏng, 1980: 82–3). The legend, though, provided a hook for the Asset appointment. Hence, the first 'holder' was Yang Hŭngdo (1900–68), a professional singer and dancer from Chindo, and her 'assistant' was Kim Kirim (b. 1927), born on Chindo but living on the adjacent mainland. With Yang's death, Kim was elevated to 'holder' alongside another Chindo singer, Ch'oe Soshim (1908–90). After Ch'oe's death, a further Chindo singer was appointed 'holder' in 1993, Pak Yongsun (b. 1938). In the 1970s, *Kanggangsullae* was standardized; both Pak and Chi Ch'unsang were involved. Dances were incorporated from elsewhere, and steps were made 'lighter' and 'more balletic'. Improvization was removed, replaced by a story linking *Kanggangsullae* to a tale of a women-only night out. On Chindo, where by 1982 rehearsals were held at the Cultural Centre between the seventeenth and nineteenth of each month, virginal white flowing *hanbok* dresses were coupled to pony-tail wigs tied with red bows.[26]

Music Maketh Chindo: The Cultural Paradise Matures

Decline in Korean folk music can be traced back to the early twentieth century. In the 1930s, during the colonial occupation, the need for metal to support Japan's ambitions of empire, meant that many percussion bands fell silent. Inroads made by missionaries and post-Korean War campaigns against superstition pushed shamanism ever further to the periphery. Chindo islanders counter this, saying that because they were distant from the mainland their bands were never silenced, and that the local shaman fraternity kept the system of controlled territories (*tan'gol pan*) in which shamans held rights to practice until the 1960s. Change, though, blew in from the mainland. Land reform in the 1950s gave tenant farmers owner-ship of small tracts of land, removing the need for communal work teams and concomitantly reducing the need for farming songs such as those preserved in Asset No. 51, *Namdo tŭl norae*. In the 1970s, mechanization accompanied the New Village Movement, effectively banishing all work songs. Missionaries sought Christian converts. And the arrival of TV spelt doom for village festivals where entertainment genres such as *Kanggangsullae* had been performed; henceforth, families would gather around TV, watching interminable festival shows.

The preservation system, for all its faults, has allowed music that no longer has any links to daily and ritual life to endure. New contexts for performance have been found, chief amongst them in Chindo being what the French Ambassador to Korea, Pierre Randy, christened the 'Moses Miracle' in 1975. In the third lunar month, and again a month later, spring tides expose a causeway, the seabed between Chindo and Modo Island (part of the adjacent mainland county). Since 1977, the Sop'o percussion band has been invited to the annual festival. The band leads people along the 2.8 km-long causeway, collecting marooned seafood, and islanders meeting mainlanders in the middle. The event has mushroomed, and recent festivals are reported by the local press to have attracted up to 400,000 visitors. Chindo is, symbolically as well as in reality, reconnected to the nation, and at the festivals, Chindo's musical Assets are performed, emphasizing the richness of local culture.

Another legend is in place, promoted as if this 25-year-old festival has been observed for five centuries. In the late sixteenth century, tigers are said to have attacked the residents of a Chindo coastal village, Hoedong, forcing them to flee to Modo Island. In their haste to flee, Granny Pong was left behind. She prayed to be reunited with her family, and in a dream was told that a rainbow would appear to allow her to cross to the island. As she prayed, the sea parted, and her family, beating drums and gongs, travelled back to Hoedong to rescue her. (The story has a rather curious ending: Granny Pong was so overjoyed she died before she could embrace her family.)

There have, though, been no tigers for as long as people can remember. The world has moved on, and the transformation of Chindo is almost complete. Today, Saturday is culture day. The massive new granite cultural hall in Chindo-ŭp offers weekly performances of local music: foreigners, today unlike 20 years ago, are a familiar sight, mixing with Koreans from across the peninsula. The focus is on Chindo's National and Provincial Intangible Cultural Assets, but samples of additional folk music – weaving songs, dry field songs, fishing songs, and so on – are also offered: some would like to repeat the island's success in garnering Asset nominations.

In May 2004, the final element in my story will be added. The National Center for Korean Traditional Performing Arts,[27] the Seoul-based government-sponsored successor to court music institutes that can be traced back at least 1,200 years, and the bastion of traditional Korean music, is building a new campus on Chindo's southern coast. Known as the *Kungnip Namdo kugagwŏn*, the Southern National Music Center, when it opens in 2004 it will celebrate the local preservation of folk music. It will employ 25 people to co-ordinate music and dance at the 'Moses Miracle', to host a summer festival and an autumn educational jamboree for Koreans and foreigners alike. So, finally, Chindo's historical legacy, as a place of banishment and as the rebel Three Elite Patrols' stronghold, will be forgiven and forgotten. Chindo is set to become a living museum for Korean music.

Notes

1. Throughout this article, I use the McCune-Reischauer romanization system for Korean words, place names and personal names, *except* where an author, writing in English, has a preferred spelling, where common usage differs (for example, 'Seoul'), or where a title appears in romanized script (for example, on a CD cover) in a hybrid romanization.
2. Chindo County (*Chindo kun*) consists of forty-nine inhabited and 212 uninhabited islands. The main island, Chindo, is the third largest in Korea, and measures 28 km west to east and 22 km north to south. Today, Chindo is a single county (*kun*) divided into six districts (*myŏn*) within which are ninety-nine administrative villages (*ri*). The villages divide further into 231 hamlets (*tong/ri*) and 770 areas (*pan*). For definitions of each unit, see Wright (1975: 63–4). Howard (1989a: 3–4) shows the village structure of one district, Imhoe.
3. In addition to fieldwork between 1982 and 1984, I have returned to Chindo six times, in 1985, 1987, 1990, 1992, 1994 and 2000. I have also worked with Chindo musicians in Kwangju, Seoul, and abroad, notably in London and Berlin. There were few materials on Chindo available in the early 1980s, but this is no longer the case, and even the local government now maintains an excellent and extensive Web site (at www.chindo.chonnam.kr).
4. Dege (1982: 62–7) gives details of crops, Korean and botanical names, national and local production levels, and 1975 market prices. Chun (1984) includes details of laver production, including a discussion about the ownership of coastal plots. Fishing techniques, based on data collected on island and mainland areas near Chindo, are discussed in Han (1977). Beyond Chindo, the speculative nature of fishing and its low status compared to farming is discussed by Brandt (1972: particularly 62).
5. Korea was a colony of Japan from 1910 to 1945. The 1925 census records that there were 170 Japanese and ten Chinese residents (cited in Kwak Ch'ungŏ, 1976) who had exclusive commercial licenses and were allowed to exploit local rice and laver production. Local people commented that most of the foreigners who had been seen since the end of the Korean War in 1953 were missionaries.
6. The last figures I have are for January 1998, when the population stood at 45,501. In September 2000, I was told by local officials that the population had dropped below 40,000. Rural to urban migration has characterized economic development, and the Republic of Korea is now one of the most heavily urbanized countries in the world, with 84 per cent of its population of 47 million living in cities with more than 100,000 inhabitants. However, since migration has been recent, many Koreans still feel close to their rural roots,

typically returning at lunar new year (*sŏllal*) and the harvest festival (*ch'usŏk*). At a conference in September 2000 organized by Seoul National University and the Chindo County Government, the journalist and scholar Kim Kwangho claimed that 20,000 Chindo islanders now live in Seoul and a further 20,000 in the provincial capital, Kwangju.

7. The New Village Movement is widely discussed in publications. For a recent analysis that focuses on the corruption that undermined the project in the 1980s, see Kim Choo Hyup, 1999. For discussions of village leadership, see Brandt (1979) and Howard (1989a: 75–7).

8. My fieldwork research was constantly monitored. This occasionally had awkward ramifications. Often, as I left a village where I had been interviewing people, a plain-clothes policeman could be seen tracing my steps. When buses arrived on the island from the mainland, an armed soldier would check for spies, and every time I was on the bus, I would be asked to produce my passport. Only once did I object: 'Look around you; everyone looks as though they could be a North Korean spy except me, so why check just me?' I was marched off the bus at gunpoint.

9. Also known as Important Tangible Cultural Assets (*Chungyo yuhyŏng munhwajae*).

10. Also known as Important Intangible Cultural Assets (*Chungyo muhyŏng munhwajae*).

11. Some of the earlier debates are summarised in Baumann 1991: 22–31.

12. See www.unesco.org/culture/heritage/intangible/html.

13. *Munhwa undong* translates as 'culture movement', but Michael Robinson (1987) usefully glosses the term to indicate cultural nationalists. This is a misnomer to many in Korea today, since a number of prominent members argued not for revolution but for learning from Japan and by the 1930s were duly considered to have sold out to the colonial power. Amongst these, the writer Yi Kwangsu (1892–1950?), the publisher and ideologue Ch'oe Namsŏn (1890–1957) and the scholar Yi Nŭnghwa (1868–1948) were most significant. However, another member, Song Sŏkha, was keen to document and promote folk arts. Indeed, Song's texts about mask dance dramas, *Pongsan t'al ch'um* and *Chinju ogwangdae*, were later published in Seoul by Ilshin Munhwasa and became models for the scholarly reports submitted to support the nominations of Intangible Cultural Assets.

14. In respect to America, Loomis (1983: iv) has demonstrated how conservation involves both preservation (planning, documentation, and maintenance) and encouragement (publication, events, and education). Conservation is often couched in terms of state policies that prescribe administrative and budgetary practices and procedures, features that characterize a series of booklets published by UNESCO (for Japan, see Shikaumi, 1970; for the Republic of

Korea, see Kim Yersu, 1976). Government strategies may obscure control and propaganda (for which, in respect to China, see Perris 1985). Identity is often at stake, to counter imperialism, colonialism or Westernization (Feintuch, 1988: 3; Lauri Honko, 1989: 16–20), and may involve the development of 'invented traditions' (Hobsbawm, 1983), 'imagined communities' (Anderson, 1983) and notions of a shared 'deep past' (Humphrey, 1992), all as part of the erection of social boundaries (Cohen, 2000).

15. Piers Vitebsky has contributed an interesting account of local strategies for the recovery of a shamanic identity in the Sakha Republic following the collapse of the Soviet Union (Vitbsky, 1995); much the same could be explored in Buryatia or Tuva. Margaret Sarkissian's account of the Portuguese settlement in Malucca (Sarkissian, 2000), and Pegg's comments on the recovery of local religions and the promotion of overtone singing in Mongolia (Pegg, 2001: Chapter 12) provide further examples of local manipulation.

16. For discussions of the distinctions, see Kim Tae-kon (1998: 29–37) and Seong Nae Kim (1998).

17. Listed in Song Pangsong, Kim Sŏnghye and Ko Chŏngun (2000). The East Coast ritual, *Tonghaean pyŏlshin kut* is the second most cited ritual. Mikyung Pak has completed an English-language PhD and a Korean-language book on *Ssikkim kut* (1985; 1996).

18. Items 628 (by Kim Yŏngmin), 813 (Kim Ilhwa), 1547 (Pak Hyogyŏng), 1890 (Shin Ûnjin), 2495 (Yi Tonghŭi), 2511 (Yi Myŏnghŭi), 3545 (Cho Ûnhŭi) and 3948 (Han Yangmyŏng) in Kim Sŏnghye 1998.

19. Kim insisted to me that she was born in 1931 in interviews in 1983 and 1990. It was common during the Japanese period for parents to fail to register a daughter's birth for several years. In Kim's case, where her official birth registration was made in 1935, the need to provide proof of marriage before registering a child may have been a further handicap, because her parents were both shamans and this was at a time many shaman unions were never formally registered.

20. The lead researcher for the 1979 and 1983 reports, Chŏng Pyŏngho, is a folk dance specialist born on the mainland in Haenam County some 50km from Chindo.

21. A similar justification is made for *Tashiraegi*, Asset No. 81, for which see Howard (1990). In this case, though, the 1980s saw considerable competition between an amateur group in Tonji Village and members of the Chindo Cultural Centre. The latter won the nomination. In 1990, I presented a critical paper reviewing what had happened at the Academy of Korean Studies, at which the scholar responsible for reports to the Office for Cultural Asset Management, Yi Tuhyŏn, argued that only the Asset form of *Tashiraegi* had ever existed. I stand by my conclusions. Recordings of the Asset versions of

Man'ga and *Tashiraegi* are listed in the discography.
22. *Ppuri kip'ŭn namu hanbando ŭi sŭlp'ŭn sori.* Cho's birthdate was probably 1924; as with Kim T'aerye, her parents did not register her birth for five or six years.
23. Items 1906 (by Shin Ch'an'gyun), 2731 (Yi Wanhyŏng) and 2954 (Yi Hyŏnsuk) in Kim Sŏnghye 1998.
24. For an affectionate obituary of Cho by a university student, see Pak Ponggu (1997).
25. The latter were recorded as part of the *Ppuri kip'ŭn namu palto sori* set. Yi Sora's extensive collection of farming songs for the Office for Cultural Asset Management resulted in five published volumes (1985, 1986, 1989, 1990, 1992).
26. Shim Usŏng (1980: 135–42) describes some of these changes, and changes in dance can also be observed by comparing the Office for Cultural Asset Management reports (Im Tonggwŏn 1965, particularly 71–5; Shim Usŏng, 1985, particularly 28–9).
27. In post-liberation Korea, a January 1950 presidential decree set out regulations for the National Classical Music Institute (*Kungnip kugagwŏn*). The Institute opened its doors in Pusan in April 1951, and after the Korean War returned to Seoul and set up in premises in Unnidong. In 1989, the Institute was renamed the Korean Traditional Performing Arts Centre (the Korean name remained as before), in recognition that it had broadened its activities from the preservation and promotion of court music and dance to folk and contemporary music. In 1995, the English name again changed, to the National Center for Korean Traditional Performing Arts. By 1999, the National Center employed 340 staff. Short accounts of court music institutes include Hahn (1990: Chapter 1) and Howard (2002: 981–90). For general information, see the National Centre's Web site (www.ncktpa.co.kr).

References

Anderson, B. (1983), *Imagined Communities. Reflections on the Origin and Spread of Nationalism*, London: Verso.
Baumann, M. P. (1991), 'Traditional Music in the Focus of Cultural Policy', in M. P. Baumann (ed.), *Music in the Dialogue of Cultures: Traditional Music and Cultural Policy,* Wilhelmshaven: Florian Noetzel, pp. 22–31.
Blacking, J. (1987), *A Commonsense View of All Music: Reflections on Percy Grainger's Contribution to Ethnomusicology and Music Education*, Cambridge: Cambridge University Press.
Brandt, V. (1971), *A Korean Village between Farm and Sea*, Cambridge MA: Harvard University Press.

Brandt, V. (1979), 'Sociocultural Aspects of Political Participation in Rural Korea', *Journal of Korean Studies*, 1: 205–24.

Chang Kwio (1982), *Namdo t'osok nongyo ŭi ŭmjojige kwanhan yŏn'gu: sŏnyul kujo ŭi punsŏgŭl chungshimŭro*, MA dissertation, Hanyang University, Seoul.

Chi Ch'unsang (1972), *Namdo tŭl norae. Chungyo muhyŏng munhwajae chosa pogosŏ* 98, Seoul: Munhwajae kwalliguk.

Chin Hoesuk (1985), *Chindo tŭl norae-e kwanhan yŏn'gu*, MA dissertation, Seoul National University.

Chŏng Aeyon, (1982), *Honam 'mu'-e taehan koch'al*, MA dissertation, Kyunghee University, Seoul.

Chŏng Pyŏngho, Chi Ch'unsang and Yi Pohyŏng, (1979), *Chindo Ssikkim kut. Chungyo muhyŏng munhwajae chosa pogosŏ* 129, Seoul: Chŏnt'ong muyong yŏn'guso/Munhwajae kwalliguk.

Chŏng Pyŏngho, Yi Pohyŏng, Yi Chuyŏng, Yi Tongyŏng and Chŏng Chun'gi, (1983), *Mu-ŭishik p'yŏn. Han'guk minsok chonghap chosa pogoso* 14, Seoul: Munhwajae yŏn'guso/Yenŭng minsok yŏn'gushil.

Chun Kyung Soo, (1984), *Reciprocity and Korean Society: An ethnography of Hasami*, Seoul: Seoul National University Press.

Cohen, A. (2000), *Signifying Identities: Anthropological Perspectives on Boundaries and Contested Values*, London: Routledge.

Dege, E. (1982), *Entwicklungsdisparitäten der Agrarregionen Südkoreas. Kieler Geographische Schriften*, 55, Kiel: Universität Kiel.

Eckert, C. J., Ki-baik Lee, Young Ick Lew, Robinson, M. and Wagner, E. W. (1990), *Korea Old and New: A History*, Seoul: Ilchogak.

Eikemeier, D. (1980), *Documents from Changjwari: A Further Approach to the Analysis of Korean Villages*, Weisbaden: Otto Harrasowitz.

Feintuch, B. (1988), *The Conservation of Culture: Folklorists and the Public Sector*, Lexington: University Press of Kentucky.

Hahn Man Young (1991), *Kugak: Studies in Korean Traditional Music*, Seoul: Tamgudang.

Han Manyŏng, (1983) 'Folksongs', in *Traditional Performing Arts of Korea*, Seoul: Korean National Commission for UNESCO, pp. 15–26.

Han Woo-keun (1970) *The History of Korea*, Seoul: Eul Yoo Publishing Company.

Han Sang-bok (1977), *Korean Fishermen*, Seoul: Seoul National University Press.

Hŏ Ogin (1986), *Chindo ŭi sogyowa pojon*, Kwangju: Kwangju ilbosa.

Hobsbawm, E. (1983), 'Introduction', in Eric Hobsbawm and Terrence Ranger (eds), *The Invention of Tradition*, Cambridge: Cambridge University Press.

Lauri Honko (1989), 'Nationalism and Internationalism in Folklore Research', *NIF Newsletter*, 17: 16–20.

Howard, K. (1989a.), *Bands, Songs, and Shamanistic Rituals: Folk Music in Korean Society*, Seoul: Korea Branch of the Royal Asiatic Society.

Howard, K. (1989b.), '*Namdo tŭl norae*: Ritual and the Intangible Cultural Asset system', *Journal of Ritual Studies*, 3(2): 203–16.

Howard, K. (1990), '*Tashiraegi*. En Corée, pas de retour après la mort si ce n'est dance un Trésor Culturel Intangible', *Cahiers de Musiques Traditionelles*, 3: 119–39.

Howard, K. (1991–2), 'Paper Symbols in Chindo *Ssikkim kut:* A Korean shamanistic ceremony', *Cahiers d'Extrême-Asie*, 6: 65–86.

Howard, K. (1996), 'Preservation and Presentation of Korean Intangible Cultural Assets', in *Methodologies for the Preservation of Intangible Heritage*, Seoul: Korean National Commission for UNESCO/Office of Cultural Properties pp. 85–114.

Howard, K. (2002), 'Social and Regional Contexts', in *Garland Encyclopedia of World Music: East Asia*, New York: Garland Publishing, pp. 981–90.

Humphrey, C. (1992), 'The Moral Authority of the Past in Post-Socialist Mongolia', *Religion, State and Society*, 20(3–4): 375–89.

Im Tonggwŏn (1965), *Kanggangsullae. Chungyo muhyŏng munhwajae chongsa pogosŏ* 7. Seoul: Munhwajae kwalliguk.

Joe, Wanne J. (1972), *Traditional Korea: A Cultural History*, Seoul: Chungang University Press.

Kim Choo Hyup (1999), *The Saemaul Movement and Korean Rural Development: A Comparative Study of Government Policy in the 1970s and 1980s*, PhD dissertation, University of Sheffield.

Kim Hey-jung (2001), '*Chindo sangyŏsori ŭi yuhyŏng kwa ŭmakchŏk t'ŭksŏng/Types of sangyeo-sori (bier-carriers' song) in Jindo Island and their musical properties*', *Asia ŭi changnye ŭmak/Funeral Music in Asia*: 137–164. Seoul: Kungnip kugagwŏn/National Center for Korean Traditional Performing Arts.

Kim, Seong Nae (1998), 'Problems in Defining Shaman Types and Local Variations', in Howard, K (ed.), *Korean Shamanism Today: Revivals, Survivals, and Change*, Seoul: Korea Branch of the Royal Asiatic Society, pp. 33–43.

Kim Sŏnghye (1998), *Han'guk ŭmak kwanyŏnhak ŭi nonmun ch'ongmok*: 1945–1995, Seoul: Minsogwŏn.

Kim Tae-kon (1998), *Korean Shamanism – Muism*, Seoul: Jimoondang Publishing Company.

Kim Yersu (1976), *Cultural Policy in the Republic of Korea. Studies and Documents on Cultural Policies*, Paris: UNESCO.

Kim Yŏlgyu (1976), *Han'guk ŭi shinhwa, minsok, mindam*, Seoul: Ilchogak.

Kwak Ch'ungŏ (ed.) (1976), *Chindo kunji*, Kwangju: Chŏnnam Chindo p'yŏnch'an wiwŏnhoe/Chŏnnam maeil ch'ulp'an'guk.

Kwon Oh-sung, (1983), 'Melodic Structure of Korean Funeral Procession Songs', *Yearbook for Traditional Music*, XV: 59–70.

Loomis, O. H. (1983), *Cultural Conservation: The Protection of Cultural Heritage in the US. Publications of the American Folklife Centre 10*, Washington: Library of Congress.

Maliangkay, R. (1999), *Handling the Intangible: The Protection of Folksong Traditions in Korea*, PhD dissertation, School of Oriental and African Studies, University of London.

Na Sŭngman, (1990), *Chindo chiyŏk ŭi tŭllorae yŏn'gu.* PhD dissertation, Chŏnnam National University, Kwangju.

Naegojang chŏnt'ong kakkugi (compilation committee) (1982), *Okchu ŭi ŏl.* Chindo: Chindo kunji p'yŏnjip wiwŏnhoe/Kwangju: Chŏnil ch'ulp'ansa.

Nettl, B. (1985), *The Western Impact on World Music*, New York: Schirmer Books.

O Changhyŏn, Pak Chinju and Shim Usŏng (1976), *Minsok nori chidojaryo*, Seoul: Samilgak.

Paek Sŏnghyŏn (1988/9), '*Han'guk minyo ŭi pogo Chindo*', *Ŭmak kyoyuk*: 134–38.

Pak Chuŏn and Chŏng Chŏngsu (1988), *Chindo musok hyŏnji chosa*, Seoul: Han'guk minsok pangmulgwan.

Pak Mikyung (1985), *Music and Shamanism in Korea: A study of selected Ssikkum-gut rituals for the dead*, PhD dissertation, University of California, Los Angeles.

Pak Migyŏng (1996), *Han'guk ŭi musok kwa ŭmak*, Seoul: Segwang ŭmak ch'ulp'ansa.

Pak Ponggu (1997), '*Cho Kongnye sŏnsaengnimŭl ch'umohamyŏn*', *Sabalt'ongŭm*, 1997/5: 10.

Pegg, C. (2001), *Mongolian Music, Dance, and Oral Narrative*, Seattle: University of Washington Press.

Perris, A. (1985), *Music as Propaganda: Art to Persuade, Art to Control*, Westport: Greenwood.

Pilzer, J. (2003), '*Sŏdosori* (Northwestern Korean Lyric Song) on the Demilitarized Zone: a study in music and teleological judgement', *Ethnomusicology*, 47(1): 68–92.

Robinson, M. E. (1987), *Cultural Nationalism in Colonial Korea, 1920–1925*, Seattle: University of Washington.

Sarkissian, M. (2000), *D'Albuquerque's Children: Performing Tradition in Malaysia's Portuguese Settlement*, Chicago: University of Chicago Press.

Shim Usŏng (1980), *Han'guk ŭi minsok nori*, Seoul: Samilgak.

Shim Usŏng (1985), '*Kanggangsullae*', in *Chungyo muhyŏng munhwajae haesŏl: nori-wa ŭishik* Seoul: Munhwa kongbobu, pp. 25–38.

Shin Kyŏngnim (1985), *Minyo kihaeng*, Seoul: Han'gilsa.

Small, C. (1987), 'Performance as Ritual: Sketch for an Inquiry into the True Nature of a Symphony Concert', in Avron Levine White (ed.), *Lost in Music:*

Culture, Style and the Musical Event, London: Routledge & Kegan Paul.

Son Sŏkchu (ed.) (1980), *Muak. Ch'egye chŏngnip charyojip 3*, Seoul: Han'guk munhwa yesul chinhŭngwŏn.

Song Pangsong, Kim Sŏnghye and Kim Chŏngun (2000), *Han'guk ŭmakhak nonjŏ haeje II*: 1980–1995, Seoul: Minsogwŏn.

Turner, V. (1969), *The Ritual Process*, Ithica NY: Cornell University Press.

Uchida, R. (1980), 'Rice Planting Music of Chindo (Korea) and the Chugoku Region (Japan)', in Blacking, J. and Keali'inohomoku, J. (eds), *The Performing Arts*, The Hague: Mouton, pp. 109–19

Van Gennep, A. (1960), *The Rites of Passage*, originally published in 1909, London: Routledge & Kegan Paul.

Van Zile, J. (2001), *Perspectives on Korean Dance*, Middletown CT: Wesleyan University Press.

Vitebsky, P. (1995), 'From Cosmology to Environmentalism: Shamanism as Local Knowledge in a Global Setting', in Fardon, R. (ed.), *Counterworks: Managing Diversity in Knowledge*, London: Routledge, pp. 183–203.

Wright, E. R. (1975), *Korean Politics in Transition*, Seattle: University of Washington Press.

Yi Chŏngnan (1984), *Nongyo sangsasori ŭi ŭmakchŏk t'ŭkching*, MA dissertation, Hanyang University, Seoul.

Yi Sora (1985, 1986, 1989, 1990, 1992), *Han'guk ŭi nongyo* I-V, Seoul: Hyŏnamsa.

Yun Igŭn (1999), *Hyangt'o minyo, irokke karŭch'yo poseyo*, Seoul: Kungnip kugagwŏn.

Recommended Listening

Ahn Sook Sun, Kim Dae Ryeh (1998), *Live Concert*, Samsung Music (Seoul) SCO-166CSS.

Ahn Sook Sun, Park Byung Chon (1998), *Ascend*, Samsung Music (Seoul) SCO-167CSS.

Chindo Sangyŏsori (1994), Samsung Nices (Seoul) SCO-044CSS.

Chin-do Ssit-kim-kut (1994), Samsung Nices (Seoul) SCO-043CSS.

Chindo Tashiraegi (1995), Samsung Nices (Seoul) SCO-067CSS.

Corée/Korea: Chants rituals de l'île de Chindo/Ritual Songs from the Island of Chindo (1993), AIMP XXVIII. Archives Internationals de Musique Populaire/VDE-Gallo (Genève) CD-756.

Dancing Winds (1997), Samsung Music (Seoul) SCO-138CSS, 1997.

Hwimori (1994), Seoul Records (Seoul) SRCD-3281, 1994.

Kim Taerye:Ch'ŏnmyŏng/Supreme (1995), Samsung Nices (Seoul) SCO-055CSS.

Kim Yong Woo: Chige sori (1996), Seoul Records (Seoul) SRCD-1354.

Kim Yong Woo: Kwenari (1998), Samsung Music (Seoul) SCO-165KYW.
Korea: Shamanistic Ceremonies of Chindo (1993), JVC (Tokyo) VICG-5412–2.
Man'ga/Bearers' Song (1994), Cantabile (Seoul) SRCD 1224.
Park Byung Chon: Kuŭm tasŭrŭm/Unrestrained Sound (1994), Samsung Nices (Seoul) SCO-024CSS.
Ppuri kip'ŭn namu palto sori/The Deep-Rooted Tree Collection of Korean Folksongs (1984), Seoul: Korea Britannica Corp./Jigu (Seoul) JLS 120166 – JLS 120176.
Ppuri kip'ŭn namu hanbando ŭi sŭlp'ŭn sori/The Deep-Rooted Tree Collection of Korean Songs of Sorrow (1989), Seoul: The Deep-Rooted Tree Publishing Company/SEM (Seoul) SELRO 138.
Salp'uri (1994), Cantabile (Seoul) SRCD-1161.
West End (1996), Samsung Music (Seoul) SCO-105CSS.
Young-Hee Shin: Jindo Sitggim-kut (2000), Seoul Records (Seoul) SRCD 3001.
Young-Hee Shin: Jindo Arirang, Man'ga (2000), Seoul Records (Seoul) SRCD.

–6–

'Chilled Ibiza': Dance tourism and the Neo-Tribal Island Community

Andy Bennett

The Spanish island of Ibiza has long been a destination for European tourists. With the advent of cheap package holidays during the 1960s, Ibiza and other Mediterranean resorts became a popular location for working-class and lower middle-class families, for whom overseas holidays had previously been unafford-able (Urry, 1994: 130). Since the mid-1980s, the appeal of Ibiza has been consid-erably enhanced for younger holiday makers through the island's danceclub culture, whose 'Balearic beat' has helped shape new genres of dance music across Europe and the rest of the world (see Melechi, 1993; Malbon, 1999). Each year, thousands of young people from western Europe and other parts of the world visit Ibiza to sample the island's characteristic blend of vibrant club culture and Mediterranean climate. The result is a seasonal, and primarily hedonistic, trans-national commu-nity whose temporal relationships are framed exclusively around the aural and physical pleasures of the club atmosphere as experienced in the exotic setting of a Mediterranean island. The trans-national and temporal nature of the Ibiza club culture is further accentuated by the global flow of DJs, musicians and producers (Laing, 1997) whose temporal associations with Ibiza ensure an ever-changing soundscape of musical moods and fragments drawn from all over the world.

Drawing on Maffesoli's (1996) concept of 'neo-tribes', this chapter examines the significance of the Ibiza club culture as a trans-national, neo-tribal community constructed through processes of late modern consumption and tourism. The chapter begins by briefly outlining the development of dance music and the place of Ibiza within this development. This is followed by a consideration of dance music's role and place within global tourism, and how a growing nexus of island resorts act as nodal points for the shifting trans-national constellation of clubbers. The second part of the chapter focuses on the Ibiza experience itself, examining how the island's club culture creates a particularized blend of local and global influences, the exoticism and seductiveness of Ibiza being experienced through and against a constantly developing global soundscape. The final section of the chapter considers how the concept of 'neo-tribe', particularly its fluid and unstable quality, can be applied in our understanding of the Ibiza club scene as a temporal and shifting island 'community'.

The Development of Contemporary Dance Music

The origins of contemporary dance music can be traced back to two distinctive musical innovations – 'house' and 'techno'. House music was the creation of DJs in Chicago gay clubs during the late 1970s (see Rietveld, 1997), who pioneered a technique referred to as 'blend mixing', whereby sections of music are manually mixed together through skilful manipulation of vinyl records using a twin-turntable record player. Using this technique, DJs are able to produce new sounds and tonal textures, and, in some cases, entirely new songs or pieces of music (see Back, 1996: 192). The term 'house' itself also has a distinctly local connection with Chicago. Thus, Rietveld notes how house derives from a particular Chicago dance club known as The Warehouse, whose setting 'away from any mainstream leisure area of Chicago, and its management policies and audience showed an attitude which enhanced its special and underground character' (Rietveld, 1997: 126).

The second major influence on the development of dance music during the late 1980s and early 1990s was techno. Although 'techno' itself originates from dance clubs in Detroit, early techno innovators being DJs Derrick May and Carl Craig, its roots can be traced back to the city of Düsseldorf in the industrial heartland of Germany. During the early 1970s classical music students Ralf Hutter and Florian Schneider began experimenting with electronic music and formed the group Kraftwerk (see Bennett, 2001). A key innovation in Kraftwerk's music was the use of industrial noise – for example, traffic sounds, the sound of factory machinery, shopping mall crowds and so on. As Schneider explains, Kraftwerk made 'sound-pictures of real environments, what we call tone films' (cited in Gill, 1997: 77). While Kraftwerk themselves have remained an essentially underground, avant-garde group, today they are generally regarded as the founding fathers of techno. Thus, as Gill (1997) writes:

> In the world of electronic music, Kraftwerk are the Kings across the water. Despite releasing no new material in over a decade, they continue to wield more influence than any of their Anglo-American peers in the arcane business of bleeps and beats. Scratch a techno whizkid or studio engineer, and nine times out of 10 you'll find a Kraftwerk fan (the tenth will be too busy sampling them to respond). (Gill, 1997: 76).

Other 1970s artists whose experiments with electronic music have had a large influence on contemporary dance music are Tangerine Dream (also from

Germany), Brian Eno and Giorgio Moroder. In addition to pursuing his own successful music career, Moroder also produced Donna Summer's 1977 hit 'I Feel Love', considered by some to be the first piece of electronic dance music due to its pioneering use of a sequencer device.

As suggested above, in addition to new techniques in DJ-ing, contemporary styles of dance music also owe much to breakthroughs in technology during the 1980s and early 1990s. Particularly significant in this respect was the impact of digital technology on the composition and recording process. Digital technology paved the way for a new era in sound recording, analogue tape machines being replaced with computers. Computers were able both to store and reproduce sound much more accurately than the old analogue recording machines that produced varying elements of white noise or 'tape hiss', partly due to imperfections in the tape itself.

Digital technology also facilitated a number of other breakthroughs in the recording process, including sampling, which allows for a recorded sound to be 'triggered' when required, using the keyboard of a synthesizer, drum pad or even a human voice in conjunction with a microphone. The triggering of samples is achieved using MIDI (Musical Instrument Digital Interface). As Negus (1992: 25) explains, MIDI 'enable[s] various instruments to be connected up together, allowing composition to take place within a computer's memory'. Sampling enables the manipulation of sound sources on a scale never before possible. Using sampling techniques, musicians and studio producers can effectively take sounds 'out' of their 'original' contexts and rework them into new pieces of music.

Club Culture

If the style of contemporary dance music and the techniques employed in its production mark a radical break with previous genres of popular music, such as rock and pop, the youth cultural groups that frequent dance music events are also seen to be different from previous youth cultures. During the early British rave scene of the mid-1980s, some observers suggested that dance music signalled an end to stylistic divisions between youth. This view is exemplified in Redhead's (1993: 3–4) observation that rave succeeded in 'mixing all styles on the same dance floor and attracting a range of previously opposed subcultures from football hooligans to New Age hippies'. Although such radical style mixing is no longer held to be true in relation to dance music (see, for example, Malbon, 1999), many theorists and researchers still regard dance music culture as a more fluid and temporal expression of collectivity than previous youth cultural groupings, whose memberships, it is argued, were tied to issues of class background and a stylistic unity based around common use and understanding of fashion and consumer items (Hall and Jefferson, 1976; Willis, 1978; Hebdige, 1979). Making a case against the application of such class-based explanations of style to contemporary club culture, Malbon (1999: 26) draws attention to the 'tactile … forms of communality' which characterize the contemporary club crowd. Similarly, in my own work I have argued that within the context of contemporary dance music culture:

> The nature of musical taste, as with music itself, is both a multi-faceted and distinctly fluid form of expression. Music generates a range of moods and experiences which individuals are able to move freely between … in many of the larger clubs which feature urban dance music nights, the desire of the consumer to choose from and engage with a variety of different musical moods has been further realised by using different rooms or floors as a means of staging a number of parallel events with club-goers free to move between these events as they please. (Bennett, 1999: 611)

Some writers argue that such qualities of fluidity and temporality were inherent in club culture from its beginning. For example, in discussing the catalytic role of Chicago's Warehouse club in the rise of house music, Rietveld argues that its underground quality and spatial isolation from the city centre night-time economy gave rise to a temporal, transient communality of clubbers. As Rietveld observes

> … in this isolated twelve-hour frenzy of the night, in the middle of the weekend, new identities could be forged that were not necessarily there to be sustained throughout the rest of the week. The dance, the music, even the club itself were built for that moment in the weekend, to disappear once it had occurred. (Rietveld, 1997: 127–8)

From its very beginnings then, house engendered a notion of temporality among those who attended house events, the latter becoming more translocally articulated as house, and the various subgenres of dance music that followed, became more globally prominent.

Contemporary club culture has also seen a major shift in the role of the DJ from 'passive "record player" to (virtual) musician' (Langlois, 1992: 230). Indeed, the apparent blurring of once highly defined roles in music production and perform-ance in the world of contemporary dance music is such that DJs can now legiti-mately claim to be composers, arrangers, producers and performers. In addition to their skills in mixing songs in a 'live' context, many DJs now routinely draw upon the facilities offered by recording studios. Thus, as Langlois (1992) notes:

> The most celebrated DJs are often involved in re-mixing other artists' recordings, providing a variety of interpretations of existing material. From the production side of studio work to composing new tracks themselves is a small step which many DJs are able to take. (Langlois, 1992: 230)

As a consequence of this shifting role, a new status has been conferred on the

DJ, the latter often assuming the status, prestige and critical acclaim once reserved for rock artists. As Langlois observes, 'the better known [DJs] enjoy considerable status and sometimes command their own following, who will go to hear *them* rather than to a particular club (Langlois, 1992: 234). Similarly, Laing (1997) points to the large trans-national networks that now exist for the production and marketing of dance music, a global flow that also facilitates extensive touring for DJs and their particular brand of club event.

If dance music DJs and promoters now increasingly operate at a trans-national level, the relative ease of long-distance travel, combined with a desire to see new DJs and experience new musical styles has engendered a growing culture of 'dance tourism' (see Carrington and Wilson, 2002), candidly described in one report as 'clubbers who travel the world less to see the sights than to experience the nights' (*Guardian*, 2000: 2). Arguably, however, this description is rather one sided in its evaluation of the dance-tourist. Thus, if a large attraction for the young traveller is indeed the promise of new clubs, DJs and music, then the location itself also plays a significant part. Indeed, in addition to clubs, many dance tourists travel to sample the flavour and excitement of dance 'parties', open-air events held in rural locations. Such events are particularly popular in places such as Goa, where dance parties begin when the sun sets and end at sunrise; during the course of the night dancers engage in a semi-ritualistic search for spirituality, combining the experience of dance, music and drugs with a sense of oneness with nature (see Saldanha, 2002). In this and similar examples, dance tourism can be seen as a form of what Desforges (1998) refers to as 'collecting places', where knowledge of the world is gained through the opportunity that travel affords for experiencing 'difference'.

Dance Tourism and Ibiza

Within the emerging sphere of dance tourism, Ibiza plays a central role, the island being regarded both as an historical reference point in the global dance scene and a place that retains an important resonance as a dance resort. In terms of its significance as a venue for dance music, Ibiza first came to prominence during the mid-1980s when young holiday makers from the UK and other European countries, desiring a change from the over crowding and commercialization of Ibiza's main resort, San Antonio, began to explore other parts of the island and discovered Ibiza Town. Melechi (1993: 31) describes Ibiza Town as 'a more upmarket resort, away from the drone of the familiar accents and the banality of the burger bar, where the tourist could enjoy the pleasure of anonymity'.

The attraction of Ibiza Town was further enhanced by the unique musical style being produced by DJs in local dance clubs, notably Club Amnesia. The particular style of dance music featured in Ibiza clubs, which came to be known as 'Balearic

Beat', collapsed the boundaries between hitherto rigidly defined musical styles, such as rap, jazz and soul, combining them with Spanish tinged melodies to produce an 'eclectic mishmash' (Malechi, 1993). According to Melechi, both the environment of Ibiza Town and the appeal of the then relatively unknown 'Balearic Beat' were judged by many to offer a more authentic experience of 'Ibiza', an experience that seamlessly combined the exotic and seductive qualities of a Mediterranean island resort with the satisfaction of sharing in a new, pioneering chapter in dance music whose disregard for musical boundaries seemed to resonate perfectly with the carefree existence of island life itself.

Since the early 1990s, when Melechi and other dance music researchers published their accounts of the Ibiza club scene, the popular image of the island's club culture has been compromised to some extent through the influx of Club 18–30 style tourists whose antics are captured in tabloid features and TV exposes of uncontrolled hedonism characterized by excessive drinking and casual sex. As a consequence, Ibiza has become something of a cliché in some quarters of the dance music scene. Nevertheless, as illustrated by the growing number of CD collections featuring Ibiza 'club anthems', the Ibiza club scene continues to thrive, attracting clubbers from all over Europe and other parts of the world. Indeed, one by-product of the Ibiza club scene's 'incorporation' (Hebdige, 1979)[1] by more mainstream entertainment concerns has been the successful commodification of the Ibiza experience, a process that draws equally on visual descriptions such 'Fantasy Island':

> There are places on this Earth that can be compared to Paradise, and Ibiza is one of them without a doubt. Famous all over the world for its unique charm and beautiful climate, this Balearic Island combines entertainment with sex, parties, women, sun, beaches, and alcohol. It has all the right ingredients for the perfect recipe to fulfil fantasies.[2]

And 'Party Capital of the World':

> Today, it seems that the international techno-house scene has chosen Ibiza as Party Central. Nevertheless, the crowds of tourists at Ibiza are sophisticated, hip, rich, young, and beautiful. You won't find Mom and Pop snapping polaroids.[3]

Embedded in such claims are a combination of visual and sensual references, designed to package up the Ibiza experience in a distinctively youthful way. In effect, Ibiza is sold to the young clubber/ tourist / consumer in two distinctive ways, as a place of natural beauty and as a prominent place on the map of musical history. A useful way of contextualizing this is Urry's notion of the 'tourist gaze'. According to Urry (1990: 13), tourists 'seek to experience "in reality" the pleasurable dramas they have already experienced in their imagination'. Thus, rather than being regarded as social/geographical spaces in their own right, particular urban and rural locations become frames of reference, based upon particular tourist expectations that are, in their turn, based upon images and information received from television programmes, books and other media. As I have noted elsewhere (see, for example, Bennett, 2002), music can play a particularly seductive role in informing understandings, and thus expectations, of particular places, with locations as diverse as the city of Liverpool in the UK and the US 'deep south' being largely understood and interpreted in terms of their musical heritages (see Cohen, 1991; Evans, 2001). Moreover, in these and other places, local tourist industries have done much to fulfil the expectations of the tourist gaze by putting in place museums and exhibitions and offering guided tours of 'relevant' landmarks.

In effect, though different to those examples described above, Ibiza is also subject to a distinctive form of 'musicalized' tourist gaze. Ibiza's role as a primary site of innovation for contemporary dance music styles is now firmly established. In the same way that respective devotees of *blues* and *country* cite Chicago and Nashville as important centres for the development of these musical styles, so devotees of dance music will note the influence of 'Balearic Beat' on the development of *house*. Similarly, during the mid-late 1980s, the Ibiza dance music scene served as an important nodal point for a trans-national community of DJs (see Laing 1997) whose paths inevitably crossed in the island's dance clubs. The musicalized 'tourist gaze' of Ibiza is further enhanced by the regular release of CD collections, pooled from music featured in the island's dance clubs. The packaging of such CDs invariably features stereotypical images of the 'island paradise' – palm trees, empty beaches, golden sunsets – while the titles of collections, such as 'Chilled Ibiza' add to the seductive quality of the Ibiza experience.

Such images also carry over into sound, suggesting a seemingly 'natural' relationship between the musical selections featured on the Ibiza CD collections and the physical beauty of the island and its environs. This powerful merging of natural images and music plays a key role in informing expectations of the Ibiza experience. Frith (1987: 142) has noted the way in which music can 'intensify our experience of the present' and provide 'the key to our remembrance of things past'. In a similar way, music can also feed into the ways in which individuals anticipate and prepare for future activities and events. The Ibiza 'experience' is one based on a series of expectations that, while they may vary, each correspond with a particular representation of Ibiza as a space in which desirable aspects of contemporary youth leisure – for example, music, dance, drugs and sex – are both readily accessible and, more importantly, the collectively accepted norm.

At the same time, the physical space of the island, and the phenomenological experience of the island 'condition' engender particular expressions of club cultural identity. Earlier in this chapter it was noted how researchers have suggested a more fluid and transient quality in contemporary club cultures. Given the transitory nature of the clubbing experience, clubbers can 'lose themselves in the crowd' (Malbon, 1999), celebrating their anonymity or assuming a different identity or series of identities. In the context of urban clubs, such escapes from the everyday into the temporal world of the club are particularly fleeting. In the context of the 'Ibiza experience', the clubber is able to extend this desire for temporality, and the personal enjoyment that follows, over a longer period of time. On Ibiza, the clubbing experience extends beyond the confines of the club itself, becoming, in effect, a total experience for the duration of the period that the clubber resides on Ibiza. The whole island becomes an extension of what Hollands (2002) terms a 'playscape' for young people; a youth lifestyle that is normally squeezed into evening and weekend leisure time is freed from such restrictions, temporarily becoming the 'norm' rather then a negotiation of it. As with the urban club, Ibiza disrupts the pattern of the individual's mundane everyday existence, but prolongs the period of this disruption. This, in turn, plays a key role in informing the individual's expectation of the Ibiza experience and of the nature of clubbing relations they will engage in while on the island. Ibiza is constructed by young clubbers as a space in which the cultural practices of youth are the 'accepted prac-tices'; a site on which routine, everyday pressures and expectations are temporarily suspended.

A Neo-Tribal Island Community

There are clear differences between the transient community of dance tourists who frequent the resorts and dance clubs of Ibiza, and the types of island communities described elsewhere in this book. Indeed, some may question the value of the term community at all in understanding the scenario thus far described. However, much depends on the way in which community is applied in the context of contemporary social life. As Anderson (1983) notes, the term community increasingly invokes a representation of collective life as this is 'imagined' by participants, rather than a thing in and for itself. Similarly, Chaney (1996) suggests that as traditional ways of life are replaced by reflexively chosen lifestyles, this in turn give rise to new 'affective' forms of community. The Ibiza experience, bringing together as it does a range of desirable youth leisure activities, may be regarded as an example of an 'affective' community. Ibiza becomes a 'space' in which the clubbing experience, based around hedonism and jouissance (Malbon, 1999), is both extended and expanded, the pleasure of the club experience being easily combined with a range of other sought after leisure activities in the context of an exotic 'island' location. At same time, however, 'Ibiza' is also a transient experience, one with which young people temporarily engage. Shields (1992: 16) has suggested that the increasing mobility of individuals between different, groups, crowds and other forms of collective social engagement has given rise to a 'postmodern "persona"' whose 'multiple identifications form a *dramatis personae* – a self which can no longer be simplistically theorized as unified.'

The Ibiza 'experience' adds a new dimension of anonymity, as well as geographical isolation from the more day-to-day experience of everyday life, allowing young people to engage in new forms of sociation, based around temporal expressions of self that such anonymity and geographical isolation afford. In this way, the Ibiza experience could be described as a new expression of community, one based around neo-tribal forms of affiliation. The concept of neo-tribes was first used by Maffesoli as a means of accounting for changes in the social structure which he perceived to be occurring due to the increasingly central role of consumerism in late modern society. According to Maffesoli (1996: 98), the consumerist sensibilities of individuals engendered new patterns of reflexivity and selectivity in the formation of identities, late modern identities effectively being 'chosen' rather than 'proscribed' by the structured experience of class, gender, race and so on. This, in turn gave rise to new forms of collective 'neo-tribal' association which, Maffesoli argues, are 'without the rigidity of the forms of organization with which we are familiar, [they refer] more to a certain ambience, a state of mind, and is preferably to be expressed through lifestyles that favour appearance and form.'

Hetherington (1992: 93) has further suggested that tribalization involves 'the deregulation through modernization and individualization of the modern forms of solidarity and identity based on class occupation, locality and gender ... and the recomposition into "tribal" identities and forms of sociation.' Shields adds to this description of neo-tribes in arguing that neo-tribal identities serve to illustrate the temporal nature of collective identities in modern consumer society as individuals continually move between different sites of collective expression and 'reconstruct' themselves accordingly. Thus, according to Shields (1992: 108): 'Personas are "unfurled" and mutually adjusted. The performative orientation toward the Other in these sites of social centrality and sociality draws people together one by one. Tribe-like but temporary groups and circles condense out of the homogeneity of the mass.'

In my own work (see Bennett, 1999), I have considered the significance of neo-tribe as substitute for 'subculture' a means of understanding the collective practices of youth grounded in consumer sensibilities such as musical taste, fashion sense and leisure preference. Neo-tribe, I suggest, is a more accurate term than subculture – with its implications of fixity, habit and community-ties – for comprehending contemporary youth cultural practices in which issues of class, gender and background are no longer the restrictive elements they once were and young people creatively use leisure and consumption in the construction of lifestyles through which they continually make and remake themselves. Thus, I argue '...

consumerism [has] offered young people the opportunity to break away from their traditional class-based identities, the increased spending power of the young facilitating and encouraging experimentation with new, self-constructed forms of identity' (Bennett, 1999: 602).

Youth spaces – clubs, bars, venues and so – become sites in which young people can collectively act out and refine consumption-based lifestyle projects (Chaney 1996). Youth spaces are also places that are characteristically temporal, a feature that is perhaps more clearly seen in relation to young people's appropriation of less obvious sites, for example, empty car parks and inner-city thoroughfares for the purposes of, for example, skateboarding (see Borden, 2000) or breakdancing. As such, young people are continually engaging and disengaging with such spaces and the collective practices that go on there. This is arguably one of the key problems with earlier studies applying a subcultural perspective in which the fact of 'youth culture' was perceived to be a permanent rather than a transient feature of being young. As McRobbie (1980: 69) argues, 'few writers seemed interested in what happened when a mod went home after a week-end on speed.'

Neo-tribe, allowing as it does for the state of transience in everyday life as individuals move between and engage with different groups, throws light on the dimension of temporality in youth identity and commitment absent from earlier youth cultural research. In more recent decades the increasing role of travel and tourism in young people's lives has opened new ways of examining and interpreting such neo-tribal associations. Thus, rather than being restricted to a young person's immediate sphere of everyday life, typically a local urban or rural setting, neo-tribal gatherings can now be viewed as taking place in a broader, trans-local or trans-national context. The possibility of travel facilitates new levels of neo-tribal collectivity, as young people from around the globe gather in particular spaces for prescribed amounts of time. In such spaces young people are free to experiment with their identities and to engage in interactions with others, in full-knowledge that they can easily disengage with those spaces and gatherings, and the identities they have constructed and acted out therein.

Viewed from this perspective, it is easy to understand the seductive appeal of Ibiza. Immersed in pre-formed images and perceptions of the island's club scene, drawn from books, Web sites, anecdotal accounts of friends and acquaintances and so on, young people arrive on Ibiza with the expectation that it is a place to 'let go', to over-indulge themselves in fun and pleasure. Given the proscribed temporality of the Ibiza experience, there are no ready barriers to the gratification of such expectations and wishes. Indeed, the pursuit of fun and pleasure, in a setting where the key elements of youth leisure – music, dancing, partying, sexual adventure and so on – are very much the norm, becomes the very essence of personal commitment to the dance-tourist gathering. Seeking out such pleasures, following them through and returning to one's everyday life with the personal satisfaction of having negotiated it, if only for a short period of time, are regarded as key to the Ibiza experience by those young people who visit the island. This quality of the Ibiza experience corresponds closely with Bauman's description of the neo-tribe: 'Neo-tribes "exist" solely by individual decisions to sport the symbolic tags of tribal allegiance. They vanish once the decisions are revoked or the zeal and determination of members "fades out". They persevere only thanks to their continuing seductive capacity' (Bauman, 1992: 137).

As Bauman observes, neo-tribes are built largely on the desires of individuals. In the case of Ibiza, the dance-tourist gatherings that assemble there comprise young people who desire an escape from the 'ordinary'. This, above all, is what holds this temporal community together; it is, to paraphrase Maffesoli (1996) a 'glue' that bonds the shifting membership of tribe throughout its seasonal existence. Temporality is assured by the constant coming and going of young dance-tourists who stay on average for one to two weeks. It is also assured by the perceptions of the dance-tourists themselves whose fascination with Ibiza appears inherently tied to their particular stage of life. Indeed, as Ludlam (2003) has noted, the notion of having 'done' Ibiza, and similar island dance resorts, is prevalent in many conversations that take place with and between those have been there on holiday. Ibiza is regarded very much as a place that one visits at a particular stage in life, usually late teens and early twenties, but grows out of with maturity.

Conclusion

This chapter has examined the relevance of the Ibiza club scene as an example of neo-tribal youth gatherings in late modern society. It has been noted how in the context of Ibiza, the fluidity and temporality identified as centrally defining characteristics of the neo-tribe by Maffesoli (1996) and Bauman (1992) are amplified due to the transience of the dance-tourist community. The geographic isolation of Ibiza from the normal everyday settings of those young dance tourists who visit the island, combined with the relative anonymity of the individual dance tourist within the Ibiza dance-tourist community, creates a situation in which temporal associations are both easily enacted and maintained beyond the direct setting of the club, the whole Ibiza experience becoming in effect a neo-tribal youth space. The club tourist community, then, is held together through a series of common expectations and investments of the Ibiza experience centred around a number interchangeable features – music, dance, drink, drugs, sex – integral to youth's conventions of fun and pleasure. Thus, the seasonal existence of the dance tourist community is punctuated by a continual process of engagement and disengagement, as young people temporarily enter the community and then leave again to return to their more routine everyday lives.

Notes

1. Hebdige (1979) coined and used the term 'incorporation' in relation to punk in order to illustrate how the latter's music and style were appropriated by the mainstream music and fashion industries and transformed from an underground scene into a commercially marketed product.
2 Taken from: www.askmen.com (accessed 19 February 2003).
3. Ibid.

References

Anderson, B. (1983), *Imagined Communities*, London: Verso.
Back, L. (1996), *New Ethnicities and Urban Culture: Racisms and Multiculture in Young Lives*, London: UCL Press.
Bauman, Z. (1992), *Intimations of Postmodernity*, London: Routledge
Bennett, A. (1999), 'Subcultures or Neo-Tribes? Rethinking the Relationship between Youth, Style and Musical Taste', *Sociology*, 33(3): 599–617.
Bennett, A. (2001), *Cultures of Popular Music*, Buckingham: Open University Press.
Bennett, A. (2002), 'Music, Media and Urban Mythscapes: A Study of the Canterbury Sound', *Media, Culture and Society*, 24(1): 107–20.
Borden, I. (2000), *Skateboarding, Space and the City: Architecture and the Body*, Oxford: Berg.
Carrington, B. and Wilson, B. (2002) 'Global Clubcultures: Cultural flows and Late Modern Dance Music Culture', in Cieslik, M. and Pollock, G. (eds) *Young People in Risk Society: The Restructuring of Youth Identities and Transitions in Late Modernity*, Aldershot: Ashgate.
Chaney, D. (1996), *Lifestyles*, London: Routledge.
Cohen, S. (1991), *Rock Culture in Liverpool: Popular Music in the Making*, Oxford: Clarendon Press.
Desforges, L. (1998), '"Checking Out the Planet": Global Representations/Local Identities and Youth Travel', in Skelton, T. and Valentine, G. (eds) *Cool Places: Geographies of Youth Cultures*, London: Routledge.
Evans, D. (2001), 'The Guitar in the Blues Music of the Deep South', in Bennett, A. and Dawe, K. (eds) *Guitar Cultures*, Oxford: Berg.
Guardian (2000) 'Travel: Clubbing all over the world', 4 November, pp. 2–4.
Gill, A. (1997), 'We Can Be Heroes', *Mojo*, 41, April: 54–80.
Hall, S. and Jefferson, T. (eds) (1976), *Resistance Through Rituals: Youth Subcultures in Post-War Britain*, London: Hutchinson.
Hebdige, D. (1979), *Subculture: The Meaning of Style*, London: Routledge.
Hetherington, K. (1992), 'Stonehenge and its Festival: Spaces of Consumption', in

Shields, R. (ed.) *Lifestyle Shopping: The Subject of Consumption*, London: Routledge.

Hollands, R. (2002), 'Theorising Urban Playscapes: Producing, Regulating and Consuming Youthful Nightlife City Spaces', *Urban Studies*, 39(1): 153–73.

Laing, D. (1997), 'Rock Anxieties and New Music Networks', in McRobbie, A. (ed.) *Back to Reality: Social Experience and Cultural Studies*, Manchester: Manchester University Press.

Langlois, T. (1992), 'Can you feel it? DJs and House Music Culture in the UK', *Popular Music*, 11(2): 229–38.

Ludlam, H. (2003) 'Sun, Sea, Sand and the Holiday Rep: A Sociological Investigation into Young Women's Holiday Experiences on Club 18–30 Style Holidays', unpublished BSc dissertation, University of Surrey.

McRobbie, A. (1980) 'Settling Accounts with Subcultures: A Feminist Critique', in Frith, S. and Goodwin, A. (eds) (1990) *On Record: Rock Pop and the Written Word*, London: Routledge.

Maffesoli, M. (1996), *The Time of the Tribes: The Decline of Individualism in Mass Society*, trans. D. Smith, London: Sage.

Malbon, B. (1999), *Clubbing: Dancing, Ecstasy and Vitality*, London: Routledge.

Melechi, A. (1993), 'The Ecstasy of Disappearance', in Redhead, S. (ed.) *Rave Off: Politics and Deviance in Contemporary Youth Culture*, Aldershot: Avebury.

Negus, K. (1992), *Producing Pop: Culture and Conflict in the Popular Music Industry*, London: Edward Arnold.

Redhead, S. (1993) 'The End of the End-of-the-Century Party', in Redhead, S. (ed.) *Rave Off: Politics and Deviance in Contemporary Youth Culture*, Aldershot: Avebury.

Rietveld, H. (1997), 'The House Sound of Chicago', in Redhead, S., Wynne, D. and O'Connor, J. (eds) *The Clubcultures Reader: Readings in Popular Cultural Studies*, Oxford: Blackwell.

Saldanha, A. (2002), 'Music Tourism and Factions of Bodies in Goa', *Tourist Studies: An International Journal*, 2(1): 43–62.

Shields, R. (1992), 'Spaces for the Subject of Consumption', in Shields, R. (ed.) *Lifestyle Shopping: The Subject of Consumption*, London: Routledge.

Urry, J. (1990), *The Tourist Gaze: Leisure and Travel in Contemporary Societies*, London: Sage.

Urry, J. (1994), *Consuming Places*, Routledge, London.

Willis, P. (1978), *Profane Culture*, London: Routledge & Kegan Paul.

Recommended Listening

Mediterranean (2002), *Ambient in Ibiza*, Universal Music Latino: CD160515.
Ministry of Sound (2000), *Ibiza Annual: Summer 2000*, Ministry of Sound: CD MOSCD011.
Various artists (2001), *Ibiza Sunset*, Pagan America: CD 842014.
Various artists (2001), *Ibiza Club Trax*, Hot Records. CD 3275.
Various artists (2002), *Cream – Balearic Collection*, Musicrama: CD 3660015.

–7–

Mainland Torres Strait Islander Songwriters and the 'Magical Islands' of the Torres Strait: Songs as Identity Narratives

Chris Lawe Davies and Karl Neuenfeldt

> ... to be an islander – even on the mainland [of Australia] – one must have an island.
> Beckett, 'The Murray Island Land Case ...'

Islands are not only physical places; they can also be metaphorical spaces for connecting with cultural and social origins, especially for diasporic populations separated by time, place and situation from their origins (Hall, 1990). In some cases, they may become 'magical islands' – that is, more imagined than real, more idealized than objectively examined. To quote E. M. Forster (1936: 48): 'In the heart of each man there is contrived, by desperate devices, a magical island.' Music is one means of artistic expression that can help construct such magical, metaphorical spaces.

As an island that is also a continent, Australia provides a unique example of 'island-ness'. It was the colony of an island-based colonizer, Great Britain, and its early migrants were primarily from the island nations of Great Britain and Ireland. Arguably, 'island-ness' was and still is at the core of the Australian worldview. On the positive side this encourages an ethos of self-sufficiency, on the negative side a xenophobic insularity. The latter is manifest currently in race or religion-based exclusionary policies designed to thwart certain groups and kinds of refugees.

Colonial era migrants to Australia invaded and occupied a vast land area, destroying, displacing or disenfranchising much of the indigenous population (Reynolds, 1987). Despite a history of colonial genocide and post-Federation legislative controls (which continued in some areas and contexts until the 1970s), some indigenous peoples survived, with varying degrees of connections to 'traditional' cultures and languages. Today there are two officially recognized indigenous groups in Australia: Aborigines (population 366,665) and Torres Strait

Islanders (26,240) as well as those who identify as both (17,630). In total they comprise approximately 2.4 per cent of the population (Australian Bureau of Statistics, 2001).

There are contemporary Aboriginal Australians who are island based (for example, Tiwi people on Bathurst and Melville islands, Yolngu people on Elcho and Groote Eyland islands off the Northern Territory). However, on a regional basis the most populous islands in Australia are those of the Torres Strait region. As the name suggests, Torres Strait Islanders (henceforth Islanders)[1] are recognized as having deep connections to the Torres Strait region.[2] Percentage-wise, the post-World War Two diaspora of Islanders, for work and educational opportunities (Arthur and Taylor, 1994) is notable. With approximately two-thirds of all Islanders now living 'down south' on the 'mainland' (Arthur, 1998), it is important for some to maintain connections with their own or their ancestors' home islands[3] and cultural practices.

This process of identification *in absentia* is what Martin has called the creation of an 'identity narrative' (Martin, 1995). Some Islanders on the mainland use songs and the process of songwriting to create and celebrate connections to their traditional country, their island homes in the Torres Strait region. They write and sing about places they may have left as children and visit only occasionally or perhaps never. However, connections to their island homes still help define them as a particular kind of Indigenous Australian from particular places with particular ways of living and worldviews. Arguably, for some being an 'Islander' is about being from an 'island' even if that island, that notion of separate-ness and thus unique-ness, may be more a metaphorical resource to draw upon rather than a physical reality, especially after years and sometimes generations on the mainland.

The first things to notice about Islander music are the cultural and political phenomena of which much of the music speaks. They are quite different from those of Aboriginal popular music, where questions of 'identity' and 'home' are sometimes specific but are also often broadly definitive of a pan-indigenous artic-ulation of post-colonial resistance (Lawe Davies, 1994). Although the danger is always to homogenize and generalize what are otherwise diverse and culturally specific musical forms in Islander music, there appears to be a more culturally specific sense of identity, if for no other reason than the home islands' physical separation from mainland Australia. Herein lies the essential paradox of the dias-poric imagination: although the geographic space known as the Torres Strait is a group of islands between Australia and Papua New Guinea, the majority of its population are mainland, not island-based, Australians. For many Islanders iden-tity is both an imagined unity (Anderson, 1983) and something celebrated and 'lived out' through cultural re-enactment or song and dance performances. Essentially, then, the diasporic imagination is both an 'intellectualization' (Safran, 1991: 87) and 'lived experience' through cultural activities.

As Gilroy (1990/91) has conceptualized it, in any immigrant society potential tensions exist between where you are now and where you (or your ancestors) have come from. It is what he calls 'the dialectics of diasporic identification'. In Anderson's (1983) terms, we can imagine a national community, but because it is 'imagined' it is always a provisional and mobile set of arrangements. Just how provisional and how mobile is not really the issue: that is a question mainly on the minds of the nationalists. For the diasporic focus, it is always a question of negotiating the tension between 'here' and 'there'.

This chapter examines the 'here' and 'there' of songs by Getano Bann (born on the mainland) and Ricardo Idagi (born in the Torres Strait region). Bann and Idagi are mainland-based Islanders who write and sing about making and keeping connections to island homes, thereby constructing an Islander identity reflecting their particular time, place, and situation. They provide good examples of how music can be used to animate identity (Frith, 1996; Stokes 1994); that is, literally to give it breath through song.

The Notion of Identity Narratives

Martin's (1995) analysis of 'the choices of identity' looks at how identity is constructed and culturally produced by groups and individuals as a narrative, a story with particular tropes and characters. The major goal of identity narratives is to stimulate positive change so that a group has more access to power and the potential to enhance life-chances of its subjects. There are two key ways to help fashion this often counter-hegemonic, often politically motivated discourse: selecting specific cultural traits, and trying to 'emancipate amnesia' of events and attitudes in the past.

Martin (1995: 7) cautions that identity narratives are not reducible to 'expressions of social homogeneity or representations of immutable realities'. Identity is seen as not being about homogeneity or permanence, in part because people can have a range of choices of identity narratives including rejecting all of them. The available identity narratives are always in flux and often politically contingent, although aspects of them may be promulgated and perceived as fixed and enduring.

Martin (1995: 12) contends the three key 'pillars' of identity narratives are relationships linked to the past, culture and space. Regarding the past, Martin suggests: 'Collective memories frequently have special chapters for traumatic events, that is real or imagined events the relation of which in the identity narrative confers them a particular weight (sometimes in glory, more usually in horror)'. Therefore present attitudes and behaviours can be directly linked to pivotal events in the past.

In regards to culture, Martin (1995: 13) asserts that the traits selected 'are frequently related to practices that gave the milieux where individuals grew up a particular flavour, and carry a strong affective load'. Some traits are privileged and others ignored because they may or may not be consonant with contemporary political, social and cultural circumstances or goals. Choosing emblems embodying or symbolizing group solidarity and distinctiveness is also essential. Martin (1995: 13) proposes that 'relationship to time helps to make these emblems look perennial; relationship to space offers them a field in which they can be displayed'. Therefore, identity narratives often transform cultures by selecting, valorizing, and mythologizing certain attributes and artefacts. Importantly in this context, Martin (1995: 11) also proposes that poets are the kind of culture brokers to whom a group will turn 'to preach the gospel of identity'. Songwriters are poets with the musical skills to articulate the uniqueness of a group and why its culture should be celebrated.

In regard to space, Martin (1995: 12) suggests it emerges in the narratives as 'the place where the necessities of life are available; where communities are able to sustain themselves and reproduce themselves, and have been doing so for a long time'. Significantly, it is where power was/is used in a specific way by a specific group of people. Space is also a place where a unique kind of sociality abides and abounds, and where customs that make up 'a good life' (such as artistic expression via music) are present.

Lastly, Martin asserts identities actually do not exist in and of themselves. Rather, it is the identity narratives that produce and construct them via the process of narrativization. Regardless of the invented-ness of traditions (Hobsbawn and Ranger 1983), they can be considered essential and enduring and treated as sacrosanct. Martin (1995: 13) summarizes thus: 'the identity narrative channels political emotions so that they can fuel efforts to modify a balance of power; it transforms the perceptions of the past and of the present; it changes the organization of human groups and creates new ones; it alters cultures by emphasizing certain traits and skewing their meanings and logic'. Thus the main goal of an identity narrative is to encourage a new explanation of the world so as to alter it. In this analysis, the songs of Getano Bann and Ricardo Idagi contain numerous examples of the process of narrativization at work in the creation of mainland Islander identity narratives. There is always an overlap of themes but for heuristic purposes the analysis is separated into Martin's three 'pillars': the past, culture and space.

Analysis: The Past

Situations and events that come to encapsulate collective memories are a key element in the 'past' component of identity narratives. A song by Ricardo Idagi dealing with a past situation is *Gaynawa Kubi* (see Example 7.1), which includes a Mer (Murray) Island *Babaneb* chant.[4] It refers to a past era in Torres Strait history, the direct albeit incomplete control of Islanders' work and life styles mandated by various Australian and Queensland race-based laws. It was the main governmental administrator, the Protector of Aborigines, operating historically through government departments such as the Department of Native Affairs and the Department of Aboriginal and Islander Advancement, who implemented the laws (Beckett, 1987: 44–55). The song begins with the chant in the Meriam Mir language of eastern Torres Strait and then cross fades into an English language narrative of exploitation and conversely resistance through musical cultural practice.

Gaynawa kubi a gaynawa kubi (Chant)

Our fathers have toiled the seas to give us a future / Diving for shells watched over by the protectorate / He has taken our labour, for his gain / Instead he supplied us with small change / jam and grain yeah

But all through that toiling the distant drums are calling / Calling them home, calling them home / Where the old men are chanting / E le eres / e poni deres / e pa tewspili ma / e pa tewspili ma / E le eres / e poni deres / e pa tewspili ma / e pa tewspili ma / This is the music, this is the sound from our past, and it's still here to stay

Chant

All the luggers are working, they're full of sand, shells and salt / But still they must work for the protectorate / He has taken our labour, for his gain / Instead he supplied us with small change / jam and grain yeah /

But all through that toiling the distant drums are calling / Calling them home, calling them home / Where the old men are chanting / This is the music, this is the sound from our past, and it's still here to stay

Chant.

Example 7.1 *Gaynawa Kubi* by Ricardo Idagi

Notably, the song is presented in reggae style, a style with overtly resistive expression in Aboriginal music inspired by Bob Marley's performances in Australia in the 1970s (Breen, 1989) and still popular today especially in remote northern Aboriginal communities (Smith, 2001/2002). It is of paramount importance to negotiate cultural protocols when presenting recordings incorporating Indigenous elements. The following excerpt from the CD sleeve notes for Idagi's *Listen to My Drum* album illustrates that acknowledgment is a crucial element of cultural protocol whether the artists resides in or outside the Torres Strait. They begin by acknowledging the traditional Aboriginal landowners in Melbourne where the recording was done and move on to more specific information highlighting Idagi's linkages to his home island of Mer:

> I would like to acknowledge that this recording took place on the traditional lands of the Kulin Nation. Nimaw. I acknowledge that the Ilok, Babneb and Taybobo chants and Sepsegur used on this recording belong to the Meryam people. Recognition goes to the Elders, Uncles, Aunty and brother whose songs I have adapted for these songs. (Idagi, 2002)

The *Babaneb* chant itself, *Gaynawa Kubi*, is also integral to a recording by another singer-songwriter with connections to Mer Island, Brian Williams. His song *One People* appeared on *Strike Em! Contemporary Voices from the Torres Strait Community* CD (2001). However, because Williams has both Islander and Aboriginal heritage, it required adherence to protocols arising from both cultures (Neuenfeldt, 2001). Such cultural (and musical) hybridity is a further example of the complexity of identity narratives. Since 1996 the Australian Census has even included a category for people acknowledging both Islander and Aboriginal descent, especially common on northern Cape York Peninsular where Islander communities were established at Bamaga and Seisia in 1948 amidst several Aboriginal communities (Singe 1989).

An example of a key event in the past is a song by Getano Bann. The event is the Coming of the Light, the landing of the London Missionary Society at Erub (Darnley) Island on 1 July 1871 from the boat *Surprise*. The processes and politics of Christianization and Missionization have had major impacts on Islander history and cultural practice (Beckett, 1987), which continue into the present (Mullins, 2001; Lawrence, 1998; Fuary, 1993). The re-enactment of the Coming of the Light, the re-telling of the narrative, forms an important aspect of the diasporic existence of many Islanders. To quote one Brisbane community leader, Islander Pastor Ted Reuben in his comments at the opening of the Coming of the Light Festival in 1999: 'this was the coming of the light ... and the sweeping away of the darkness ... our darkness'. Although celebrated by many Christian Islanders in the Torres Strait and on the Mainland as a day of deliverance, Gaetano Bann's song *Darkness* (Example 7.2) presents an alternative reading of the event, one of a day of enslavement. Its very title is oppositional to the binary of 'light' and its closing refrain 'From darkness / the darkness' interrogates the end result of the arrival of Christianity.

Square rigging on the horizon / first of July 1871 / what is your cargo that has no price / black of face, white of mind / From darkness / sailing out of the night / from darkness / coming into the light

Athei Maino[5] what had you seen / to choose this course your destiny / who were the markai[6] in dressing gowns / who preached the truth / lay your icons down / From darkness / sailing out of the night / from darkness / coming into the light

We bring salvation / the gift of Christ / so free your minds of your pagan lies / with rice and biscuits we'll enmesh you / to seek the way, the light, the truth / From darkness / sailing out of the night / from darkness / coming into the light

Square rigging on the horizon / first of July 1871 / your zealous chapters promised new life / you shamed our hearts with your coated lies / From darkness / the darkness.

Example 7.2 *Darkness* by Getano Bann

As suggested earlier, the Coming of the Light festival is almost universally accepted among Islander communities as the starting point of social modernity. But Getano Bann is contesting this naturalization, indeed overturning it. Clearly part of the diasporic imagination is a dialogic relation to its history, enabling cultural identity to move beyond essentializing tendencies that might be set in place through any reification of the events in 1871. As Singe (1989: 57–63) has noted, the arrival of Christianity in Torres Strait did have a dark side, such as the excesses of the mainly Polynesian missionaries ('black of face, white of mind') who came to regulate communities (and local leaders such as Maino) and eradicate or alter pre-Christian cultural practices more so than the *markai* ('white') missionaries. *Darkness* alludes to past excesses and the song envisions a different religious and narrative trajectory than many Islanders profess. As well, Bann uses 'mainstream' musical production, English language and 'Western' instrumentation to address a defining Islander historical event.

Analysis: Culture

The cultural traits emphasized by Islander songwriters are frequently linked to affective memories of childhood and the personal and cultural contexts of the transmission of particular practices or of a more general social ambience. The sleeve notes to Getano Bann's album point out that he was raised on the mainland in Mackay, Queensland by his Islander mother and Scottish father, 'but always had the feeling he was living between two worlds'. The CD came about through successful funding applications in 1996 from Arts Queensland and the Australia Council for the Arts. The sleeve notes say the project was funded to enable Getano 'to find out more about these disparate cultures'. The album also celebrates his Torres Straits heritage: of pearling, fishing, schooldays and characters in his childhood. Several songs attest to his childhood suffering, though, ending with the explanatory last song *For Life Is ...*, addressed to his father: 'Oh father it's hard / but these things I have to say / you robbed me of your loving / while you drank our lives away'.

Significantly the parent who receives entirely positive treatment is his Islander mother, not only through the song that explicitly connects her to him, *I Wear My Mother's Face*, but also the title track *Solwata* (Example 7.3). It traces out a kind of re-birthing sequence where the saltwater is emblematic of the physical environment central to the sense of place in the Torres Strait Islands. At the same time it suggests the amniotic waters in his mother's belly while he was safe inside her and to which he somehow returns through the act of reiteration in song.

Hush little child / rest beneath your mother's smile / for soon enough you will grow / then you'll make your way / in the world some day / but for now just let it go / and breathe / inside saltwater

I look at you/ all alone and confused / you know the mirror never lies / come and name your grief / let it go, set it free / for fear offers no peace of mind / All my life / I've sought the next best thing / but once I held it / what joy did it bring / I hope you're never ever, ever bothered / by your skin colour / I hope your life is filled with joy / and the lessons you'll learn in life return / reflect the special gifts you bring / and breathe / inside saltwater

Father tried long and hard to reconcile / sons conceived belied his skin / mother comfort me / through my pain and grief / please tell me who and what I am

For all my life / I had to justify / who I am, how I identify / why can't people just let me be / let me breathe / inside saltwater.

Example 7.3 *Solwata* by Getano Bann

The foetus is able to 'breathe' within saltwater; like an amphibious creature; a Darwinist return to origins, no less. Taking the images suggested by *I Wear My Mother's Face* and *Solwata*, and given the fact that he was raised in Mackay, not the Torres Strait, Getano's yearning for homeland is not necessarily literally for his own home but his mother's, arguably the motherland of the diasporic imagination. The narrative also provides a personal recounting of a clash of cultures within one family but is perhaps applicable to the broader process of hybridity underlying both cultural and biological recombinations encountered by diasporic populations.

Another example of a biologically based narrative connection to island homes is Idagi's song *Nibe Nibe* (Example 7.4) based on a Mer Island *Ikok* chant, which features structured vocal sobbing and dancing (Beckett 2003). It is the first song on his CD and importantly incorporates the voice of Eddie Koiki Mabo, to whom the recording is dedicated: '... for his struggle to have our people's land and sea rights recognized by Australian law'. It also includes excerpts from radio broadcasts. Mabo was one of the Mer (Murray) Islander claimants in a landmark court case, commonly known as the Mabo Decision, in which the High Court of Australia recognized the existence of some indigenous land and sea rights. It overturned the legal fiction of *terra nullius*, that Australia was uninhabited at the time of European invasion (Loos, 1996). The song is presented in a folk-rock style (drums, bass, acoustic and electric guitar, accordion) with no overt Islander aural signifiers such as percussion or choral singing. However, regardless of its external 'Westernness', its internal content is decidedly Islander in perspective.

There's a pagan moon rising from the Coral Sea / Red as the embers of his fire / The old man sits alone while the village people sleep / Dreams of his children are so dire / Yesterday is truly gone / Memories are history now / But it's told by his story songs / Sung by his people from before his time

O nibe nibe adudum ya e / O adudum ya sigadudum ya e

[Eddie Koiki Mabo, spoken excerpt: '... according to my tradition, those fishes, the prawn, what ever is there in that sea belongs to me and my people. That is important and that of course ought to be claimed, that I am claiming in the High Court [of Australia] ...'

I was born in the Straits, raised in the city but I still have inherited traits / They have taken me away from my island home / but they'll never take my island away from me

O nibe nibe adudum ya e / O adudum ya sigadudum ya e

[Radio excerpts mentioning land rights]

My son's mother's people call him a native / I will say outright, they have no insight / Cos when that tree shall bear its fruit, he'll search for his roots / Where is my father's people homeland? yeah

O nibe nibe adudum ya e / O adudum ya sigadudum ya e

[Radio excerpts mentioning potential impact of the High Court decision on mining]

Yesterday is truly gone; memories are history now / But it's told by his story songs, sung be his people from before his time.

Example 7.4 *Nibe Nibe* by Ricardo Idagi

The lyrics of *Nibe Nibe* and *Solwata* address consistent themes of mainland Islanders' songs: recognition of an almost inherent biological connection to island homes, and the necessity for individuals and groups to negotiate between the purported 'timelessness' of particular cultural practices (and places) and an awareness of the need to live in the present in quite different social, cultural and even economic milieu from one's ancestors'. In many of the songs of Bann and Idagi, the contemporary is balanced with and situated within the historical via a blend of 'traditional' and 'modern' approaches to words and music. It would be interesting to speculate on what kinds of songs (and themes) would result from a collaboration of the two songwriters with their different yet linked experiences of Islander life on the mainland.

Analysis: Space

Reflections on the importance of space, in the senses of locality and socio-cultural ambiences, are common in identity narratives. In the 8 minutes and 38 seconds of *Way E* (Example 7.5), Idagi provides a wide-ranging comment on the challenges of relating to and living in at least two different though interrelated Australian cultures. One is 'Anglo', urban and 'mainstream', the other Islander, rural and 'isolated'; one is temporal, the other 'timeless'; one monolingual, the other multilingual. As a narrative the song is simultaneously personalized and generalized, arguably encapsulating the experiences and yearnings of other Islanders negotiating their engagement with Australian society.

This world tells me you will not find what you're searching for here / So I left my home and the safety of my island / Walking around lost in the tall city skylines

Going to a job interview I pace the floor / Nervous hesitation to open the door / I'm sinking to the bottom chained to my homesickness rock / It's hard to surface, oh I'm in culture shock

So scared of fast cars and the electric train / I find myself in a totally foreign domain / Standing all alone watching the city breathing black smoke in / factories and freeways / I'm working in the bowels being a slave to the system / Shovelling shit uphill just to pay the bills

To the man who is the master his scheme is to get rich faster / He said, for me, he said 'to be part of it boy, you got to climb on the roller coaster'

O nole, o nole, ma kole nali, mari tonartonar / O nole, o nole, ma kole nali, mari tonartonar / Ka Meryam nali, kari tonartonar, ka meryam nali kari tonartonar /

It's a living, moving, consuming dragon / Beckoning me controlling me to follow on

I didn't know I have what I have been searching for / Given to me at birth by grandparents before them / In the shape of a dugong my mother's totem / Beckoning me wanting me to go back home

Way e way e atayba mir / Way e way e yaba sagim / Way e way e maysor mena mir igali /

When I go home I'll sit with my brothers / When I grew old I'll sing to others / oh oh oh

Mi tu Stanley sidawn lisen sing to kaba ata / Mi tu Danny ene Stolin stap lo kabi ata / Mi tu Debes stap lo Apau ene Siko ata / Mi tu Sigar stap lo Ariko ene Mani ata /

When I walk home I recall the scenes from my childhood days / yeah Bakoi ata yu mi go Tawmagerem / Kanay ata yu ol taym apo mi go naw I wan man I wokbawt go Bawz oh oh oh

Way e way e atayba mir / Way e way e yaba sagim / Way e way e maysor mena mir igali /

Where ever I may go I will always remember / Atayba kodomir a yaba sagim / Like the beat of the drums on the distant shores / Deep in my heart the maysor[7] will roar / Given to me at birth by grandparents before them / In the shape of a dugong where I belong / I Magaram le grassroots Meryam le

Way e way e atayba mir / Way e way e yaba sagim / Way e way e maysor mena mir igali /

Maysor mena mir igali

Example 7.5 *Way E* by Ricardo Idagi

Way E's lyrics provide a poignant comment on the diasporic experience and suggest that for Idagi the mainland is a place of temporary even if long-term residence, an impermanent space because it is not directly linked to key components of an Islander 'good life' such as family, language and totem.

Conclusions

In a sense, songwriters such as Getano Bann and Ricardo Idagi provide artistic role models for other Torres Strait Islander songwriters by giving public expression to what may be the private thoughts and personal reflections of many other Islanders. Such a 'one-is-many' perspective is commonly a key role of musicians as a particular kind of 'cultural poet' (Martin, 1995) who navigate the confluence of 'here' and 'there' of their own lives but also those of other diasporic Islanders. As such they enunciate the general condition of diasporic identity through their own identity narratives.

At the beginning of this chapter it was suggested that Australia's 'island-ness' manifested itself in two ways – 'self sufficiency' as the positive and 'xenophobic insularity' as the negative. While these positive and negative readings are clearly extremes on a continuum, seen in terms of the situation for colonized indigenous people, the 'xenophobia' that excludes them from the mainstream is in some sense also associated with cultural and territorial dispossession.

But what is often forgotten, and what often manifests itself in homogenizing ideological structures such as the key governmental representative organization, the Aboriginal and Torres Strait Islander Commission, is that the Torres Strait Australians have a different history from Aboriginal Australians. What in general terms is seen as the colonizing moment in indigenous politics – the 1788 British arrival in Botany Bay – has little resonance above the twenty-sixth parallel. Even below that latitude colonization constitutes not just a concrete struggle by a dispossessed and repressed series of cultures, but is itself an ideological and textual struggle.

While for mainland indigenous people whose cultural dispossession and physical displacement was axiomatic of white arrival in Australia, for Torres Strait Island people the white arrival is celebrated (albeit not unproblematically) through the Coming of the Light festival noted earlier. Also, the fact that the physical displacement of approximately three-quarters of the current population to mainland Australia is largely tied to issues of employment and middle-class advancement, suggests that both Bann's and Idagi's music resonates more at the individual level than the general level. Their intonations of diasporic identity operate as a nostalgic hearkening to island homelands and as critiques of colonization, but within a complex history of colonisation. Ang (1993: 3) suggests a useful description of the diasporic imagination as one encompassing: 'Sprawling socio cultural formations of people, creating imagined communities whose blurred and fluctuating boundaries are sustained by real and/or symbolic ties to some original 'homeland' ... It is the myth of the (lost or idealised) homeland, the object of both collective memory and of desire and attachment, which is constitutive to diasporas'.

Such a description is particularly relevant to the song-based identity narratives examined here. To quote Ang (1993: 7): '[it is] precisely that complexity and flexibility of the space between which makes out the vitality of diaspora cultures'. Both Getano Bann and Ricardo Idagi – as songwriters 'in-between' – create songs that are complex and flexible, just like the cultures they arose from and that they celebrate from a physical but not necessarily emotional distance.

Notes

1. The term 'Islanders' is also sometimes used to refer to descendants of Melanesians brought to Australia to work primarily as labourers in the sugar cane industry, especially in Queensland and New South Wales. They are known as Australian South Sea Islanders and only recently gained official recognition as a distinct group (Mullins *et al.*, 1996).
2. The major Torres Strait Islander communities in Torres Strait are located in the following areas: Top Western area (Boigu, Dauan and Saibai); Central area (Coconut, Warraber, Yam and Yorke); Western area (Badu, Mabuiag and Moa); Eastern (Darnley, Murray and Stephen), Near Western (Hammond, Horn and Thursday). On northern Cape York Peninsula there are Islander communities at Seisia and Bamaga. Most of the communities and islands have indigenous and non-indigenous names. On the mainland, there are large and active Islander communities in regional cities such as Cairns, Townsville, and Mackay and also communities in capital cities such as Brisbane, Melbourne and Sydney.
3. The song *My Island Home* was written by Anglo-Australian Neil Murray about Aboriginal musician George Rrurrambu from Elcho Island. Indigenous and non-indigenous Australians have adopted (and adapted) it as an unofficial anthem. Islander singer and actor Christine Anu recorded a popular version (Connell, 1999).
4. Beckett (personal communication with Karl Neuenfeldt, 2003) considers it to be a *Taap* chant because the singing features a descending scale.
5. Maino was an Islander chief at the time of Christianization.
6. In the Kala Lagaw Ya language of Western Torres Strait, *markai* translates as 'white man' or 'ghost'.
7. In the Meriam Mer language of Eastern Torres Strait, *maysor* refers to 'the rumble when the ocean waves meet the reef'.

Acknowledgments

Thanks to Getano Bann and Ricardo Idagi for permission to quote their lyrics at length and thanks to Bua Mabo for Meriam Mir and Kala Lagaw Ya translations.

References

Anderson, B. (1983), *Imagined Communities*, London: Verso.

Ang I. (1993), 'Migrations of Chineseness'. *SPAN Journal of the South Pacific Association for Commonwealth Literature and Language Studies,* 34–35: 3–15.

Arthur, W. (1998), *Access to Government Programs and Services for Mainland Torres Strait Islanders.* Discussion Paper 5, Centre for Aboriginal Economic Policy Research, Canberra: The Australian National University.

Arthur, W. and Taylor, J. (1994), *The Comparative Economic Status of Torres Strait Islanders in Torres Strait and Mainland Australia.* Discussion Paper 72, Centre for Aboriginal Economic Policy Research, Canberra: The Australian National University.

Australian Bureau of Statistics (2001), *Census*, Canberra: Australian Government Printing Service.

Beckett, J. (1994), 'The Murray Island Land Case and the Problem of Cultural Continuity', in W. Sanders (ed.) *Mabo and Native Title: Origins and Institutional Implications*, Monograph No. 7, Canberra: Australian National University Centre for Aboriginal Economic Policy Research, pp. 2–24.

Beckett, J. (1987), *Torres Strait Islanders: Custom and Colonisation*, Cambridge: Cambridge University Press.

Breen, M. (1989), *Our Place, Our Music*, Canberra: Australian Institute of Aboriginal Studies.

Connell, John (1999), '"My Island Home": The politics and poetics of the Torres Strait', in King, R. and Connell, J. (eds), *Small Worlds, Global Lives: Islands and Migration*, London: Pinter, pp. 69–88.

Forster, E. M. (1936), *Abinger Harvest*, Ringwood: Penguin.

Frith, S. (1996), 'Music and Identity', in Hall, S and Du Gay, P. (eds), *Questions of Cultural Identity*, London: Sage, pp. 108–27.

Fuary, M. (1993), 'Torres Strait Cultural History', in Loos, N. and Osanai, T. (eds) *Indigenous Minorities and Education*, Tokyo: Sanyusha, pp. 165–86.

Gilroy, P. (1990/91), 'It Ain't Where You're From, It's Where You're At ... The Dialectics of Diasporic Identification'. *Third Text*, 13: 3–16.

Hall, S. (1990), 'Cultural Identity and Diaspora', in Rutherford, J. (ed.), *Identity, Community, Culture, Difference*, Sage: London, pp. 222–37.

Hall, S. (1996), 'Introduction: Who needs Identity?', in Hall, S. and Du Gay, P. (eds), *Questions of Cultural Identity*, London: Sage, pp. 1–17.

Hobsbawm, E. and Ranger, T. (1983), (eds) *The Invention of Tradition*, Cambridge: Cambridge University Press.

Lawe Davies, C. (1994), 'Aboriginal Rock Music: Space and Place', in Bennett, T., Frith, S., Grossberg, L., Shepherd, J. and Turner, G. *Rock and Popular Music: Politics, Policies, Institutions*, London: Routledge, pp. 249–65.

Lawrence, H. (1998), '"Bethlehem" in Torres Strait: Music, Dance and Christianity in Erub (Darnley Island)', *Australian Aboriginal Studies* 2: 51–63.

Loos, N. and Mabo, K. (1996), *Edward Koiki Mabo: His Life and Struggle for Land Rights*, Brisbane: University of Queensland Press.

Martin, D. (1995), 'The Choices of Identity'. *Social Identities*, 1(1): 5–20.

Mullins, S. (2001), 'Kastom, Syncretism and Self-Determination: The reconciliation of *Bipotaim* and *Pastaim* in the Church of Torres Strait'. *Queensland Review*, 8(1): 21–30.

Mullins, S., R. Cox, K. Fatnowna, C. Gistitin, R. Kennedy, J. Warkill. (1996), *After Recognition: Access and Equity for Australian South Sea Islanders*, Rockhampton: Rural and Social and Economic Research Centre, Central Queensland University.

Neuenfeldt, K. and Oien, K. (2001), '"Our Home, Our Land ... . Something to Sing About": Indigenous popular music as identity narrative'. *Aboriginal History*, 20: 27–38.

Reynolds, H. (1987), *Frontier*, Sydney: Allen & Unwin.

Safran, W. (1991), 'Diasporas in Modern Societies: Myths of Homeland and Return'. *Diaspora,* 1(1): 83–104.

Singe, J. (1989), *The Torres Strait: People and History,* St. Lucia: University of Queensland Press.

Smith, R. (2001/2002), 'Music as "Boys Business" in Indigenous and Other Settings', *Music Forum* 8(1): 24–6.

Stokes, M. (ed.) (1994), *Ethnicity, Identity and Music: The Musical Construction of Place*, Oxford: Oxford University Press.

Recommended Listening

Bann, Getano (2000), *Inside Solwata*, Independent Production, Brisbane Australia, c/o Box 127, Morningside, Queensland 4170, Australia.

Dan, Seaman (2001), *Follow the Sun*, Hot Records 1075, Box 326, Spit Junction, New South Wales 2088, Australia.

Dan, Seaman (2002), *Steady, Steady*, Hot Records 1075, Box 326, Spit Junction, New South Wales 2088, Australia.

Idagi, Ricardo (2002), *Listen to My Drum: King Kadu from Werbadu*, Magadog Records, c/o Box 421, Williamstown, Victoria 3016, Australia.

Mills, Rita (2002), *Mata Nice,* Zuna 001, c/o Box 7832, Cairns, Queensland 4870, Australia.

Strike Em! Contemporary Voices from Torres Strait (2001), c/o Torres Strait Islander Media Association, Box 385, Thursday Island, Queensland 4875, Australia.

Our Home, Our Land. (1995), CAAMA 253 c/o Central Australian Aboriginal Media Association, http://www.caama.com.au/.

−8−

Music in The Diasporic Imagination and the Performance of Cultural (Dis)placement in Trinidad

Tina K. Ramnarine

When the violin whines its question and the banjo answers,
my pain increases in stabs, my severances
from odours and roots, the homemade shac-shac *scraping,*
the dip and acknowledgement of courteous country dances,
the smoke I would hold in my arms always escaping
like my father's figure, and now my mother's;
... My fingers are like thorns and my eyes are wet
like logwood leaves after a drizzle, the kind in which
the sun and the rain contend for the same place
like the two languages I know – one so rich
in its imperial intimacies, its echo of privilege,
the other like the orange words of a hillside in drought –
but my love of both wide as the Atlantic is large.

Walcott, 1997

Crisis talks are taking place in Trinidad and Tobago as I write this chapter.[1] The two major political parties in the Republic of Trinidad and Tobago, the People's National Movement (PNM) and the United National Congress (UNC) are struggling to resolve post-election political tensions resulting from both parties winning an equal share of seats. What is depressing about this current situation is that it reveals yet again the ways in which issues of ethnicity are configured into the island's struggles over power. Focusing on the musical practices associated with these island spaces gives us insights into the play of power and into ideas about musical and social differences and similarities. Contrapuntal discourses on politics, ethnicity and music are continuously shifting, creating and dissolving concordant and discordant social textures. They reveal fundamental concerns about the

integrity of island spaces, the extent to which they can be demarcated as geographically, socially and politically distinct, and the role of music in the construction of
local identities.

In an earlier analysis of the popular music, chutney, I considered the ways in
which musical performances are implicated in political processes and argued that
the interactions and relationships between musical traditions found in a post-colonial Trinidad serve as a vehicle for political aspirations towards national unity.
Even if chutney is largely identified and labelled by its practitioners and audiences
as being 'Indian-Caribbean', the musical exchanges that characterize the genre can
be seen as serving to establish both a sense of 'home' in the island and of multi-
local belonging (to various places). To elaborate briefly, chutney refers to a
heritage beyond the Caribbean (in India), but this musical genre can be used in the
expression of two very different senses of cultural placement (where one, the
Indian Diaspora is also a displacement) because of the ways in which the music
itself is put together. Chutney draws on folk and religious traditions from India. It
also draws on other contemporary Caribbean musics. It thus simultaneously references a heritage elsewhere and people's sense of belonging in the Caribbean. The
importance of considering musical exchanges is that they reveal the ways in which
musicians are imaginatively and creatively involved in the re-conceptualization of
what constitutes contemporary Trinidadian society, and in the affirmation of political aspirations for national unity (Ramnarine, 1998, 2001).

This kind of analysis was an attempt to address issues of ethnicity through a close
examination of musical practices but also, and perhaps more importantly, to suggest
moving beyond the confines of 'ethnicity' by taking into account the multiple
creative processes that produce such a popular music. Through their musical practices and the interweaving between polyphonic discourses of diaspora and of nation,
musicians throw into question notions of cultural essentialisms, fixed identities, and
belonging as territorial affiliation (cf. Gilroy, 1997). Such an analysis, drawing on
the idea of musical exchanges within the framework of specific historical processes,
can be read as being an attempt to ground 'creolization-as-process in empirical sites
of creative cultural recombination' that moves towards 'removing culture change
from the premise of cultural essence' (Khan, 2001: 293). In Trinidad, ideas about
'cultural essence' are still strong, however, and are expressed through discourses on
ethnicity juxtaposed with those on diaspora. Thus chutney is 'Indian-Caribbean'.
Musical exchanges of the kind noted in chutney practice, however, assume a potential political significance in offering ways of thinking through post-independent
stasis perceived in terms of oppositional 'ethnic groups'. Exchanges as creative
musical processes do not necessarily entail the loss of diasporic legacies in ongoing
processes of cultural transformation. Chutney is still regarded as having something
'Indian' about it. I would suggest that these kinds of musical processes, drawing on
ideas about exchange and transformation, the past and the present, cannot, however,

be mapped wholesale onto 'ethnic groups'. Neither are they simply explained by, or reducible to, creolization models (so often applied to Caribbean contexts). Even with a warning against simple readings at the poles of either essentialism or creolization, the term 'musical exchange' is itself hazardous. It can be too easily misread in terms of 'cultural essence', of the meeting of musical differences related to ethnic, political, social or cultural particularities. While difference is often fixed in musical performances, even in contexts of musical exchanges, I would suggest that the important question, really, (and the one that I want to pursue in this chapter) is the extent to which musical practices offer ways of challenging the various sorts of boundaries ('political', 'social', 'ethnic', 'cultural', 'geographic') that people insist on marking.

If current party politics do not testify to the potential for island 'harmony', cultivating such a vision is nevertheless still a worthwhile project and one that will be rehearsed with some variation here. In the calypso tradition of providing socio-political commentary through song, the calypso monarch competition in Carnival 2002 featured prize-winning songs that explored party political dynamics and raised questions about ethnicity. Sugar Aloes won the competition with 'Jubilation Time', a calypso about the PNM's rise to power and Denyse Plummer (national calypso monarch of Carnival 2001) won third place with 'No Winners': 'when you vote race, no-one wins'. Music provides an apt medium for reflecting on socio-political processes and the transformational opportunities afforded by them for as Slobin observes, 'music harbors the habitual, but also acts as a herald of change' (Slobin, 1996: 1). I do not intend to dwell much further on the island political moment here. But I introduce it because, like the complex scenarios of musical exchange that characterize a genre such as chutney, it also offers a commentary (gripping current national attention) on the politics of location. Such is the diasporic imagination that musical performances, and the discourses that surround them, serve to demarcate specific spaces that point to the different kinds of histories that shape contemporary Trinidadian sensibilities. These performances interrogate the notions of 'islander' and of 'home' and can be far removed from the rhetoric of 'island harmony' and 'rainbow society' (descriptors celebrating ethnic plurality). By focusing on Carnival genres, this chapter will explore the diasporic imagination that looks to Africa, to India, and to Trinidad (through the Caribbean Diaspora). By showing how musical performances in Trinidad draw on imageries of other places, reach out to audiences in a global sphere, and are deeply implicated with political processes that relate to the island space but resonate beyond these geographic parameters, my aim is to consider how they might strike against the core of ideas about 'boundaries' – musical or otherwise. This is the ambiguity of cultural (dis)placement. Ultimately, I wish to emphasize that although the performance spaces of Carnival are implicated in the struggles over ethnicity in Trinidad (Yelvington, 1993) and in contestations over national culture (Reddock, 1995), they share a performance politics devoted to the exploration of displacement *and* placement. Of diaspora and home. Of particular interest are the discourses of locality, given the difficulties in thinking about the island as a bounded musical space, and the ways in which musical performances are implicated in the negotiation of cultural (dis)placement in Trinidad.

The Island in a Global Context

Modification of insular ecosystems, development of plantation economies and the importation of labour forces from around the globe have characterized the Caribbean since 1492. The histories of colonialism, slavery and indentureship have left their marks on these island societies. Knight and Palmer note that since the late fifteenth century the region 'has oscillated between the center and periphery of international affairs' (Knight and Palmer, 1989: 1). Through their performances and recorded repertoires, musicians in Trinidad have explored the interstices of diasporized conditions: the spaces of island home and the ties of its inhabitants to the wider global ecumene. Influential calypso and chutney song texts refer to the imagery of the boat: the different ships that sailed across the Middle Passage (Africa to the New World) and the Other Middle Passage (from India). Brother Marvin sang about the 'brotherhood of the boat' in a calypso competition and the chutney singer, Sundar Popo (1944–2000), composed a song for the 1995 Indian Arrival Day celebrations about the *Fath Al Razack*, the ship bringing the first indentured Indian labourers to Trinidad (extracts cited in Ramnarine 1996: 144 and 1998: 10–11). 'The journey don't stop', sings the calypsonian, Chris Tambu Herbert. An understanding of contemporary migration patterns from the Caribbean to former colonial centres and to the USA depends, as Richardson observes, on the past – in taking into account earlier migrations (Richardson 1989: 227).

Songs like those of Marvin, Popo and Herbert offer reminders of the historical and economic circumstances that have shaped musical practices on the island and point to the difficulties of drawing musical boundaries that correspond with island identity. Music in the diasporic imagination highlights the problems associated with mapping musical practices onto geographic entities (cf. Ferguson and Gupta, 1992). These problems are compounded by the dissemination and practice of musics particularly associated with Trinidad – calypso, steel pan and chutney for instance – in contemporary transnational music scenes and tourist economies. These musics have found audiences and performance spaces outside the island in various centres of the Caribbean Diaspora and in world music scenes. Steel pans have become a feature of such diverse musical landscapes as London, Plymouth, New York, Switzerland, Finland, France and South Africa. Travelling to Trinidad, tourists participate in major island musical spectacles such as Carnival. Diasporic and touristic intercultural networks, inter-island movements of people and music, recording opportunities and transnational music markets have all played their parts in establishing performance arenas for the island's musical traditions that extend beyond its geographic setting. A study of musics in Trinidad, then, immediately presents a challenge to ideas about the island as a clearly demarcated space. The musical references to diaspora, to boats, journeys, origins and homelands elsewhere, are but some of the ways in which our views are stretched regarding what the boundaries of island identity might be. If Trinidad's musical practices are tied in various ways to global soundscapes, how, then, might they be analysed usefully in relation to defined geographic parameters?

While Trinidad's musics are located in the global domain, musical transnationalism, particularly through the networks of the Trinidad Diaspora and the island's tourist industry, offers a context for reflecting on island music practices. Practitioners in other geographical settings, for example, refer to island aesthetics in evaluating their own performance practices. Steel bands in Europe compete in the European Pan Festival for the opportunity to perform in musical events in Trinidad. They are judged by a team appointed by organizers of the World Steelband Festival in Trinidad. British calypsonians continue to follow the Trinidadian calypso scene at the same time as making their sung commentaries relevant to the British context (see Ramnarine forthcoming) and chutney singers from Trinidad are major contributors to the musical shows organized for London's and Amsterdam's Indian-Caribbean communities. Both non-islander and Trinidad Diaspora receptions to its various musics have impacted on local developments within the island context. Calypso, steelband and chutney have been promoted as island-specific sounds in part because of their successes in global arenas.

Theatre of the Calypso

In view of the musical flows between global and island spaces I would like to explore an example of the discursive association of particular genres with the island by considering a drama trilogy about calypso written by the Trinidadian playwright, Rawle Gibbons (1999 [1991]). The first part of the trilogy is *Sing de Chorus* and it draws on calypsos from the 1930s and 1940s. It explores how the calypsonian 'became something of a national, cultural symbol when his championing of nationalist causes embroiled him with the colonial authorities' (Regis, 1999: x). As well as capturing the public imagination through voicing the political sentiments of the era, calypsonians gained prestige because of the attention paid to their art outside of the island context. Recording companies such as the RCA Victor Company in the USA and the Gramophone Company HMV in England and France began to market recordings of calypso. The USA was a popular destination for Caribbean migrants from the early twentieth century and calypsonians also sought opportunities in metropolitan cities such as New York. From early in the twentieth century, then, calypso was an island music that was being established as an important genre within Trinidad but that was also reaching beyond the island space. A passage from Act One, Scene Two of *Sing de Chorus* explores the moment when major recording companies began to demonstrate interest in calypso and depicts the responses of its practitioners to the possibilities afforded by such international undertakings. The year is 1934.

Gomes: Gentlemen, the Decca Company of New York is interested in making recordings of Trinidad calypso. They've asked me to select the best calypsonians to send to New York.

Battler: You mean America?

Radio: How much New York it have? All you hear the man? You know what that mean? We calypso on record just like Rudy Vallee, Bing Crosby! The world waiting on we song!

Saga: That mean money in we pocket. They have to pay we for we songs, not so, Pa Gomes?

Gomes: Of course. The rate will be ten dollars a song. But that's only for the best.

Battler: Ten whole dollars!

Gomes: Plus your passage to New York, of course.

Saga: When we starting, Pa Gomes?

Timer: Mr. Gomes, if you don't mind, how come Decca choose you to conduct this business?

Radio: How you mean, Timer? Pa Gomes have big business connections all over the place.

Gomes: Let's say, it's a collaboration of interests. Including the calypsonians.

Timer: And how you plan to select the best calypsonians, Mr. Gomes?

Radio: Timer always asking some damn fool question. Like you getting dotish with age? It must be the king of the tent that get pick first. Not so, Pa?

Gomes: Well, I'm more interested in the calypso than the calypsonian. If the people like a song and it's a hit, then the record should sell well. That's the way I'm seeing it. You boys better get on the move. Destination USA.

Saga: Imagine. Mighty Saga stepping off this ocean liner in fine style, dressed to kill and waltzing through New York not without a bevy of beauties in train, which one to shine his shoes, which one to comb his hair, which one to keep the fans at bay. I enter the studio ...

Radio: And have to wait in line, because the masters of the art already in there recording!

(Gibbons, 1999 [1991]: 42–3)

The character Pa Gomes is based on a retailer who dealt with records, radios and other goods, Eduardo Sa Gomes. Gomes set up his store in 1930 in Duke Street, Port of Spain, and one of his main suppliers was the American Record Corporation (ARC). Cowley (1993) notes the importance of Gomes's initiatives in the promotion of calypso. While vocalists making records of Trinidadian musics in the USA from 1912 onwards had been vaudevillians rather than 'skilled calypsonians with reputations gained in the competitive atmosphere of Carnival calypso tents', Gomes helped calypsonians to gain access to these recording opportunities. In 1934, he sponsored two renowned calypsonians, Atilla the Hun and the Roaring Lion, to travel to New York and record for ARC. Trinidadian calypsonians continued to record in the USA until the Second World War, under a partnership between Gomes and Jack Kapp (who moved from ARC to set up USA Decca Records). These recordings, featuring well-known island based calypsonians, reached receptive markets in Trinidad, in other British West Indian territories and in Harlem's English-speaking Caribbean communities. American tourists to the Trinidad Carnival were also interested in the recordings and bought them as souvenirs (Cowley, 1993).

Gomes's initial interest was in selling the recordings made in the USA to audiences in Trinidad. In this he was following established marketing practices. The 1912 New York recordings by the calypsonian, Lovey (George Bailey) with his band, for example, were marketed to audiences in Trinidad, not to New York's Caribbean communities. During the mid-1930s, however, calypsonians began to turn their attention to North American themes. The Roaring Lion (Rafael De Leon) and Atilla the Hun (Raymond Quevedo) sang about the reception they received from influential American musicians like the singer and orchestra leader, Rudy Vallee: 'We were making records for the Decca Company, when we were heard by Rudy Vallee. Well he was so charmed with our rhythmic harmony, he took us in hand immediately' (Decca, 1938). The Duke of Iron (Cecil Anderson) sang: 'I am happy just to be, in this sweet land of liberty ... Now where can you roam when you ain't got a home? Oh where can you flee to a land that's free? USA' (Varsity, 1939). Together with the introduction of North American themes was a change in calypso performance contexts. While calypso in Trinidad was an integral part of Carnival, in New York the song genre was heard mainly through recordings, radio and club performances. Through these performance contexts, calypso entered a mainstream popular entertainment scene. Calypsonians performed for Caribbean and African-American audiences but by the late 1930s they were also singing for 'middle-class white listeners' (Hill, 1998: 79). By the 1950s, the stage was ripe for a singer like Harry Belafonte (a New York singer born of Jamaican parents) to establish calypsos and Caribbean folk songs as popular music (and a passing fad) and to achieve greater commercial success than Trinidadian calypsonians. Hill observes that by the late 1940s in New York, 'calypso was, on the one hand, folding into a broadly Caribbean culture in the United States, while on the other it was about to become a popular style of music performed by North Americans as well' (Hill 1998: 89).

Harry Who?

Ah Wanna Fall is the second play in Rawle Gibbons's calypso trilogy. Gibbons draws on calypso texts from the 1930s to the 1970s in a presentation of calypso history of this period. The third scene of Act One takes place in a street in Port of Spain where calypsonians, taxi drivers and vendors approach a group of tourists. A calypsonian, Figs, sings for them and amidst applause, one of the tourists asks, 'Great! That some kind of folk song?' The question prompts Figs and his colleague, Kitch (Kitchener) to reflect on and assert a national claim to the calypso genre and also to the steelband. The scene continues as follows:

Figs: Calypso. We native song.

Tourist 2: Calypso? The agent told us Jamaica was the land of Calypso and this here's the land of ...

Kitch: The steelband?

Tourist 1: Naw, the hibiscus, he said.

Tourist 2: Yeah, and Tobago the land of the Humming Bird. Or was it the other way around?

Tourist 3: Who cares? Hey can you guys do a real Harry Belafonte calypso? I mean, like the genuine thing?

Kitch: Harry who? Listen mister, Calypso come from right here in Trinidad. We make
it and we make the steelband too ...

While Kitch does not recognize Harry Belafonte as a calypsonian there have
been discussions about rights to calypso performance spaces within the island
context itself. The markers of gender, class and ethnicity have provided some of
the barriers to calypsonian status in the past. Women have been seen as intruding
into a male space. Indian-Trinbagonians (citizens of the Republic of Trinidad and
Tobago) have been exploring the boundaries between calypso and chutney.
Whereas chutney has at times been interpreted as the Indian version of calypso and
at others as the Indian alternative to calypso in local discourses, musicians have
laid claims to both genres without perhaps distinguishing so clearly between them.
Generally, calypsonians have asserted their claims to calypso performance on the
basis of their islander identities. Thus Denyse Plummer, for example, challenging
the ascription of non-African male status, sings: 'This woman is a whole
Trinidadian ... I mix up like *callaloo* [a dish made of various ingredients], boil
down the coconut with pasta, chow mein and aloo; I ain't no Syrian, Indian,
African, White or Chinee, I'm just simply a Trini you see' (track five of the CD
recording, *Whole Trinidadian*, 2001).

And what about the steelband? Dudley notes that the late 1950s 'was a time
when steelbands were reveling in the eclecticism of their repertoire', which
included Latin popular songs, American film songs, classical pieces like
Beethoven's Minuet in G as well as arrangements of Trinidadian calypsos (Dudley
2001: 187–8). After Independence, steelbands were expected to promote calypso
music during Carnival. Indeed, steelband competitions (especially the one known
as Panorama) required arrangements of calypsos. This did not diminish the interest
of players in a wide repertoire. What is striking about Dudley's discussion of
Panorama is that musical considerations as well as nationalist ideals of promoting
'local' music helped to establish steelband arrangements of calypsos. The 1963
calypso arrangement of the steelband North Stars featured structural complexity,
elaborate variations on the calypso melody (Mighty Sparrow's *Dan is the Man*),
several modulations and counterpoint. A member of another steelband, Starlift,
reminisced about the impact of this arrangement on future competition entries:

[Tony Williams] did things that people hadn't thought of. Just the way he arranged.
Those days calypso was just verse and chorus. You play your tune, you might put in a
rev (a flourish or run), but just chords. Tony wouldn't play just chords. Our second pans
would be strumming, right? But he wouldn't do this, he was running up and down,
countermelody and thing. So they won, and everybody sat up and took note ... By the
following year, 1964, he won with 'Mama Dis is Mas'. Tony changed three keys! First
time ever in a Panorama competition ... (Starlift member, Eddie Odingi, cited in
Dudley 2001: 191)

Drawing on a range of such musical techniques, steelbands explored the possibilities of arranging calypsos within musical frameworks that interested them at the same time as promoting their repertoires as 'indigenous'.

Why were the Classics so popular anyway? As Dudley notes, European art music was part of the island's soundscape. While steelband arrangements could be read in terms of resistance, the reversal of colonial order, the appropriation of power through knowledge of culturally valued forms, these politically informed readings are not sufficient to account for the 'experience of pleasure', the aesthetic dimensions that direct musical choices. Following the character, Kitch's discourse of steelband in the national space, Dudley analyses arrangements of classics (as one player puts it, 'disarranging and rearranging') in terms of the 'need to generate a musical structure and feeling that were more familiar and energizing to carnival dancers than the structure and feeling of the original'. Steelband arrangements can be interpreted, therefore in relation to the performance aesthetics of other Carnival genres and draw 'attention to the differences between local and foreign musical aesthetics' (Dudley, 2002: 157–8). Such an analysis, with its distinctions between 'local' and 'foreign' would seem to place performance firmly within the bounded national space. Despite discussion on 'Trinidadian' aesthetics, Dudley concludes with an interpretive stance that moves beyond us/other distinctions that I find altogether more convincing in accounting for what is going on in the social and musical activities found in this island space. The Classics performed in calypso style from the 1960s onwards now find a 'mirror image' in the Panorama competition, which features calypsos performed in a classical style. Dudley describes these as 'ten minute theme and variation arrangements, elaborate modulations and re-harmonizations, introductions and codas, strictly memorized and performed by an orchestra of one hundred players ... judged by formally trained musicians' (Dudley, 2002: 160). The variety of different meanings that people find and the range of opinions they express about this music 'reflect an ongoing tension between the undeniable social forces that have shaped the art form, and visions of steelband performance as an aesthetic enterprise' (Dudley, 2002: 160). Dudley's observation can be extended to analysis of Carnival as a whole. Discourses about the Trinidad Carnival reveal much about what is happening at social and political levels but they do not necessarily correspond with actual musical practices and may not provide the best maps to reading the island's soundscapes. For musicians, the importance of performance as 'an aesthetic enterprise' cannot be overstated and the processes of music making shows how musical (not social or political) considerations are privileged. While Carnival musics encompass a wide spectrum of styles and genres, recent socio-political commentaries have debated Carnival's origins, variously sought in Africa (Smart and Nehusi, 2000; Liverpool, 2001), in India (Persad, 2001), or in Europe and Africa (NCC, 2001), asserting particular claims about to whom the event 'belongs'. Discourses focusing on musical origins and preservations can tell us much about the workings of musical transmission in diasporic contexts, but when they are used in claims of exclusivity and the affirmation of island difference they also tell us about the playing out of contemporary politics and reveal those tensions between the musical and the social.

'Between the Vision of the Tourist Board and the True Paradise'[2]

While Harry Belafonte was drawing new audiences to calypso in the USA, singing about his 'island in the sun', Trinidadians insisted on the genre as an island expression. In the Gibbons extract cited above, the calypsonians, taking on the role of public educators, exhibit a certainty about the cultural island origins of the Carnival genres, calypso and steelband. The tourists encourage the moment of self-reflection. With their questions about place (Jamaica or Trinidad) and about authenticity (a real Harry Belafonte) they provoke assertions about these specific genres as being the island's musics. Calypsonians continue to think about tourists who assist them in reflecting on their musical practices. Lady Wonder sings, 'Calypso history should be part of school curriculum; It should also form the base of parent child relation; Every child throughout sweet Trinbago; Whenever them tourist ask about calypso you feel proud to show yuh know yuh cultural heroes' (from the calypso, *Calypso Pledge*, 1990). The tourists continue to be represented as requiring explanations about island practices. Shadow's 2001 calypso song, *Stranger* features the narrative voice of the tourist in the first verse: 'I'm a stranger … I came down here for the Carnival. Kaiso music have me in a trance, want to play *mas* [masquerade or Carnival processions], teach me how to dance'. In an impromptu performance, a tourist jumped on stage as Shadow competed for the title of Soca Monarch 2001 (which he won). But an array of discourses about tourism and about Carnival, calypso and steelband as island genres shows conflicting perspectives regarding performance motivations and island orientations. I shall turn now to considering some of these perspectives.

Trinidadian commentators have pointed out the national significance of Carnival and its potential to represent the island in global forums since the early 1930s (Belgrave, 1978 [1932]). Carnival literature continues to describe the Trinidad and Tobago Carnival as being at the centre of 'the cultural confidence of Trinidad and Tobago' (Springer, 2000: 17) and as 'the best folk festival in the Western world, and the best show on earth' (Claude Clarke in NCC, 2001: 2). In a recent study of the Trinidad Carnival, van Koningsbruggen explores the importance of this event to discourses about the nation and about the role of the tourist in island self-scrutiny. He writes about the continued importance of the tourist (North Americans in particular), suggesting that the efforts of the Tourist Board and of the National Carnival Commission to promote tourism are not just designed to appeal to the tourists' tastes but are also reflections of the world of middle-class

Trinidadians (Van Koningsbruggen, 1997: 194). The concerns of Van Koningsbruggen's 'middle-class Trinidadians' are outlined in relation to objections towards the dominance of American shows on television, the perception of culture as 'a thing', which centres on connections to Carnival, the Africanization of Carnival and the illusory self-images of Trinbagonians as the 'most beautiful people in the world who live in a tropical paradise of sand, sea and sun' (Van Koningsbruggen, 1997: 194–209). Van Koningsbruggen is critical in his assessment of islanders' self-images:

> People try to maintain the monopoly of a particular way of looking at things and to reject vigorously anything which contravenes it. Tourism is to be encouraged, the steelband and the calypso are to be promoted internationally, the masquerade costumes are to be sold to foreign museums, the carnival festival as a whole is to be extended worldwide and exported by satellite television, and Trinidad is to be profiled as a tropical paradise on earth. The ideal image of self is both a source of inspiration and an obstacle with respect to all these goals because of the high level of ambivalence, which boils down to the need to propagate and protect Trinidad culture at the same time. (Van Koningsbruggen 1997: 209–10)

Van Koningsbruggen's emphasis on island motivation for Carnival performances in relation to tourist markets and island representations of a tropical paradise perhaps overshadows the various routes whereby Carnival genres reach global performance spaces. Carnival certainly provides a medium for some of the most intense self-scrutiny in Trinidad, but islander discourses about this musical spectacle centre on a profound appreciation of the manifold ways in which its genres traverse the globe. In contrast to Van Koningsbruggen's focus on tourism promotion, Liverpool (2001) looks at the diasporic networks between Caribbean island and Caribbean Diaspora, and on the musical networks that link the Caribbean with Africa. This is a perspective tied up with island history and ongoing political strategies of engagement with the past. As Liverpool notes, 'while for most tourists it [Carnival] is the greatest show on earth, for Africans in Trinidad and Tobago it is a ritual of power and resistance' (Liverpool, 2001: 69).

While several writers have focused recently on the African dimensions to Carnival (Liverpool, 2001; Smart and Nehusi, 2001; Adeyinka, 2001), Indian claims to this performance space have also been made. These claims have been made in part by chutney musicians who have entered Carnival, setting up, amidst much heated debates and controversy, competitions and tents following calypso models (Ramnarine, 2001). In a recent commentary, Persad went so far as to locate the origins of Carnival in Saivism and urged islanders not to forget its Indian past (Persad, 2001). The extremes of diasporic imaginations displayed through such visions of Carnival as 'African' or 'Indian' have all the hallmarks of the political around them – a politics of difference within the nation state. Differences configured and transposed in terms of ethnicity. While diaspora as history is vital to an understanding of the past and its effects on the present, does anyone really want to be confined by the 'ethnic' any longer? Is not the island home an appropriate place to begin challenging these boundaries as Gilroy (1987) does in his book *There Ain't No Black in the Union Jack*? Differences are, as Catherine Hall notes, 'always socially constituted, and they always have a dimension of power' (Hall, 2000: 16). Moreover, they have to be *'continuously and vigilantly crafted'* (Hall 2000: 20, emphasis mine). Without necessarily seeking to establish the 'origins' of Carnival in one place or another, some musicians have argued through their song texts for a more inclusive view of Carnival. Rikki Jai sang, 'I sing chutney and calypso for I'm a Trinbagonian'. Lady Wonder observes, 'Calypso has played itself in cosmopolitism; not only Africans but Indians, Chinese and Syrians; some say mafia will take over but calypso has a built in stamina; don't care who's the godfather this artform will prosper' (from the calypso, *Calypso Pledge*, 1990). Like Gibbons's character Kitch, when he exclaims: 'Harry who? Listen mister, Calypso come from right here in Trinidad. We make it and we make the steelband too', and Denyse Plummer as she sings 'I'm a whole Trinidadian', both Rikki Jai and Lady Wonder are exploring the intersections between the diasporic and the national, and in striving for an island 'harmony' privilege the latter. Resolving internal island differences, such a stance nevertheless returns us to broad questions about the island in a global context and about the historical, social and creative webs that connect disparate geographic spaces. The dramas of the island space are, after all, the human dramas played out everywhere.

Concluding Remarks

Two calypsonians have the following conversation in the third part of Gibbons's Calypso Trilogy, *Ten to One*:

Melody: All you calypsonians ain't playing good, nah. What you say? Tankabouli?

Blakie: Check the Arabian dictionary. If you don't know a lil bit of everybody language you can't call yourself a cosmopolitan calypsonian.

(Gibbons 1999:173–4)

The dialogue between Melody and Blakie resonates with Blacking's views that patterns of music provide a 'means for people to bridge gaps of communication and understanding between their lives in societies that prescribe certain ideas, sentiments, and definitions of experience' and that the artist who reaches universal experience through the expression of a personal one does so 'because he or she has been able to live beyond culture, and not for culture, and to re-tune particular cultural conventions to the common experiences of human beings by using modes of thought that every individual possesses' (Blacking, 1995: 240–2).

Music in the diasporic imagination shows one way of bridging the island space and the wider world ('re-tuning to the common experiences of human beings') within temporal as well as geographic frameworks. Chris Tambu Herbert sings about an ongoing journey. Sundar Popo sings about Indian migration to Trinidad. Brother Resistance sings about African migration to Trinidad. Singing about specific experiences these songs about ships and journeys are also comments on a common experience of migration and on the ongoing significance of the historical moments of arrival. They are also songs about colonial and post-colonial politics. They reference the island space and reveal its contemporary dramas. They draw on 'different' historical narratives (the 'epics of arrival') and musical repertoires, but highlight the fact that almost 'every person in the Caribbean cast of dramatic personae has been a newcomer' (Lewis, 1983: 4). Lewis notes that Caribbean history has been a violent history, and that the region still carries the imprint of a heritage of upheaval, social and cultural shock. The 'moral earthquakes' of post-Conquest slavery, post-Emancipation society and post-colonial national sovereignty with their creeds of proslavery, antislavery and nationalism 'add up to the accumulated moral deposit of Caribbean society and culture' (Lewis, 1983: 15). The ongoing dramas of ethnic frictions in Trinidad that are played out through various Carnival genres (as well as party politics with which I began this chapter) must be understood within those moral and ideological frameworks. But tired ideas about ethnicities ('the result of ancient human survival strategies, outdated but still determining the worldview of many' – Kubik, 1994: 22) must be discarded if, as Shepherd suggests, the twenty-first century should see the Caribbean aligning itself to a project of 'true emancipation' (Shepherd, 2000: 65). Throwing 'ethnicity' out of the picture leads to taking another look at knowledge of peoples and places and at reified domains of cultures. Creolization models (the spectre of ethnicity lurking around them) have been used to account for the Caribbean as a 'consummately global place'. But as Khan argues, 'creolization' is not specific to the Caribbean. The reputed specificity of the concept to the Caribbean 'is a particular fiction that invents the region', distinguishing it from the rest of the world and thus affirming preconceived ideas about culture (Khan, 2001: 272–3). If, as Khan suggests, anthropologists have not gone beyond the trope of culture-place and that applications of the concept of creolization to globalization processes at worst 'privileges a relatively safe counterhegemonic revision of the way we understand culture, power, and culture change' that 'supports some of the very assumptions and approaches it is meant to dismantle' (Khan, 2001: 272), considering music 'as the most important aspect of music-making' (Blacking, 1995: 227) may yet force us to get rid of that ideologically laden interpretive stance. The practices of musicians in 'picking up, transforming and re-interpreting various genres', as seen in the Carnival examples, show how 'musicians often appear to celebrate ethnic plurality in problematic ways' (Stokes, 1994: 16). Beyond problematic celebration of ethnic plurality, if these practices are creolization processes exemplified they also show how musicians may be striking against the very concept of 'ethnicity' and the 'continuous, vigilant crafting of difference'. For Melody (in the extract cited above), the calypso performance is no good because he does not understand the text. 'What you say? Tankabouli?' I like Blakie's response and the idea of tuning into his vision that we can always check out 'tankabouli' because 'if you don't know a lil bit of everybody language you can't call yourself a cosmopolitan calypsonian'. That goes beyond bounded cultures. It is another way of expressing the idea of 'living beyond culture and re-tuning to common human experiences'. And such re-tunings come without the dull prospects of creative uniformity. The musical processes at work in the island space of Trinidad – Carnival genres in and musical legacies from global spaces, musicians' emphasis on working with specifically musical features, the ways in which music is created, put together, aesthetics and reception – are 'anthropologically problematic' (Blacking, 1995: 227) in that they prompt us to rethink our ideas about the mapping of 'culture' onto geographic spaces and/or onto 'ethnicities', about cultural diversity and/as the unique, special or signifying traits of different regions. Island boundaries are sonically blurred through the juxtaposition of various musical elements and through the versatile approaches of musicians to a variety of musical traditions and repertoires in which musical and aesthetic considerations override all others. Music in the diasporic imagination and the ambiguities of performing cultural (dis)placement in the island setting of Trinidad offer us another route to questioning the 'place' of 'culture' altogether.

Notes

1. This chapter is based on field research undertaken in Trinidad during February 2001. The fieldwork, which involved studying Carnival events, was supported by a British Academy award, which I gratefully acknowledge. The elections to which I refer took place in December 2001 and were followed by intense debates and media reportage in Trinidad and Tobago.
2. This is the line with which Walcott begins The Bounty (1997).

References

Adeyinka, O. N. (2000), 'A Carnival of Resistance, Emancipation, Commemoration, Reconstruction, and Creativity', in Smart, I. I. and Nehusi, K. (eds), *Ah Come Back Home: Perspectives on the Trinidad and Tobago Carnival*,

Washington DC and Port-of-Spain: Original World Press, pp. 105–29.

Belgrave, J. (1978) [1932], 'Reflections on Carnival', in Sander, R. W. (ed.), *From Trinidad: An Anthology of Early West Indian Writing*, New York: Africana Publishing Company, pp. 40–4.

Blacking, J. (1995), *Music, Culture, and Experience: Selected Papers of John Blacking*, Chicago and London: University of Chicago Press.

Cowley, J. (1993), '*L'Année Passée*: Selected Repertoire in English-speaking West Indian Music'. *Kiskidee*, 3: 2–42.

Dudley, S. (2001), 'Ray Holman and the Changing Role of the Steelband, 1957–72'. *Latin American Music Review*, 22 (2): 183–98.

——— (2002), 'Dropping the Bomb: Steelband Performance and Meaning in 1960s Trinidad', *Ethnomusicology*, 46 (1): 135–60.

Ferguson, J. and Gupta, A. (1992), 'Beyond "Culture": Space, identity, and the politics of difference'. *Cultural Anthropology*, 7(1): 6–23.

Gibbons, R. A. (1999), *A Calypso Trilogy*, Kingston, Jamaica: Ian Randle Publishers and Tunapuna, Trinidad: Canboulay Productions.

Gilroy, P. (1987), *There Ain't No Black in the Union Jack: The Cultural Politics of Race and Nation*, London and New York: Routledge.

——— (1997), 'Diaspora and the Detours of Identity', in Woodward, K. (ed.), *Identity and Difference,*. London: Sage Publications, pp. 301–43.

Hall, C. (ed.) (2000), *Cultures of Empire: Colonizers in Britain and the Empire in the Nineteenth and Twentieth Centuries*, Manchester,: Manchester University Press.

Hill, D. (1998), '"I am Happy Just to be in this Sweet Land of Liberty": The New York City *Calypso* craze of the 1930s and 1940s', in Allen, R. and Wilcken, L. (eds) *Island Sounds in the Global City: Caribbean Popular Music and Identity in New York*, New York: The New York Folklore Society and The Institute for Studies in American Music.

Khan, A. (2001), 'Journey to the Center of the Earth: The Caribbean as master symbol'. *Cultural Anthropology*, 16(3): 271–302.

Knight, F. W. and Palmer, C. A. (1989), 'The Caribbean: A regional overview', in Knight, F. W. and Palmer, C. A. (eds), *The Modern Caribbean*, Chapel Hill and London: University of North Carolina Press.

Kubik, G. (1994), 'Ethnicity, Cultural Identity, and the Psychology of Culture Contact', in Behague, G. H. (ed.), *Music and Black Ethnicity: The Caribbean and South America*, Florida: North-South Center Press at the University of Miami.

Lewis, G. K. (1983), *Main Currents in Caribbean Thought: The Historical Evolution of Caribbean Society in its Ideological Aspects, 1492–1900*. Kingston and Port of Spain: Heinemann Educational Books (Caribbean) Ltd.

Liverpool, H. (2001), 'Reexportation and Musical Traditions Surrounding the

African Masquerade' in Regis, H. A. (ed.) *Culture and Mass Communication in the Caribbean: Domination, Dialogue, Dispersion*, Gainesville: University Press of Florida.

NCC (National Carnival Commission of Trinidad and Tobago) (2001), 'Carnival History ... Who Gets the Credit?', in *Before and Beyond Mas*, Trinidad: NCC.

Nurse, E. 'Prince' (ed) (2001), *Downtown Mas 2001: Souvenir*, Trinidad: Edmund Prince Nurse.

Persad, K. (2001), 'Carnival and Shivratri', *Sunday Express* (Trinidad), 25 February 2001, p. 16.

Ramnarine, T. K. (1996), 'Indian Music in the Diaspora: Case studies of Chutney in Trinidad and in London'. *British Journal of Ethnomusicology*, 5: 133–53.

—— (1998), 'Brotherhood of the Boat: Musical dialogues in a Caribbean context' *British Journal of Ethnomusicology*, 7: 1–22.

—— (2001), *Creating Their Own Space: The Development of an Indian-Caribbean Musical Tradition*, Barbados, Jamaica, Trinidad and Tobago: University of West Indies Press.

—— (forthcoming), 'Imperial Legacies and the Politics of Musical Creativity'. *World of Music*.

Reddock, R. (1995), 'Contestations Over National Culture in Trinidad and Tobago: Considerations of Ethnicity, Class and Gender', in Deosaran, R. and Mustapha, N. (eds), *Contemporary Issues in Social Science: A Caribbean Perspective*, pp. 106–45. University of West Indies: Ansa McAl Psychological Research Centre.

Regis, L. (1999), 'Building Bridges of Song: An Introduction', in Gibbons, R. A. (ed.), *A Calypso Trilogy*, Kingston, Jamaica: Ian Randle Publishers and Tunapuna, Trinidad: Canboulay Productions.

Richardson, B. C. (1989), 'Caribbean Migrations, 1838–1985', in Knight, F. W. and Palmer, C. A. (eds), *The Modern Caribbean*, Chapel Hill and London: University of North Carolina Press. pp. 203–58.

Shepherd, V. A. (2000), 'Image, Representation and the Project of Emancipation: History and identity in the Commonwealth Caribbean', in Hall, K. and Benn, D. (eds), *Contending with Destiny: The Caribbean in the 21st Century*, Kingston: Ian Randle Publishers.

Slobin, M. (ed.) (1996), *Retuning Culture: Musical changes in Central and Eastern Europe*, Durham and London: Duke University Press.

Smart, I. I. and Nehusi, K. (eds) (2000), *Ah Come Back Home: Perspectives on the Trinidad and Tobago Carnival*, Washington DC and Port-of-Spain: Original World Press.

Springer, P. E. (2000), 'Carnival: Identity, Ethnicity, and Spirituality', in Smart, I. I. and Nehusi, K. (eds). *Ah Come Back Home: Perspectives on the Trinidad and Tobago Carnival*, Washington DC and Port-of-Spain: Original World Press, pp. 17–27.

Stokes, M. (ed.), (1994), *Music, Ethnicity and Identity: The Musical Construction of Place*, Oxford and Providence: Berg.

Van Koningsbruggen, P. (1997), *Trinidad Carnival: A Quest for National Identity*, London and Basingstoke: Macmillan Education Ltd.

Walcott, D. (1997), 'Homecoming iii', in *The Bounty*. London and Boston: Faber & Faber.

Yelvington, K. A (ed.) (1993), *Trinidad Ethnicity*, London and Basingstoke: Macmillan Press.

Recommended Listening

Kitchener (1997), *Kitch: Reflections of a Legend*, New York: J. W. Records Production Inc. JW121CD.

Plummer, Denyse (2001), *Whole Trinidadian*, CD, Port of Spain: Crosby's Music Center. JWDP002.

Popo, Sundar (1995), *Cool Yourself with Cold Water*, cassette, New York: JMC Records Inc. JMC-1113.

Shadow (2001), *Just For You*, Mount Hope: McGarland Music. CRCD008.

Tambu (n. d.), *... Once Upon a Time*, Petit Bourg: Bangaseed Limited. BSCD104.

–9–

Between Mainland and Sea: The *Taarab* Music of Zanzibar

Werner Graebner

Nyota nakuamini dira na ramani
Nimo safarini siwasili asilani
Wasemao siponi wasisibu ya Manani

My guiding star, I trust in you, my compass and my map.
I am journeying, I would never arrive.
Those who say I will not escape do not trust in what is
    foretold by the Beneficent.[1]

Zanzibar – comprising the islands of Unguja and Pemba and a few smaller islets just off the East African coast – is one of the centres of what is generally called Swahili culture, an Islamic urban culture moulded by monsoons and contacts across the Indian Ocean.[2] This culture flowered in the towns along the East African Coast at least since the tenth century AD, communication across the sea, to Arabia, India and beyond, being assured by the *dhow*, the characteristic lateen-sailed boats of the Indian Ocean. Even today the Zanzibari orient their lives more across the ocean and to the Islamic world rather than to the African mainland or the West, an outlook that is also very much apparent in the islands' music and song. The characteristic sound, defining the islands' aural landscape, is *taarab* music: traditionally in Zanzibar a lush orchestral sound produced by a variety of Oriental, African and Western instruments. Swahili language lyrics, heir to an old tradition of poetry, form a most important ingredient of *taarab*.

Islands and the sea cannot be thought of in isolation, and images of the sea are pervasive in coastal culture, language, and song. Lyrics like those of *Nyota* (*The Guiding Star*) are an expression of this ethic, stars formerly being a major guiding principle in *dhow* navigation across the open sea. Tropes relating to the sea abound in language in general; for example, when speaking about the field of poetry,

171

Swahili language would render this as *bahari ya mashairi*, literally 'the sea of poetry', or *taarab* in general would be *bahari ya taarab*. The designation 'Swahili' is a legacy of the mercantile history of the coastal urban civilization. Now firmly integrated into the Swahili language's Bantu context, it originally derives from the Arabic *sahil*, with the meaning of 'margin' or 'coast'. In older Arabic geographer's texts it can usually be rendered as 'port of trade'. While we can speak of a basic identity of coastal culture and coastal society, the identity of what are sometimes called the Waswahili ('Swahili people') is an elusive one, one that has always been shifting and on the move.[3] It has often been contested in the course of its history, especially since the nineteenth century, with the onslaught of the Omani sultans and then colonization by European powers. The challenge has continued and is continuing into the post-colonial era and contemporary times. This short history of *taarab* music in Zanzibar throughout the twentieth century will try to show how a coastal or Swahili identity is negotiated, constructed and upheld in a musical form in the face of political and social obstacles. This music, as acoustic and verbal text, occupies a highly contested intermediary ecological niche between the African continent and the expanse of the Indian Ocean and respective musical cultures.

The Production of History

In most discussions about the music nowadays, the time in the second half of the 1950s when Ali Abdalla Buesh composed *Nyota* is portrayed as the golden age of *taarab*. The style of lyrical development, as well as Zanzibar's orchestral style are described as the 'real *taarab*'. However, this peace was soon to be challenged by the pre-independence political awakening, the turmoil erupting after the 1964 revolution and by the subsequent experiment in scientific socialism. If these developments left *taarab* somehow subdued – there are tales of censorship, demand for political lyrics, the critique of *taarab* as a supposedly bourgeois entertainment not in line with socialist development – the style asserted itself as the most popular with the audience and by becoming the islands' quasi-national sound.

By the mid-1990s the classical picture of *taarab* was seriously challenged by what came to be known as 'modern *taarab*' or *mipasho*. The latter term translates as 'backbiting', referring to the stingy popular lyrics that are the rage of the day. Modern *taarab* is a development that basically results from the entertainment circuit in Tanzania's capital city Dar es Salaam. But even there, many of the featured stars of *mipasho* actually hail from Zanzibar, and the ever fashion-conscious female Zanzibari *taarab* audience, of course, has lent its support to local favourites East African Melody, and more recently, Zanzibar Stars Modern Taarab, all championing the new dance-focused style.

In the face of this and the earlier challenges, propagators of a 'pure' *taarab* tradition have united behind the banners of an argument that posits *taarab* as

adhering strictly to a concert setting without dance. One that points to the importance of thought-heavy lyrics, and squarely bonds *taarab* with the palace of the
Sultan of Zanzibar and, more generally, propounds an Egyptian derivation:

> *Taarab si ngoma ya kucheza ni muziki wa kumliwaza mtu na kumfanya fikra na mawazo*
> *ya dunia, mapenzi, na mengi mengine yanayomtokea mwanadamu katika maisha.*
> *Katika Taarab mtu hupata maliwazo kupata ya mashairi, muziki nyororo kwa ala zake*
> *zinazotumika ambazo hutoa sauti zake zenyewe.*

> *Taarab Unguja ilianzishwa na Mfalme ajulikanae kwa jina la Seyyid Bargash bin Said*
> *(1870–1888) naye alikuwa mtu wa anasa na apendaye starehe za aina mbali mbali.*
> *Pia mfalme huyu ndiye aliyeanzisha Unguja na baadaye ilienea afrika ya mashariki*
> *kote. Aliagiza kikundi maalum kutoka Misri ili wapige taarab katika kasri yake ya Beit*
> *El Ajaib. Baadaye aliamua kumpeleka Misri Moh'd Ibrahim ili akajifunze muziki na pia*
> *alijifunza chombo kijulikanacho Kanuni au Ganun.*

Taarab is not like *ngoma*, to be danced to. It is music to soothe the listener and to make
him ponder the world, love, or many other things that happen to man in his life. In
taarab man gets words of comfort out of the lyrics, the soft music with the instruments
that are used and give this particular sound.

In Zanzibar the Sultan known by the name of Seyyid Bargash bin Said (1870–1888)
started *taarab*; he was a man who liked luxury and the pleasures of life. It was this ruler
who started it all in Zanzibar and later it spread all over East Africa. He imported a
taarab ensemble from Egypt, to play in his Beit el-Ajab palace. Later on he decided to
send to Egypt Mohamed Ibrahim to learn music and he also learned to play the instrument known by the name of *kanuni* or *ganun*.[4]

Most existing histories of Swahili *taarab* so far focus on Zanzibar and are
implicitly or quite explicitly the history of one social club by the name of Ikhwani
Safaa (Saleh, 1980, 1988a, 1988b; Khatib, 1992; Mgana, 1994). The Egyptian
attributions given to the style are usually equally strong its origin in the Sultan's
palace in the 1880s with the invitations of Egyptian musicians, and the later
training of a Zanzibari musician in Egypt. However, the earliest existing recordings of Swahili *taarab*, commercial recordings made between 1928 and 1930, do
portray a style, that is firmly integrated into an Indian Ocean musical world and is
not overly tributary to Egyptian influence.

In 1928, HMV's representatives in Zanzibar had sent a group of musicians to
Bombay for a studio recording. The group included the well-known singers and
instrumentalists Maalim Shaaban, Budda Swedi, and Mbaruk Talsam (the latter
originally from Mombasa). The same group of musicians, including the female
singer Siti bint Saad, did two more recording sessions in Bombay for HMV in
1929 and 1930. Other companies entered the market soon after: Columbia

recorded the same group of musicians in Zanzibar later in 1930; the German Odeon did recordings in Mombasa in the same year, inviting over the group of Siti bint Saad, and also recording a number of Mombasa-based *taarab* artists. The recordings proved to be popular all along the Coast, the companies recorded and released hundreds of songs and by mid-1931 72,000 copies had been sold.[5]

For the purpose of analysis I played recordings from this period, and recordings made along the coast in the late 1940s and early 1950s, to a number of professional musicians in Mombasa and Zanzibar and asked them to comment on the styles, rhythms, modes, and so forth. The results of this inquiry reveal a musical style that is actually quite heterogeneous and exhibits the following features (see also Table 9.1):

1. The integration of local dance rhythms and melodies, which can be attributed to a Swahili musical sensibility (dances like *msondo*, *goma*, and *kumbwaya*);
2. relationships to musics of the Arabian Peninsula (Yemen, Gulf Countries) – musical contacts across the Indian Ocean, that result from migration, trade and cultural exchange in a pre-media age;
3. several examples show influences that can be termed Western, Indian, Pan-Arabic; some of these could be the earliest influences of recorded music which spread in East Africa in the 1920s;[6]
4. with very few exceptions all lyrics are in Swahili, some in the general variety of Zanzibar, others identifiable as Kiamu or Kimvita.

A most surprising result of the test was my experts' astonishment that the music was so kaleidoscopic and that it featured quite a number of elements from local *ngoma*-dances. In their memory, historical *taarab* had had more of an Egyptian or Indian disposition, than was now apparent from the recordings. An Egyptian and Indian bent can be attributed to the spread of the recording medium and especially to the rise of the song-film genres so popular in these two countries.[7] However, this influence came in more predominantly at a later time in the later 1940s and the 1950s.

In conversations about their early experience of this kind of music, a number of elderly practitioners and other witnesses recall a pre-1950s performance style whose description supports the impression garnered from analysing the extant recordings: Musical instruments featured were the *'ud*, occasionally a violin, and small drums. The manner of performance described seems to be more akin to what we know today from *kidumbak* or *ngoma*-dances like *chakacha* (the musicians sit in a circle and take turns in singing, including members of the audience). The lyrics are not yet in the standardized form we have come to know from later *taarab* – that is, the words are strings of short songs, single verses and choruses contributed by a number of singers and the audience. Social occasions are

Table 9.1 Stylistic features of taarab recordings 1930–50

	1930 Zanzibar	1930 Mombasa/Lamu	1947 Mombasa	1950 Dar-es-Salaam/ Mombasa
a) Swah. Ngoma	7	8	0	0
b) Kitarab[8]	6	0	0	0
c) Arabia/Gulf/ RS	3	4	6	3
d) Arabic (general)[9]	3	3	1	13
e) 'Indian'	5	0	8	5
f) European	1	0	0	3
g) Latin	0	0	0	2
h) Kimanyema	0	0	1	2

weddings, *jando* ('initiation') but also loose social get-togethers in the evening hours just to play music. We can thus imagine the social and musical contexts in which the songs we know from the recordings were performed. These descriptions also make more perceptible the relationships that existed between the performance of this early form of *taarab*, and the various *ngoma* dances whose rhythms and melodies feature in the recordings.

The analysis of the early recordings of Swahili music shows a number of linkages between the East African Coast and music and dance on the Arabian Peninsula. Actually, a number of relationships point both ways between the Gulf, Yemen and the East African coast. Many musical instruments of East African origin can be found in the Gulf area, in southern Iraq, along the Persian Coast, and on the Makran Coast of Pakistan. The same goes for complete musical forms, and lyrics. Some of the latter are definitely Bantu or Swahili (Oman, Makran). We do have here a regional sphere of interdependence – of links and cultural exchange via trade, travel, and migration – antecedent to the spread of media like the phonograph, film or later technologies. The early recordings are witnesses to this earlier system of exchanges across the Indian Ocean. An early document of musical interrelationships across the Indian Ocean is the spread from the thirteenth century onwards of a stringed lute called *gambus*. This instrument was also played on the East African coast until the early decades of the twentieth century but has since disappeared. It can still be found today on the Comoro Islands, in Malaysia and Indonesia.[10]

What are we to make of the results of this inquiry? I hold that the early Egyptian attributions are possibly the result of later retrospective thinking, trying to root the world of 1950s *taarab* clubs and their style derived from Egyptian film orchestra in a more remote past. Moreover, it is the history of the Ikhwani Safaa club that is often generalized as the history of *taarab*. Most local writers have been associated with this club and have based their histories on the reminiscences of club members. Most of these reminiscences are in turn based on a short written club history, authored by Shaib Abeid Barajab, one of the club's founders.[11] It is to this original report that I would now like to turn.

Actually Shaib Abeid gives us a more diversified picture than later chroniclers, who have based their accounts on this source. Moreover those later readings are often discernible in the original text, as some of them have added their remarks or highlighted certain passages. The document covers a time from the last years of the nineteenth century to World War I. The club was officially founded in 1905, yet the text devotes quite a number of pages to anecdotes and initial activities that lead up to the club's foundation.

The account informs us that the initial members were young Hadhrami (*Washihiri*), hence more recent immigrants and less affluent members of Zanzibar's Stone Town. These men – many of them working as coolies in the town's port – were engaged in competition with groups of other young men (one rival group identified as Hadhrami youth as well), a competition that was regularly brought into the open in the course of competitive *ngoma*-dances. The text mentions: *tari la diriji* (a Swahili *ngoma*-dance also known from the northern coast), *kinanda cha marwas* (a reference to a song and dance genre accompanied by the *gambus* (lute) and small *marwas* (drum)). Other references are to the Hadhrami *sharah* dance and a number of unidentified dances from South Arabia or the Gulf.

Further on in Shaib Abeid's text one club member is singled out as playing the *gambus*, another as playing an Indian-made *'ud*. This is an interesting piece of information, since the traditions of Bahrain relevant to the *sawt*-genre mention this instrument as well. This Indian *'ud* is a lute which is made from a solid piece of wood, rather than small strips of wood as in the classical Arabic *'ud* usually identified with Syria or north Africa. Another *'ud*, Egyptian-made, was given to a club member later on by an elderly woman who had played in a *takht* (musical group) that entertained an earlier Sultan (Seyyid Bargash 1870–88), but the instrument was soon stolen. A contradictory statement is made by Shaib Abeid in that he says that the club members practised '*taarab*' in secret, since it was the exclusive domain of the Sultan, and was otherwise unknown or not permitted outside the palace circle. However, he then writes about an itinerant singer and *'ud*-player from Aden who entertained about town at the invitation of a local patron, and whose music he classifies as '*taarab* of the highest levels'.[12]

The club was officially founded in 1905 and named Ikhwani Safaa ('Brothers who love one another'). Some of the musicians playing in the bands of the Sultan's palace gave them tuition in '*taarab*'. In 1907 the club ordered a set of musical instruments from Egypt, *'ud*, *qanun* (trapezoid zither), *nai* (flute), and *daff* (tambourine). More tuition on these instruments was received from the Sultan's musicians. Contrary to later historians who report that only Arabic songs were sung – and well into the 1950s – we learn that Swahili songs in the Lamu style were practised because these were common fare at the time and much in demand at local weddings (Abeid, n.d.: 26, 29).

Shaib Abeid also records the foundation of a rival club by the name of Nadi Shuub at about the same time (1907), and a number of competitive performances by the respective musical groups. However, Nadi Shuub soon faltered, and the same possibly happened to Ikhwani Safaa, since Shaib Abeid's club chronicle ends in 1911. As Jahadhmy (1966) reports, Ikhwani Safaa had a renaissance later on in the 1940s at the same time as the foundation of musical clubs in the towns along the coast, with the larger orchestras modelled on Egyptian film music. Shaib Abeid's 'history' was most probably written at this later point, sometime in the 1940s or 1950s.

Actually Shaib Abeid's notebook is not a regular historical text, but rather a collection of anecdotes and little stories that are rooted in oral rather than written genres. In terms of formal properties the text comes closest to the well-known Swahili town chronicles of Kilwa, Lamu or Pate. Much of the writing could also be classified as being in a genealogical mode. Genealogical reasoning when dealing with the history of *taarab's* early practitioners is exemplified by a number of further details in Shaib Abeid's and in other peoples' texts, whether they draw directly on him or not. One is predilection with the life times and reigns of Sultan's, both by Shaib Abeid himself and by later commentators of his text. Another is the care that is taken to outline the origin of musical instruments ordered at different times, and especially of the *qanun*, which seems to be especially valued.[13] In anthropological parlance we could maybe speak of the *qanun* as a cargo instrument, in the same way as some later practitioners mention the presence of strings or their imitation on the synthesizer as essential to *taarab*.[14] Incidentally on Ngazija (Grande Comore) early *taarab*, reported to have been imported from Zanzibar, was called by the name of *fidrilia* (from English fiddle, Swahili *fidla*), because some of the most prominent early practitioners on the island played this instrument (Graebner 2001a, 2001b).

A. A. Suleiman writing in 1969 about the life story of Siti bint Saad mentions that while recording in Bombay she met the great Egyptian singer Umm Kulthum who was also there for recording. So far I have not been able to trace any documentary evidence for a recording session by Umm Kulthum in India in 1929 or 1930. The recording industry was well developed in Egypt, and studios readily available, hence there would have been no need for her to go all the way to Bombay for a recording. Perhaps lacking other evidence to link Siti bint Saad and group to the dominant Sultan/Egyptian/Ikhwani Safaa-centered story, Moh'd Seif Khatib in his *Taarab in Zanzibar* (1991) lists Siti bint Saad's first teachers and musicians in her group as among the founding members of Ikhwani Safaa. These names, however, do not appear in Shaib Abeid's writings on the club's early history.

Moving back to Shaib Abeid's text and taking some of its formal properties, namely the diverse episodes and the genealogical way of reasoning, as a starting point, we could outline a lineage for *taarab* that comes remarkably close to stylistic features isolated in the recordings from the 1930s to the 1950s:

1. links to coastal *ngoma*-dance practices;
2. links to dances from Yemen, the Gulf and Red Sea area;
3. links to the classical traditions of the northern Swahili coast (Lamu):
4. the *gambus* genre (*kinanda cha marwas*);
5. Swahili songs and poetic traditions;
6. links to the Yemeni and Gulf *sawt*-genre;
7. links to Egyptian instruments and musical forms practised in and in the vicinity of the Sultan's palace (subsequently extended and amalgamated to later media-derived Egyptian forms).

Shaib Abeid's account ends with the onset of World War I. For the following decades until the later 1940s we loose track of Ikhwani Safaa's further activities. The late 1920s recordings of Siti Bint Saad and others document a popular musical style that seems to be uniformly spread in the coastal towns, and suggests a deeper involvement with local musical and verbal culture, as well as links to musical currents around the Indian Ocean. We can glimpse the onset of the media age, however, with the occasional reference to Western, Indian or Pan-Arabic musical elements in these recordings.

Siti bint Saad's biographers mention that she sang Arabic and Hindustani songs at the behest of her upper-crust patrons at the Sultan's Palace. Her songs and those of Maalim Shaban in Kiunguja (the dialect of Zanzibar) were favoured over the Kiamu and Kimvita (the dialects of Lamu and Mombasa respectively) songs usually performed by Mbaruk, another group member. This is in contrast to earlier decades, when the court brought in singers from Lamu 'by the boat load' (Jahadhmy, 1966: 69), or, as we have heard, when Ikhwani Safaa practised Lamu songs to be performed because of their popularity.[15] Otherwise Siti bint Saad is well remembered in oral history as a singer whose songs addressed the concerns of her lower class neighbors in Zanzibar's Ng'ambo community (cf. Fair, 1998, 2001).

Siti bint Saad may rightly be termed the first media star in East Africa. In the 1950s, Shaaban Robert devoted a partly fictional account to her life story (Robert, 1967) and she is remembered to this day as the ultimate Swahili *taarab* singer. It is difficult to explain why her name is so well remembered. Possibly the timbre of her voice suited the recording technology of the time best, as her sharp voice cuts across the din even of heavily used and scratchy shellac records. Maybe it was a coincidence that she was there at the right time, for the brief period of commercial recording between 1928 and 1930, before the general world recession brought recording in East Africa to a halt until the late 1940s.

By that time however, musical fashions had already changed. Egyptian films were the rage of the day and *taarab* clubs modeled their large-scale orchestras along the lines of the *firqah* ensembles starring in these films and on the recordings by the stars being readily available:

Zama zilikwenda zikigeuka na tarabu za vikosi vilivyo na intidhamu na ala nyingi sana zilianza kubuniwa Unguja, Mvita na Dar es Salaam: mtindo ukawa wa nyimbo za Umu Kulthumi na Muhammad Abdulwahab na Farid Atrash wa Misri: michezo yao ya senema ilifika hata huku na rekodi za nyimbo zao zikipatikana kwa urahisi, na kwa hivyo, vijana wa utamaduni wakaanza kupenda ama dansa na nyimbo za kizungu au nyimbo za kiarabu: Akhawan Safa ikajiunda upya huko Unguja, Young Egyptians na Ahli-Liwtan Dar es Salaam, na Mombasa Zamzam na kisha chama cha Johari; vyote vyama hivi vilipiga muziki kwa nadhumu ya kisasa, wakavaa nguo rasmi wakipiga na wakatumia vikuza sauti na ala nyingi ...

(Jahadhmy, 1966: 69)

The times were beginning to change though and the *taarab* groups featuring many instruments were created in Unguja, Mombasa and Dar es Salaam. Their style was tributary to the likes of Umm Kulthum, Mohamed Abdulwahab and Farid al-Atrash from Egypt, whose films were shown even here and whose recordings were easily available. So the youth liked either to dance and European songs, or Arabic songs. Ikhwani Safaa re-united in Zanzibar, Egyptian and Al-Watan in Dar es Salaam, in Mombasa Zamzam and later Jauhar Club were formed. All these clubs played music in the contemporary style, they wore uniforms on stage, used amplification and many instruments ...

No *taarab* recordings were made in Zanzibar at this time, however, the style can be imagined by reference to recordings of Mombasa's Jauhar, or Dar es Salaam's Egyptian and Al-Watan Musical Clubs. While most of the songs recorded were in the Swahili language the musical structure owes much to the influences of Egyptian film orchestras. Sometimes whole arrangements are copied from the repertoire of famous singers and film stars like Moh'd Abdel-Wahhab or Umm Kulthum. According to their own historians, Ikhwani Safaa sang Arabic songs exclusively until the second half of the 1950s. Some of the first Swahili ones were *Nyota (The Guiding Star), Vingaravyo vyote si dhahabu* (All that Glitters is not Gold), and *Nipepee* (Fan me some Fresh Air).[16]

However, Ikhwani Safaa does not represent the whole picture of Zanzibari *taarab* of the time. Smaller groups along the lines of the old-style violin-'*ud*-percussion set-up continued to play for weddings and evening pastimes. Women's *taarab* clubs like Royal Air Force, Navy, Nuru l'Uyun were active as well. The Michenzani Social Club, in addition to their theatrical activities featured a small *taarab* ensemble as well, and was soon to rise to popularity with the songs of Bakari Abeid, who was to become Zanzibar's most popular post-World War II singer. In 1958 Bakari Abeid was also recruited into Ikhwani Safaa and he continued to sing for both groups well into the 1960s. Many social and cultural clubs, featuring both *taarab* and *michezo* (theatrical plays) were founded in the late 1950s and early 1960s, like Ghazzy, a splinter group from Ikhwani Safaa, the Miembeni Social Club, and Shime Kuokoana.[17]

Ikhwani Safaa did not record because the bandmaster A. A. Buesh was against recording. Otherwise, the surviving recordings from this time – by Bakari Abeid with either Michenzani Social Club, or some Ikhwani Safaa renegades, or slightly later, by Shime Kuokoana – portray a quite energetic and rhythmically marked style, that to today's ears sounds closer to *kidumbak* rather than to the received orchestral *taarab* tradition. *Kidumbak* is a musical form that can be located at the interface between *taarab* and local *ngoma* dance traditions. Today's *kidumbak* often makes use of the latest *taarab* hit songs and many youngsters hone their musical skills in *kidumbak* groups before being admitted into a *taarab* musical club. *Kidumbak*, therefore, is now sometimes called *ki-taarab*, 'a diminutive kind of *taarab*', as 'derived from *taarab*'.[18] Against this view of *taarab* as the great tradition, a number of older musicians hold that the most celebrated model of Swahili *taarab* in earlier decades of this century, the group of Siti bint Saad, was not so much different even from today's *kidumbak*: 'In the time of Siti bint Saad [the 1920s/30s], the musicians used to squat on the floor, their instruments were two small drums, a tambourine, violin and *udi*. The audience danced. Thus, this old-time *taarab* was much more akin to *kidumbak* rather than today's *taarab* with its big orchestras and the aloof character of *taarab* reception.'[19]

There are no recordings of *kidumbak* from the early days and we do not know what *kidumbak* sounded like in the 1950s. Violin and/or *'ud* were used as the melodic instruments, while the genre's name *kidumbak* refers to the two small clay drums that form the basis of the ensemble. Today another prominent instrument is the *sanduku* (a one-stringed box bass, akin to the tea-chest basses utilized in a number of places in southern Africa). The *sanduku* is said to have been a cheap locally made substitute for the double bass. On some of the recordings of Bakari Abeid with the Michenzani Social Club, the double bass sounds rather more like a *sanduku*, sounding short staccatoed phrases. Otherwise the early Michenzani sound is characterized by accordions and *'ud*, the accordion voice being covered by a small violin section. The few other recordings surviving from this period in Zanzibar music are some political songs by Shime Kuokoana, preserved at the national radio. Shime's sound is squarely based on one accordion and the *sanduku* plays a prominent role, not surprising since the group originated as a *kidumbak* ensemble:

Shime Kuokoana was founded as a drama group within the Afro Shirazi Youth League; to raise support for the party in the fight for independence from Britain. Swahili drama needs music, but Shime had neither instruments nor musicians. They thus hired Khamis Kombo's *kidumbak*, and we started to play at their functions. Gradually, the club received help from parties and coastal social clubs, so from 1959 onwards there was a gradual transition from *kidumbak* to *taarab*, with the inclusion of accordion, later violins and the percussion used in *taarab*.[20]

The January 1964 revolution (shortly after independence in December 1963) led by Abeid Karume and the Afro-Shirazi party left *taarab* somehow subdued. All *taarab* clubs were first put under the umbrella of the Ministry of Culture and the local party organizations: *Taarab* was suspect as a music linked to the former powers, and also because the government wanted to control the lyric output of the clubs. During the early revolutionary period many of the earlier recordings were destroyed at the national radio station. Individual musicians were all recruited into a national *taarab* orchestra run by the Ministry of Culture. The clubs continued with their activities yet almost none of the smaller clubs survived the national phase. From the 1970s and into the early 1990s the *taarab* scene was dominated by Ikhwani Safaa (intermittently called Malindi CCM) and Culture Musical Club, which evolved out of the national orchestra and incorporated former members of Shime as a prominent stock.[21]

The political and ideological situation surrounding music-making in Zanzibar at this time is perhaps best characterized by two incidents from the 1970s. On a visit to Guinea, Zanzibar's second president Aboud Jumbe saw a *ballet africain* and asked for Sekou Touré's help in setting up a similar group in Zanzibar. It was intended that the *ballet*, as 'a true African art form', would replace *taarab* as the national music style, as the latter was still considered to be a bourgeois entertainment, a foreign import, linked to the former ruling Arab elites and entertainment at the Sultan's palace. As was to be expected the *ballet* did not really hit the nerve of the Zanzibar audience and came under serious critique of the religiously inclined because of the scantily clad dancers. After Jumbe's term in office the *ballet* was closed down, Guinean tutors left for home. In the late 1970s intellectual circles posited the theoretical question whether *taarab* with its aforementioned associations could really be 'oral literature', hence 'African' and 'of the people' (Khatib, 1981). Maybe Khatib's own biography answers the query best. While being a staunch and upcoming CCM party functionary, he was and is also a poet writing *taarab* lyrics and member of Ikhwani Safaa.

In the 1980s and into the 1990s the sound of Zanzibar *taarab* was defined by the orchestral line-ups represented by both Ikhwani Safaa and the Culture Musical Club: While both clubs feature a large membership going into the hundreds, active musicians are about 30 to 50. Of these about 25 to 30 might be on stage or participate in recording. The typical line-up is thus five to eight violins, *qanun*, one or two *'ud*s, *nai*, two accordions, keyboard, electric guitar, cello, double bass, *dumbak*, two bongos, *rika* (tambourine), a host of female and male solo singers, plus a female chorus of about ten. While orchestras in this mould were popular all along the coast from the 1950s and into the 1960s almost all these organizations went out of business in subsequent years. Ironically, the economical stalemate after the revolution and the subsequent socialist austerity policy may have generated the right conditions to sustain this old-style 'pure *taarab*'. In Mombasa, Tanga (on the northern Tanzanian coast) and Dar es Salaam the sound of smaller ensembles was dominated by keyboards, electric and guitars and bass guitars and a generally heavier beat, closer to the sound of urban dance bands. While this was still considered a natural evolution out of the earlier stylistics – the keyboards subbing for the string sound or replacing the accordion – a new development emerging from the Dar es Salaam scene in the mid-1990s, so-called 'modern *taarab*' or *mipasho*, took the world of Swahili *taarab* by storm. *Mipasho* means 'backbiting' and the style is so called because of this song characteristic that has become its major feature and attraction.[22]

Zanzibar now also has its protagonists of 'modern *taarab*' above all a group called East African Melody. The group features a line-up of two keyboards, guitar, bass guitar, and drum machine; it is especially popular among the younger generation which considers the string sound of Culture and Ikhwani Safaa old-fashioned. Besides the *mipasho*, 'backbiting songs' so popular among the female audience, the popularity of modern *taarab* is also based on the fact that it is more danceable.[23] Musically the Zanzibar version of modern *taarab* includes many elements of both *kidumbak* and *beni* (from the English 'band'). The latter grew out of the colonial marching band and this brass band sound has been integrated into the circuit of Zanzibar wedding entertainments, along with *taarab* and *kidumbak*. Like *kidumbak*, *beni* uses melodies, words and choruses of contemporary and older *taarab* songs and strings them together into long medleys. Purists denounce 'modern *taarab*' as non-*taarab*, as not in line with what is accepted and what to them is the essence of *taarab*. Definitions of *taarab* usually include a laid-back instrumental performance that allows for the contemplation of thought-heavy lyrics, a seated audience and no dancing. These are characterizations that specifically apply to middle and late period orchestral *taarab*. Yet they include neither female *taarab*, nor the performance style of smaller groups operated on the Isles. Comparing modern *taarab* to the earliest documented style encountered on the 1928–30 recordings we find that the contemporary style might not be so devious after all.

Taarab song

Swahili *taarab* is unthinkable without its song lyrics, generally cast in a shape that relates strongly to received traditions of classical Swahili poetry. These traditions have been strongest in the Lamu Archipelago on the northern Kenyan coast and quite a number of the oldest epic forms have been discovered in that area. Until the turn of the twentieth century poetic conventions of the north coast dominated lyrical production all along the Swahili Coast, into the north of Mozambique and as far as the Comoros. The same can probably be said for song production: In his chronicle of the founding of Ikhwani Safaa, Shaib Abeid acknowledges the popularity of Lamu songs in Zanzibar in the early 1900s to the extent that no musical group could do without these songs:

Sisi tuliwanza kujifunza Nyimbo hizi za Kiarabu na zakiswahili ... na nyimbo za Kiswahili kwa mahadhi ya Lamu nyingi Maana wakati huwo sana tukitumia Mahadhi yatokayo Lamu na Masharii ya kiasli na nyimbo za Mikassa na tarab za arusi aghlab huwa Kucha.

(Shaib Abeid, n.d.: 26, 29)

We started to learn these Arabic and Swahili songs ... and many Swahili songs in the Lamu style. Because at the time we used these melodies from Lamu very much, and their original poetry, and for a wedding *taarab* they were absolutely necessary.

We do not know much about the musical and performance style of these early songs but a number of written samples survive. Some later renditions are available in the form of recordings, like *Kigalawa* ('the outrigger'), a text originating in Lamu, but still sung in Zanzibar in the late 1920s by Mbaruku who belonged to the group of musicians playing with Siti bint Saad (see example 9.1 below).

Kigalawa	*si sawa sawa na chombo?*
Baharini	*chenda mirengo mirengo*
Sivuweni	*shuga lasitiri mambo*

Kigalawa	*kumbe kina vitu ndani*
Unitweke	*hata kwa mwenye Huseni*
Jabu moto	*'menitiya kisimani*[24]

The small outrigger, isn't it a boat as well?
In the sea it moves from side to side.
Don't take it away, the 'shuga' (women's covering) hides matters.

The small outrigger, so there are things inside.
Put the load on my head, even for Mwenye Huseni.
The neck is hot, you have put me into a well.

Example 9.1 *Kigalawa* ('The Outrigger')

The composition of *Kigalawa* illustrates the major principles of Swahili lyrical form. That is, usually two half-lines per line, fixed number of syllables per half-line and strict rhyming schemes.[25] In this case it is four by eight: four syllables for the first half-line and eight for the second. The three-line form is called *wimbo* ('song') (see example 9.2 below).

Ki-ga-la-wa   *si sa-wa sa-wa na cho-mbo?*
Ba-ha-ri-ni   *che-nda mi-re-ngo mi-re-ngo*
Si-vu-we-ni   *shu-ga la-si-ti-ri ma-mbo*

Example 9.2 Three-line form of song called *wimbo* ('song')

The figural language used in *Kigalawa* also aptly characterizes the style of Swahili *taarab* poetry, properties preferably employed until today. Topics are rarely addressed in a straightforward way, but are customarily veiled in allusions. The language generally abounds in tropes.

Jahadhmy (1966), a chronicler of the lives of Siti bint Saad, Mbaruku and their group, describes *taarab* practice in the late 1920s. Mbaruk is singled out as purveyor of the Lamu style of Swahili song, yet fashion is moving towards a the adaptation of Arabic and Hindi songs and towards Swahili lyrics in the Kiunguja dialect of Zanzibar:[26]

Mbaruku hakupendeza sana nyumba ya Mfalme wa Unguja; mapenzi ya huko yalikuwa ya Siti binti Saad na Mwalimu Shaaban ambao walipendwa kwa sababu ya maimbaji yao ya kiarabu na ya kiunguja. Nyumba hiyo haikujua kiamu wala kupenda nyimbo za kiamu, kinyume cha wafalme waliotangulia ambao wakiwaagizia waimbaji wa Lamu kwa meli nzima.

(Jahadhmy, 1966: 69)

Mbaruku was not much liked at the house of the Sultan of Zanzibar. Their favorites were Siti Bint Saad and Mwalimu Shaaban who were liked very much for their singing in Arabic and the Swahili of Unguja. This house did not know the Swahili of Lamu, nor did they like the songs in the Lamu language or style, contrary to earlier Sultans who invited singers from Lamu by the 'boat load'.

This statement in particular refers to preferences at the court of Zanzibar, where the group was often invited for performance, yet a general change was in the air. The recording medium exposed musicians and their public to a wider sphere of musical models, which were adapted to local performance practice. While the musical style – the playing of *bashraf* instrumental introductions, the adaptation of Arabic or Indian melodies, Western or Latin rhythms – points towards an internationalization caused by the newly available media, the songs surviving from this time point towards an increased localization of song topics and style. Many of the songs recorded by Siti bint Saad and her group specifically address the lives of Zanzibar's Ng'ambo community, the lower class suburban housing area where Siti and her group also lived. The song *Kijiti* for example, is a thorough critique of the colonial legal system, enforcing law at will. In the *Kijiti* case the murderer of a young woman is acquited and flees to the mainland, while two women witnesses are convicted of the murder because they organized a party and bought some alcohol (see example 9.3).[27]

Tazameni tazameni	*alivyofanya Kijiti*
Kumchukua mgeni	*kumchezesha foliti*
Kenda naye maguguni	*kamrejesha maiti*
Kijiti alinambia	*ondoka mama twenende*
Laiti ningelijua	*ningekataa nisiende*
Kijiti unaniua	*kwa pegi moja ya tende*
Jaji amekasirika	*kitini alipoketi*
Kasema biladi fuli	*mashahidi wa Kijiti*
Takufunga Sumaili	*na K biti Subeti*

Look, look all what Kijiti has done.
To take a guest and force her to 'play' his game.
He went with her into the bush, and brought her back as a corpse.

Kijiti told me: Come on Mama, let's go.
If only I had known, I would not have gone.
Kijiti you are killing me for a single shot of liquor.

The judge was mad in his chair where he sat.
And he said: 'Bloody fools!' to the witnesses against Kijiti.
We will put you in jail Sumaili, K. the daughter of Subeti.

Example 9.3 *Kijiti* (*Kijiti*; a personal name)

The topics and the verbal delivery of *taarab* songs would completely change with the advent of the new style of the 1950s. Henceforth songs on the human condition and especially romantic love songs would dominate the repertoire. While the earlier style had thrived on social commentary and verses often composed on the spur of the moment, the new verbal style, like the music, came to be much more formal in terms of presentation, as well as textual construction. Composers reverted to the received forms of classical poetry strictly following the rules with a regular outline of verses, lines, syllables and rhyme. *Nyota* (*The Guiding Star*) one of the early Swahili songs composed for performance by the new Ikhwani Safaa in the 1950s fittingly demonstrates the features of the new style (see example 9.4 below).

Nyota nakuamini	*dira na ramani*
Nimo safarini	*siwasili asilani*
Wasemao siponi	*wasisibu ya Manani*
Nyota tokea zamani	*naelewa ni sukani*
Sibaini sioni	*I wapi pwani pwani*
Huu leo mtihani	*nasubiri yake shani*
Dharuba na matufani	*zivumazo baharini*
Nyota tena sizioni	*nahiliki mawimbini*
Sioni sionekani	*nimefunikwa gizani*
Bandarini 'taegesha	*nipokewe kwa bashasha*
Rabi 'taniwasilisha	*na khatari kunivusha*
Anivushe vya kutisha	*na salama kunivesha*[28]

My guiding star, I trust you, compass and map.
I am journeying, I would never arrive.
Those who say I will not escape do not trust in what is foretold by the Beneficent.

My guiding star, since long ago I know you are my steering wheel.
I cannot distinguish, cannot see the shore.
Today this is my trial, I patiently trust in God's mysterious ways.

When tempests and hurricanes rage across the sea.
The stars I do not see, the waves destroy me.
I do not see nor am I seen, covered by darkness.

I will steer into port, so a vivacious crowd may receive me.
The Almighty will make me arrive, and take all hazards away from me.
May he take away all that bothers me, and clothe me in peace.

Example 9.4 *Nyota* (*The Guiding Star*)

While not adhering strictly to the syllable count in the first two verses, the song is otherwise a model of a *taarab* song of the times. With regular rhyming patterns at the end of half-lines, and then by verse three the fully realized eight-by-eight syllable meter that would become the standard for *taarab* compositions in the decades to come. Also note the artful shift from the –ni rhyming sound to the –sha for the final verse, a shift that also signals a general change of mood with the safe arrival in port. Throughout, the text abounds in subtle shifts in the choice and meaning of words: Like the variations on the meanings of the verbs *–vusha* ('remove'/'relieve of something') and *-vesha* ('put on'/'clothe') both from the same stem, and implied meanings from homophonic form *-vusha* ('carry, ferry across' [from the stem *–vua* meaning 'save, preserve, get out of difficulty']). The general meaning of the song aims towards a moral teaching, the trust in the guiding principles of religion, and more specifically Islam. For our topic of island musics, of course we savour the emplotment in terms of seafaring and the sea, imagery that abounds in both Swahili poetry and *taarab* song.

In his book *Taarab Zanzibar* M. S. Khatib (1992: 44–54) termed the time from circa 1950 to 1964, as an era of *taarab* song that was impregnated by capitalism. Hence the domination of such mundane topics as romantic love, especially in the figuration of praise songs (usually addressed prospective female lovers) in terms of 'things' such as *Tini* ('Fig'), *Zabibu* ('Grape'), *Nanasi* ('Pineapple'), and *Ndege Wang* ('My Bird'). As already sketched in the previous section *taarab* came under suspicion after the revolution as a purveyor of bourgeois mentality. Hence the collectivization of clubs under the guidance of the Ministry of Culture and the party branches. Overambitious functionaries destroyed many *taarab* records and tapes at the national radio station in the years following the revolution. There is talk of action against love songs, and of the banning of songs from the airwaves of the national radio, yet much of this seems to be overstressed. The fact, however, is that a censorship board screening lyrics was active well into the 1990s and that all public performances still have to be licensed by the respective government offices.[29]

Few recordings survive from the immediate post-revolutionary time, few political ones at that. One of these is *Walosema Hatuwezi* ('The Ones who Said we Could not Do It) by Shime Kuokoana and singer Juma Sheha (see example 9.5).

Tulipotweka jahazi	*tumelivusha salama*
Wenyewe wafanyakazi	*mara tumesimama*
Karume ndiyo kiongozi	*sukani kashika vyema*
Wapo wapi walowezi	*walio wakitusema*
Wee melio na jahazi	*kufuka si la mrama*
Dhoruba la kipuuzi	*sasa hana lawama*[30]

When we set sail on the dhow, we ferried it across in peace.
We workers, for once we have stood together.
Karume is our leader; the steering wheel is secure in his grip.
Where are the squatters, who were gossiping about us?
Between a steamboat and a dhow, to emit smoke is not swaying.
It's been a foolish talk about storm, now he [Karume] has no blame.

Example 9.5 *Walosema Hatuwezi* (*The Ones Who Said We Could Not Do It*)

The song is performed in a basic *kidumbak*-inspired style with just accordion, *sanduku* and percussion. The lyrics surprise in that the imagery is almost the same is in *Nyota* portrayed earlier. Despite the *ballet afrain* intermezzo, and contradicting all theoretical and political arguments, *taarab* and the Swahili poetic sensitivity instituted itself as the basic medium of expression in post-revolution Zanzibar, even for politically inspired lyrics. *Taarab* orchestras would be invited for important political functions. On the occasion of important anniversaries or to outline specific political or social programmes special songs would be composed. Quite a number of songs from the immediate post-revolutionary period into the 1980s would come to explain and praise the political union between the islands comprising Zanzibar and mainland Tanganyika: *Jamhuri*, the Republic of Tanzania formed in April 1964, later the union of Zanzibar's Afro-Shirazi Party with mainland's TANU (Tanganyika African Union) to CCM (Chama cha Mapinduzi).[31]

Muungano umetimu	*Unguja na Tanganyika*
Tumeishika hatamu	*wananchi kwa shirika*
Tunaujenga kwa hamu	*kwa umoja twatumika*[32]

The Union has been fulfilled between Zanzibar and Tanganyika
We the people have taken control in working hand in hand
We build it with desire, cooperating in unity.

Example 9.6 Song excerpt

Yet the basic outlook, whether socially or in music was and still is still more favourably across the ocean and especially to the countries of the Gulf. Large numbers of Zanzibari emigrate for work or to do trade, the latter gaining momentum especially after the liberalization of the economy from the second half of the 1980s onwards.

Images of the sea can be found in the new 'modern *taarab*' as well. Thus *Love in Sea Express* by Abdallah Issa brings the imagery up to date following the introduction of the first regular speed boat service between Dar es Salaam and Zanzibar in the early 1990s.[33] Part of the lyrics have been adapted and taken even further by DJ Cool Para – a pioneer of what he calls *taa-rap* – bridging the gap between the classical *taarab* tradition and current youth musics rap and hip hop. For *Raha ya Moyo Wangu* he has taken over the chorus section of an old Ikhwani Safaa song. In the rap section he gives his own take of a modern love story. The original chorus is left intact and rendered by specially hired *taarab* singers; the instrumental underpinning is drum machine, synthesizer and bass guitar (see example 9.7 below).

Raha naona raha   chorus
Moyo wangu
Mimi kupendwa na wewe

Uliyepewa sauti na sura iliyo jamali
Habibi ya noor-al-ayn, mtoto macho laini
Kumbuka mara ya kwanza kwenye Sea Express ndipo tulipokutana
Nimeketi kwenye class si mbele si nyuma sana
Ukapita kwa kasi kiumbe rahimu sana mtoto mzuri sana
Tutaweza kupendana zimeandikwa mbinguni ndoa zote[34]

Happiness! I feel at ease.
My heart,
To be loved by you!

You have been given a voice and face of incredible beauty,
Beloved light-of-eyes, child with the soft eyes!
Remember when we first met in the Sea Express:
I was seated in the middle rows, not too far ahead nor to the back.
You went by really fast, you Godly creation, beautiful child!
We will love each other, all marriages are already written in heaven.

Example 9.7 *Raha ya Moyo Wangu* (*Comfort of My Heart*)

    The song evokes a whole web of intertextual relations: The chorus part refers us back to the original splendor of the acoustic *taarab* orchestra and for insiders conjures the original song text. Otherwise the partly Arabizing sections of the rap part (*jamali, nour-al-ayn, rahimu*) and the reference to the traditional concept of destiny stand in marked contrast to the contemporary hip-hop rooted musical accompaniment and the song setting in a Russian-made speed boat. Yet this eclectic mix possibly brings current Zanzibari 'modernity' to a point. The 1990s have seen an unprecedented opening up of the political, economic, and hence social and cultural landscape. On one side the political stalemate between the ruling CCM and the opposition CUF has resulted in an increasing political integration into the national Tanzanian framework. On the other hand the economic liberalization has generated new possibilities for business ventures, especially in the import-export business, and the renewing of the old trade network to the Gulf States and to south Asia. There has also been much local and foreign investment in developing tourism facilities on the island, profiting from Zanzibar Stone Town's status as a gazetted UNESCO world cultural heritage site. While generating much needed business incentives after three decades of socialist austerity policies, many developments are seen as a threat to Zanzibari identity by a large

segment of the local population. Thus tourism and related industries have generated new occupations as beach boys, tourist touts, drug dealers with a large influx
of questionable characters from the streets of Dar es Salaam or Nairobi, and it has
attracted substantial numbers of prostitutes from as far away as Uganda or Zambia
as well.

Local conditions for performance have decreased since the mid 1990s, because
few people are nowadays able to afford the performance of a live *taarab* group, let
alone a large orchestra, for their wedding celebrations. Wedding festivities have
become less extravagant affairs and live music has been replaced in large part by
so-called *rusha roho*, the playing of music cassettes of various styles over a small
sound system, thus collapsing a number of different musical events into a single
one. Otherwise, the developing tourism industry has generated new possibilities
for *taarab* artists to perform. Possibly a major incentive in times of economic hard-
ship, where before music making had been an evening pastime in the social club,
with negligible financial gain. Fewer people now have the leisure to indulge in this
kind of diversion, either because daytime jobs and financial pressures leave less
time, or because new forms of leisure activities, media like satellite TV, video,
internet cafes, to name but a few, keep people from spending time with practice or
social get-together at the music club. Internationally, the developing market niche
for so-called 'world music' since the later part of the 1980s, has also had its effect
on Zanzibari *taarab* music. The recognition of the old-style acoustic *taarab* on the
world music scene, with regular touring and recording of some of the major
ensembles since the early 1990s, has lent support to a style that locally had been
under pressure by new fashions, especially the 'modern *taarab*' developing in the
past decade.

Conclusion

Among islands the location of Zanzibar exhibits a very particular characteristic.
Positioned in the very vicinity of the African continent geographically and culturally, it is contiguous with the east African coast and so-called Swahili cultural
sphere spanning a stretch of almost 2000 kilometers from the south of Somalia, all
along the Kenyan and Tanzanian coasts into northern Mozambique. In the history
of the coast Zanzibar occupies a very special position. In the early nineteenth
century the Sultan of Oman transferred his residence to Zanzibar, subsequently
conquered most of the Swahili city-states along the coast, and through caravan
trade opened up the interior of the continent for commerce. While severely
contested and despised at the time, this time of Zanzibari overlordship of the coast
now has a certain nostalgic currency. Thus even non-Zanzibari inhabitants of the
coast now like to see *taarab* music as originating in the palaces of the Sultan,
linking it with Egypt as another powerful place of the coastal imagination. Yet as

my analysis has shown, *taarab* probably owes more to centuries of exchange across the Indian Ocean than to one Zanzibari attending music lessons in Cairo. Belonging to this Indian Ocean music culture has also informed the later trajectory of the style. Thus while political and media policies were to a large extent governed by British imperial power, the coast preferred to tune into Radio Cairo, or watch Indian or Egyptian films, rather than step in style with Hollywood and Fred Astaire.

New political agendas engulfed Zanzibar and the coast in post-independence times. The Coast Protectorate was integrated in the new Republic of Kenya, and shortly after independence and the revolution of 1964, Zanzibar was married to mainland Tanganyika to form the United Republic of Tanzania. Coastal culture and agendas were somehow marginalized in the new states, yet, as the review of Zanzibari *taarab* history has shown, Swahili musical and verbal sensibilities prevailed even in the face of serious challenges. The development of co-called 'modern *taarab*' shows the validity and vitality of the genre for an ever-expanding audience. It is a question of conjecture what will happen to the classical form of *taarab*, in the face of the more recent economic and social developments in Zanzibar, and by its inclusion into local tourism and international world music circuits. Is the future just another fake folk music?

Swahili music and culture, the island or coastal experience begs the question of the specificity of island, coastal or sea musics. I envisage an approach that moves beyond an analysis of genres directly linked with the sea, like for example fishers' or pearl divers' songs, sailors' songs, but rather an outline of the distinct musical and aesthetic correlates of larger scale historical processes that may be thematized around the seas. We might take inspiration in these contexts from Braudel's (1972–3) landmark work on the Mediterranean, Gilroy's (1992) sweeping *Black Atlantic*, and more recent work that recognizes the Indian Ocean as a similar historical sphere of interaction (McPherson, 1998). Such an access to islands – music and the sea as a particular musico-ecological space – could offer a truly historical corrective to much contemporary popular music research that is engulfed by current mass media-based post-modernist and globalizing paradigms.

Notes

1. Excerpt from Ikhwani Safaa Musical Club. *Nyota* (ca. 1957). Words and music by Ali Abdalla Buesh.
2. Seyyid Said, Sultan of Oman and Zanzibar transferred his court to Zanzibar in the early nineteenth century and Zanzibar became the most important commercial entrepot for the East African trade in the course of the century. Zanzibar became a British Protectorate in 1890. In January 1964, just after

independence, a revolution toppled the Sultan. In April of the same year, Zanzibar joined Tanganyika to become part of the United Republic of Tanzania. The population of both islands is estimated to be 966,906 (2000) with the population of Zanzibar town standing at close to 200.000. About 95 per cent of the population are Muslim.

3. For more information on Swahili culture and history cf. Horton and Middleton (2000).
4. Statement read by Idi Abdallah Farahan at a workshop on '*Taarab* Traditions', Zanzibar 1 July 2000. Idi Farahan is prominent elder of the Zanzibar *taarab* community, a seasoned musician and educator, currently bandmaster of Ikhwani Safaa Musical Club.
5. On the record trade cf. Evans (1931); Graebner (1989).
6. Indian recordings were widely available throughout East Africa as many shops were owned by Asian businessmen. European and Arabic recordings were also sold. Mbaruk Talsam, one of the prominent musicians on these recordings is said to have befriended European soldiers during World War I, he supposedly played a number of English songs and was very much liked for this.
7. The first Egyptian sound film was premiered in the spring of 1932.
8. *Kitarab* – in the classical Swahili *taarab* style. This refers to a generalized style, that cannot be properly located and may contain older Swahili forms as well as Arabic ones from Southern Arabia or the Gulf.
9. Refers to a general conception of Arabic music, contains popular and classical Egypt styles.
10. Recent experience on the Comorian island of Anjouan and research on the history of the *gambus*, or the *kibangala* or *kinanda* as it is called in Swahili, reveal a style that could be called 'pre-*taarab*' (cf. Graebner 2002a,b and the literature cited therein).
11. Saleh (1980, 1988), and Khatib (1992) were or are members of Ikhwani Safaa, others like Mgana (1994) and Topp-Fargion (1992) base their work on information supplied by Maalim Idi Farahan, a prominent member and a self-appointed historian of the club. Farahan is the current owner of Shaib Abeid's historical text, a little notebook containing about thirty pages of handwritten text.
12. This touring musician is described as travelling to Bombay after his stay in Zanzibar, a further pointer to activities and exchange of musical ideas in pre-media times.
13. A later reader of the text has marked these and added later dates when *qanuns* were ordered.
14. Conversations with Zein l'Abdin, Mombasa, April 1993, members of Jauhar Musical Club, Mombasa, January 2001.

15. The northern dialect of the Lamu area was also the erstwhile Swahili literary and art language; north coast features were common also in written poetry all along the coast in the last decades of the nineteenth century and into the twentieth century.

16. The composition of *Nipepee* (by Shaib Abeid) is usually dated to the 1940s. Some even say that it originally dates to the 1920s, and was later adapted and rearranged by Shaib Abeid, still later by Seif Salim Saleh. (Mohamed Ahmed, personal communication September 2002). Recording of *Nipepee* by Seif Salim on: Ikhwani Safaa Musical Club. *Music of Zanzibar: Taarab 2.* (GlobeStyle CDORBD 040; recorded 1988).

17. Conversations with Abbas Machano, Mombasa, April 1987; Bi Kidude, Hamburg, July 1989 and Zanzibar, July 1994; Said Nassor, Hamburg, July 1989 & Zanzibar, January 2001; Khamis Shehe, Zanzibar, July 1994 & January 2001; Idi Farahan, Zanzibar, August 1995 & January 2001; Seif Saleh, Hamburg, July 1989 & Zanzibar, July 1994; Said Mwinyi, Zanzibar, September 1995.

18. In Swahili specific noun classes are linked to particular semantic concepts. A specific noun class prefix may thus be used to shift the original gender of a noun, for example to form a diminutive, as in this case (Schadeberg, 1992: 12).

19. Conversation with Makame Faki, Zanzibar, August 1996; the point was reiterated on different ocassions by Khamis Shehe and Said Nassor, Zanzibar, January 2001.

20. Conversation with Abbas Machano, Zanzibar, April 1996.

21. Only a few recordings were made in the 1970s. Some by 'Culture' as the quasi national orchestra were released by the mainland-based Tanzania Film Company on 45 rpm singles.

22. Since the mid 1990s Dar es Salaam has become the major center of musical production, and of stylistic development as well. A more liberal political and economical regime, together with a liberalization of the media landscape has resulted in a stylistic departure from the received forms. For more information on *mipasho* and related developments cf. Graebner (1999, 2003); Lange (2000), Khamis (2001); Askew (2002).

23. Like Swahili wedding *taarab*, the new dance-hall *taarab* is an entertainment especially geared towards female audiences, men take part only in marginal roles.

24. Lyrics of *Kigalawa* composed by Sheikh Swaad from Lamu. As a *ngoma* dance song the song is still sung nowadays in Zanzibar.

25. For a short introduction to Swahili prosody, cf. Allen (1967).

26. Mbaruku was born and grew up in Mombasa. He later moved to Lamu to learn from the master poets of the time like Mohamed Kijuma, Bwana Zena

and Sheikh Swaad.

27. The song is still remembered in Zanzibar today and often performed by Bi Kidude, an elderly lady who knew Siti bint Saad as a child growing up in her neighborhood. A recording of the song by Bi Kidude is available on RetroAfric RETRO12CD. For the full song lyrics and an outline of the case as well as for further songs characteristic of the times cf. Fair (1998, and 2001).

28. *Nyota*, words and music by Ally Abdalla Buesh, ca 1957. Original performance by Nadi Ikhwani Safaa, singer Mohamed Juma Dunia. Currently no easily available release of the song exists. Amani Studio (Zanzibar) does have a wobbly concert recording of Ikhwani Safaa with the original singer Moh'd Juma, dating to the 1970s. I would like to thank Maulidi Mohamed 'Machaprala' (a later singer and interpreter of the song) for lending me a copy of a private recording by the composer A. A. Buesh with *'ud* as the sole accompaniment. The transcription of the lyrics follows this latter recording.

29. All performing groups have to be registered at the department of culture.

30. Excerpt from: Shime Kuokoana *Walosema Hatuwezi*, singer Juma Sheha, composed shortly after the revolution. Recording in the archives of Sauti ya Tanzania Zanzibar (Voice of Tanzania, Zanzibar).

31. *Jamhuri*, 'Republic'. While the Union seems to pose no problem for the mainland side, there have been frequent moves on the Zanzibar side, even under the Isles' CCM governments, to act contrary to agreed Union policies. The situation was exacerbated with the new multi-party constitution inaugurated in the 1990s, with the opposition CUF (Civic United Front) openly campaigning for withdrawal from the Union.

32. Excerpt from: Ikhwani Safaa Musical Club. *Muungano*. Words by M. G. Khatib; music: I. Farahan. (Cited after Saleh 1980:41).

33. Abdallah Issa and Dumbak Music Masters present *Love in Sea Express*. Dubai: Dumbak Music Masters. 'Sea Express' was the trade-mark of the new speedboats introduced at the time

34. Excerpt from: DJ Cool Para. *Raha ya Moyo Wangu*. Zanzibar: Alakeifak Y2K Music Store 2001. The original song is: Ikhwani Safaa, *Raha*. Words and music: Yussuf Mohamed.

References

Abeid, S. n.d. 'Ikhwani Safaa' (Unpublished notebook). Zanzibar.
Allen, J.W.T. (1967), 'Swahili Prosody',. *Swahili* 37 (2):171–179.
Askew, K. (2002), *Performing the Nation: Swahili Musics and Cultural Politics in Tanzania*, Chicago: University of Chicago Press.
Braudel, F. (1972–3), *The Mediterranean and the Mediterranean World in the Age*

of Philip II,. 2 Vols, London: Collins.

Fair, L. (1998), 'Music, Memory and Meaning: The Kiswahili Recordings of Siti binti Saad', in Beck, R. M., Geider, T. and Graebner, W. (eds), *Swahili Forum V*, Köln: Institut für Afrikanistik. [AAP No. 55], pp. 1–16.

(2001), *Pastimes and Politics: Culture, Community and Identity in Post-abolition Urban Zanzibar*, London: James Currey.

Gilroy, P. (1992), *The Black Atlantic: Modernity and Double Consciousness*, Cambridge: Harvard University Press.

Graebner, W. (1991), '*Taarab* – Populäre Musik am Indischen Ozean', in Erlmann V. (ed.) *Populäre Musik in Afrika*, Berlin: Museum für Völkerkunde, pp. 181–200.

—— (1999), 'Tanzania/Kenya – *Taarab*: The Swahili Coastal sound', in *World Music, Volume 1: Africa Europe and the Middle East*, London: The Rough Guides, pp. 690–7.

—— (2001), 'Twarab ya Shingazidja: A First Approach', in Beck, R. M., Geider, T. and Graebner, W. (eds), *Swahili Forum VIII*, Köln: Institut für Afrikanistik. [=AAP No. 68], pp. 129–43.

—— (2002a.), 'An Ocean of Sound: Swahili *Taarab* and the Musical Imaginary of the Western Indian Ocean.' Paper presented at the *International Conference on Cultural Exchange and Transformation in the Indian Ocean World*, University of California, Los Angeles, 5–6 April 2002.

—— (2002b), 'The Kibangala Connection: Pre-*taarab* Roots on the Northern Kenya Coast?.' Paper presented at the Fifteenth Swahili-Colloquium, Bayreuth, 10–12 May 2002.

—— (2003a), 'Give Them Their Medicine: *Taarab* as a Vital Language in East Africa', in Probst, P. and Spittler, G. (eds) *Between Resistance and Expansion: Approaching Local Vitality in Africa* [forthcoming].

—— (2003b), 'The Interaction of Swahili Taarab Music and the Record Industry: A Historical Perspective', in Beck, R. M. and Wittmann, F. *Close-up: Contextualizing African Media*, Köln: Koeppe. [forthcoming].

Horton, M. and J. Middleton. (2000), *The Swahili: The Social Landscape of a Mercantile Society,* Oxford: Blackwell.

Jahadhmy, A.A. *et al.* (1966), *Waimbaji wa juzi: Mwalim Shabaan, Mbaruk Effandi, Siti bintSaad, Budda bin Mwendo,* Dar es Salaam: Chuo cha Uchunguzi wa Lugha ya Kiswahili.

Khamis, S. A. M. (2001), 'Re-defining *Taarab* in Relation to Local and Global Influences', in Beck, R. M., Geider, T and Graebner, W. *Swahili Forum VIII*, Köln: Institut für Afrikanistik. [=AAP No. 68], pp. 145–56.

Khamis, S. A. M. (2002), 'Wondering About a Change: The *Taarab* lyric and global openness'. *Nordic Journal of African Studies,* 11(2): 198–205.

Khatib, M. S. (1981), '*Taarabu* ni Fasihi Simulizi?', in *Makala za semina ya fasihi simulizi*, iliyoandaliwa na Taasisi ya Uchunguzi wa Kiswahili, Dar es Salaam, Juni 1981,. Dar es Salaam: Chuo Kikuu cha Dar es Salaam, pp. 16–25.

—— (1992), *Taarab Zanzibar,* Dar es Salaam: Tanzania Publishing House.

Lange, S. (2000), 'Muungano and TOT: Rivals on the Urban Cultural Scene' in Gunderson, F. and Barz, G. (eds), *Mashindano! Competitive music performance in East Africa*, Dar es Salaam: Mkuki na Nyota, pp. 67–85.

McPherson, K. (1998), *The Indian Ocean: A History of People and the Sea*, Delhi: Oxford University Press.

Mgana, I. (1991), *Jukwaa la taarab – Zanzibar*, Helsinki: Mediafrica.

Robert, S. (1967), *Wasifu wa Siti bint Saad: Mwimbaji wa Unguja.* (Diwani ya Shaaban 3), Nairobi: Nelson East Africa.

Saleh, S. S. (1980), 'Nyimbo za *taarab* Unguja'. *Lugha Yetu* 37: 35–47.

—— (1988a.), 'Historia na muundo wa *taarab*', *Lugha na Utamaduni* 1: 8–11.

—— (1988b.), 'Historia na muundo wa *taarab*. (Sehemu ya pili)'. *Lugha na Utamaduni* 2: 9–11, 24.

Schadeberg, T. (1992), *A Sketch of Swahili Morphology*, Koeln: Koeppe.

Shariff, I. N. (1988), *Tungo zetu: Msingi wa mashairi na tungo nyinginezo*, Trenton NJ: The Red Sea Press.

Suleiman, A. A. (1969), 'The Swahili Singing Star Siti bint Saad'. *Kiswahili* 39 (1/2): 87–90.

Topp-Fargion, J. (1992), *Women and the Africanisation of* Taarab *in Zanzibar*. Ph.D. dissertation. School of Oriental and African Studies, University of London.

Topp-Fargion, J. (1994), 'A History of *Taarab* Music in Zanzibar: A process of Africanization', in Parkin, D. (ed.) *Continuity and Autonomy in Swahili community*, Wien: Beiträge zur Afrikanistik and London: School of Oriental and African Studies.

Recommended Listening

Bi Kidude. *Zanzibar*, CD, London: RetroAfric RETRO12CD.
Culture Musical Club. *Waridi: Scents of Zanzibar/Parfums de Zanzibar*, 1 CD, Paris: Jahazi Media/Virgin 724359 44982
Ikhwani Safaa Musical Club. *Music of Zanzibar: Taarab 2*, 1 CD, London: GlobeStyle CDORBD 040
Kidumbak Kalcha. *Ng'ambo: The Other Side of Zanzibar,* 1 CD, Todtnauberg: Dizim Records 4501.
Mila na Utamaduni / Culture Musical Club. *Bashraf: Taarab Instrumentals from Zanzibar*. 1 CD. Todtnauberg: Dizim Records 4509.
Mila na Utamaduni / Culture Musical Club. *Spices of Zanzibar,* 1 CD, Frankfurt: Network Medien 24210.

V.A. Zanzibar: Soul and Rhythm/De l'âme à la danse, 2CDs, Paris: Jahazi Media/Virgin 724359 57370.

–10–

British Islands:
An Obsession of British Composers

Fiona Richards

In the first chapter of *Peter Pan*, J.M. Barrie describes his island 'Neverland' as a reflection of the workings of a child's mind. One among many such literary islands, the Neverland is an amalgam of real and imagined experiences:

> I don't know whether you have ever seen a map of a person's mind. Doctors sometimes draw maps of other parts of you, and your own map can become intensely interesting, but catch them trying to draw a map of a child's mind, which is not only confused, but keeps going round all the time. There are zigzag lines on it, just like your temperature on a card, and these are probably roads in the island; for the Neverland is always more or less an island, with astonishing splashes of colour here and there, and coral reefs and rakish-looking craft in the offing, and savages and lonely lairs…there is also first day at school, religion, fathers, the round pond … and either these are part of the island or they are another map showing through it, and it is all rather confusing, especially as nothing will stand still. (Barrie, 1988: 12–13)

As an island nation, the British have long betrayed a fascination with the notion of the 'island'. It is no isolated episode that one of the most popular and compelling BBC television programmes of 2000 was the series *Castaway*, in which a carefully selected group of men, women and children were sent to form a community on an uninhabited Scottish island. A desire to visit and create real and imagined island worlds of secrets and adventures is a deep-rooted part of British culture. There have been many examples of this urge in literature, most famously in works such as Defoe's *Robinson Crusoe*, Stevenson's *Treasure Island* and Ballantyne's *Coral Island*, but also in extraordinary tales such as Muriel Spark's *Robinson* and D. H. Lawrence's *The Man Who Loved Islands,* and in the numerous accounts of fantastic islands in children's literature, such as Enid Blyton's little Kirrin Island and Arthur Ransome's halcyon Wild Cat Island (the summer residence of *Swallows and Amazons*).

What is this fascination?

Is it perhaps some half remembered magic of childhood that we take with us into adult life? Dreams of a treasure island where one can live an adventurous life in a glorious sunlit land teeming with cockatoos, luscious fruits and coconuts, bordering on a golden strand leading to an ever blue sparkling sea. Maybe it is just the hope that if only we could cut ourselves off from the mainstream of life all problems would be resolved, all frustrations would melt away. (Atkins, 1976: 7)

When contemplating the important part that islands have played in literature, children's laureate Quentin Blake posed the suggestion that 'there must be something that both focuses and stimulates the imagination in a place that you can draw a line round' (Blake, 2000: 80).

This chapter looks at some of the different ways in which British composers have found their imagination stimulated by and focused on particular British islands, and have then attempted to express their fascination in musical terms. Judith Weir (*b*. 1954), for example, has been drawn to the Western Isles of Scotland, attracted not by the landscape but rather by Hebridean folk songs and legends, reworking and revisiting the myths of South Uist in her music, initially without having visited the island. Conversely, Sir Peter Maxwell Davies (*b*. 1934) has adopted the culture and landscape of Orkney as a part of his work and life in an actual, physical sense, moving to live there and to embrace life within the island community. Of an earlier generation, John Ireland (1879–1962) repeatedly visited the Channel Islands, creating musical fantasies of places that were at once real and a product of his memories and imagination. Arnold Bax (1883–1953) and E. J. Moeran (1894–1950) were lured to Ireland, the former producing his orchestral piece, *The Garden of Fand*, a tone poem about an enchanted island, the latter settling in Kenmare. Benjamin Britten's (1913–76) *On this Island* was less a romantic vision than a response to the questioning of nationality issues prevalent in the 1930s.

More recently, in 1995, Andrew Hugill (*b*. 1957) wrote an *Island Symphony*. This was composed on St George's Island, a tiny place off the Cornish coast south of Looe. In many ways St George's Island is an archetypal 'fantastic' island, with a long history complete with medieval chapel site and ancient caves. An electro-acoustic piece, the *Island Symphony* uses natural, sampled and synthesized sounds within its four movements. Hugill presents the various aspects of the island through different compositional approaches. Incidentally, St George's Island has a history of attracting musicians, and had previously been a source of inspiration for the aforementioned Arnold Bax.

Each of these figures has different ways of attempting to depict island aspects musically. Memory and imagination play important roles in the recreation of the place in sound. Some island pieces are hazy impressions, while others have a strong sense of topography: for Hugill, for example, a structural and timbral picture of the place matches the notion of the geographical map of an island. A number of the composers fascinated with islands are also captivated by their inhabitants, the people encountered encapsulated in the music. This feature has literary correlatives, for example with Muriel Spark's *Robinson*, where the main protagonist, a woman named January, says of her time as a castaway: 'All the time I was on the island I set considerable store by faces ... ' (Spark, 1978: 137).

This chapter will focus on three of the composers named above: Ireland, Weir and Hugill, and will look at some of the different ways in which British islands resonate in their music.

John Ireland and the Channel Islands

As a young man John Ireland (1879–1962) studied at the Royal College of Music and on leaving established himself as a pianist and organist and as a composer primarily of chamber music, piano miniatures and songs, but also of a number of large-scale choral works and orchestral pieces, including a piano concerto. Places, among them London and the Sussex Downs, had a significant impact on his music. For Ireland the Channel Islands were his Arcadia, a refuge, both physically, from his house in London, and mentally, from problematic personal relationships, and also a place of vivid memories. These islands, with their glorious rocky and sandy bays, have warm springs and mild winters. From May onwards the sheltered lanes are luxuriantly fern-and flower-clad. Ireland was drawn to the Channel Islands over many years, from at least as early as 1906. He was a regular summer visitor to Jersey from 1908–14, and then settled on Guernsey for a brief time, from September 1939, until the German invasion of the island in 1940 forced his departure. These periods in his life stimulated a number of musical works, which in different ways respond to the notion of the 'island'.

From the two years prior to the outbreak of the First World War there are two major compositions associated with an aspect of the island of Jersey. These are the piano piece, *The island spell* and the orchestral prelude, *The Forgotten Rite*. And there are other works that have fleeting and retrospective connections with Jersey. From the year on Guernsey there are a further two works, one a simple choral setting for the local choir of St Stephen's church, located in the island's capital, St Peter Port, the other a suite of movements for piano, completed on Ireland's enforced return to London, with the title *Sarnia*, this being the Roman name for Guernsey. The three movements that make up the suite: *Le Catioroc*, *In a May morning* and *Song of the springtides*, all have literary and historical associations with the island, as well as being attached to real locations.

The first of Ireland's Jersey pieces is *The island spell*, begun in 1911 and completed the following year during a halycon summer holiday on the east coast of the island. In this piece, Ireland's manner of capturing the essence of the island was to focus on its French aspects; hence there is a strong influence of Debussy in terms of the piece's structure, harmonies and stylistic piano writing. The piece opens with a repeating motive, based on a pentatonic (five-note) scale starting on D-flat. Above this a melody, marked 'as if a chime', is picked out. The central section develops the chime-like motive, and makes much of rapid piano runs, before closing with a reference to Debussy's *La Cathédrale Engloutie* (*The Submerged Cathedral:* another secret, this time submerged, island place) and a rising scale featuring the successive whole tones favoured at the time by contemporary French composers.

Jersey was also the inspiration for *The Forgotten Rite*, of which Ireland wrote to a friend, Kenneth Wright, on 10 September 1928:

> It's a work I felt much about. I wrote it after being alone for 6 weeks in Jersey, and one felt so intensely, painfully, in fact, the indescribable beauty of the light, the sea, and the distant other islands. At that time, one felt that the very thinnest of material veils separated one from the actual Reality behind all this smiling beauty … (Wright, 1928)

The Forgotten Rite is essentially an evocation of Pan the goat-god. Like *The island spell* it has strong French connections and shows the influence of Debussy in the orchestration in particular, which features muted French horns, flute solos and harp glissandi. The static nature of the opening chords, which oscillate slowly around a second inversion chord, and the sensuous nature of the string writing establish this as a dream-world akin to Debussy's *Prélude à l'Après-midi d'un faune*. So Ireland's essential means of capturing this island in music was through a deliberate, sensuous musical 'Frenchness', Jersey for him at this time a place of vivid and magical colours, a rosy escape before the start of World War I. It is also the case that he was at this time a young man, carrying none of the scars of turbulent personal relationships that can be heard in his later music.

Ireland's piano suite, *Sarnia*, completed some years later, in 1940 and 1941, conveys a rather different image of the Channel Islands. During the 1920s and early 1930s the composer suffered a series of personal traumas, involving relationships with much younger men and women, and a failed marriage. After a few years recovering, spending much of his time on the coast at Deal, in Kent, Ireland decided to move to Guernsey. For most of his time on the island he lived on the west coast, very close to two significant pagan sites. Le Creux ès Faies, a burial chamber in the immediate vicinity of Fort Saumarez, was associated with the fairy tradition in Guernsey. Near by was Le Catioroc, a headland on the west coast, on which a neolithic stone-covered burial chamber, Le Trépied dolmen, is situated. This was reputed to be the scene of witches' sabbaths in the sixteenth and seventeenth centuries, and the last surviving site of pagan rituals on the island.

Whereas the Jersey pieces are openly ardent, eulogizing the landscape and resonating with the headiness of a balmy summer dream, the Guernsey pieces are much more complex, closely bound up with specific places, actual people and literature. Each of the three miniatures that make up *Sarnia* is dedicated to a Guernsey inhabitant, and each has some connection with a novel or poem. Thus *Le Catioroc* is attached to the headland mentioned above, is dedicated to a local flautist, and has a structure influenced by a section of a novel by Arthur Machen, *The Great God Pan.*

The central movement, *In a May morning* has equally complex extra-musical island connections. In April 1940 Ireland moved from the west coast of the island to the capital, St Peter Port, where he met a young boy, Michael Rayson. The beauty of this youth, together with the aura of the island in the spring of 1940, was the inspiration for *In a May morning.* A year after his departure from the island, Ireland wrote to his close friend, the Reverend Kenneth Thompson:

> I think you referred to Michael, in connection with my new piano pieces. Well of course he was just a part of the whole flood of beauty in Guernsey – those last 6 or 7 weeks were really an extraordinary revelation – there was *everything at once* – the unbelievable beauty of the Channel Islands in Spring, the delightful surroundings and feeling of heart's ease – the joy of that lovely Church where I played the organ – and Michael constantly about the house and garden, fitting in so well with everything – it was almost too wonderful to be true & certainly far too wonderful to last … alas, how fragile, how transitory! And yet, how eternal & true! Well, I have expressed some of it in my new piano work, 'SARNIA'. (Ireland, 26 June 1940)

In a May morning is an attempt to capture in music the atmosphere of a person, a place and a time. The movement is prefaced by a quotation from Victor Hugo's novel of 1866, *Les Travailleurs de la Mer.* Hugo spent some time living in exile on Guernsey, where he wrote and located this work. Ireland intended the quotation not to describe the music, but rather the beauty of Michael Rayson and the Guernsey spring, to which the music was his reaction. The last movement of *Sarnia, Song of the springtides*, took its title from a work by the English poet Swinburne, another writer who spent some time living on Guernsey.

There is one last example of a work with island connections. In 1941 Ireland wrote a tiny piano piece with the title *A Grecian lad.* The theme was the youth Narcissus, the inspiration a long-ago, remembered holiday in Jersey. Thus for Ireland his Channel Island pieces are differentiated by island and by time. The Jersey pieces are French impressions with a single mood, the Guernsey pieces retrospective nuggets with complex personal and literary associations. In both cases these works are imbued with nostalgia. Ireland was a profoundly sentimental man, given to reminiscing about an imagined, happier past, and the theme of remembrance runs deep in his output.

Judith Weir and the Western Isles

Born in Aberdeenshire, Scottish composer Judith Weir (*b*. 1954) studied composition with John Tavener, at Cambridge and at Tanglewood. Her output is wide-ranging, embracing small-scale piano pieces, vocal music and several successful operas. Weir's island fascination is quite different from that of Ireland, stemming not from the actual experience of landscape, but from a removed perspective. For her, the appeal of the Western Isles of Uist and Barra (part of the Outer Hebrides) came from literature, particularly Scottish folklore, recorded memories and documented island traditions. She has described the reason why folklore holds particular attractions for her as a composer:

> [a] very specific reason that I personally like to use it in my work is that it has a terrific bareness and simplicity, and this allows me as a composer to, as it were, weave something around these very bare bones. If I were to work with more, as it seems, complicated literature, I think there would soon be a confusion and a clash between what I'm doing and what the writer does. But with folk tales, all you get is the story and that leaves me a lot of space to work. (Weir, 1996)

Through many years of reading folk tales, one theme that stood out for Weir was the story of a person who leaves home never to return again. The reason why this particular myth so appealed to Weir was its timelessness and the fact that it recurs in many different guises. Over a period of three years she produced three works based on the prevalent Hebridean myth of a mortal stolen by the fairies, but during all this time Weir never actually visited the Hebridean islands she evoked. The fascination was a literary one, the impact of her Scottish heritage.

The first of these pieces was *The Song of a Girl Ravished Away by the fairies in South Uist*, for voice and piano, part of her *Songs from the Exotic* (1987). In this tale, a girl goes out one night to collect in her cattle, is stolen by the fairies and sings to her mother from captivity. Weir found the words of the song in a collection by Margaret Fay Shaw, with the title, *Folk Songs and Folk Lore of South Uist*, a compendium of all sorts of things, including riddles, proverbs, stories, poems and music. Weir has described this as a book which has 'absolutely resonated' through her life as it seems to contain 'so many people's lifetimes within it' (Weir, 1996).

The words of *The Song of a Girl Ravished Away by the fairies in South Uist* were originally sung to a very simple tune, as printed in Shaw's book. Weir's melodic line uses this as a starting point, and plays with just a few notes within a contained structure. Her own version makes small but crucial changes to the original folk tune. The tempo is now considerably slower, and some of the notes are chromatically altered. Much of Weir's piano part simply consists of single notes from the song tune, picked out and sustained in order to build up a spare yet sonorous harmony, the sustaining pedal used to create the sound of distant bells. Essentially the song has one atmosphere to match the unchanging situation.

In 1989 Weir wrote a piano quartet, *Distance and Enchantment*, in which she refashioned this song into a more complex instrumental work on the subject of disappearance, the viola meditating on the earlier folk-derived tune while the violin, cello and piano elaborate around this line. And then in the following year, 1990, her three-act opera, *The Vanishing Bridegroom*, laced together three Gaelic tales concerned with disappearances, this time drawing on two significant folk sources: J. F. Campbell's *Popular Tales of the West Highlands*, collected and produced in four volumes between 1860 and 1862, and Alexander Carmichael's *Carmina Gadelica* (the Latin for Gaelic songs/hymns/incantations and so forth / *Ortha nan Gaidheal*), six volumes of Hebridean charms and incantations collected at around the same time, in the 1860s and first published in 1900.

Each act of Weir's opera takes a version of the vanishing myth, and, as is the manner in folk tales, tells this in a precise manner within a formal framework. Each act is a separate and complete story, but together they tell a story that unfolds across the whole opera, connecting the acts, concerning three episodes in the life of a particular family who live on a remote Scottish island. To enhance the evocations of islands visited only through words, in this work Weir drew extensively on elements of traditional Scottish musics. Thus in *The Vanishing Bridegroom* she features *pibroch* (piping / *piobaireachd*), traditional *waulking-songs* (songs to accompany work on the island) and the eerie psalm singing of the Western Isles.

Act I, *The Inheritance*, is a parable which tells two tales, the one of a missing legacy, the other of a woman married against her will. The act has a number of borrowings from Scottish folk music traditions. The opening of the piece, which takes place at a funeral, was directly inspired by the tradition of Gaelic psalm singing in Presbyterian churches in the West of Scotland. The singing in these churches is unaccompanied, led by a precentor, with a staggered sound as the congregations join in. To emulate this staggered sound Weir wrote gently overlapping vocal lines. Later in the act, as the woman is married, a group of fiddlers play a similarly smudgy version of Scottish folk music featuring extravagant glissandi, open strings and dissonances.

Act II is the 'lyrical interlude' (Griffiths, 1990) of the opera, in which the bride of Act I has a child, and in which her husband is seduced by magic fairy singing to disappear into a fairy knoll for 20 years. This act contains many different types of musical associations with traditional Scottish elements, and returns to Margaret Fay Shaw's book of folklore, folk songs and descriptions of island traditions, as noted in a small community in South Lochboisdale, South Uist, between 1929 and 1935. One of the most powerful descriptions in the book is of the *waulking song*, sung to accompany the preparation of island tweed:

When word came that it was ready it was collected and preparations were made for the great event of a *luadhadh*, or waulking, which is when the cloth is shrunk and made ready for the tailor ... A lantern hung from the rafters and shone down on the singers in their rough aprons, their heads tied in kerchiefs, their sleeves rolled high. The air was potent with the smell of hot urine, but no substitute will give the soft-ness of texture nor set the colour, especially of indigo. When finished the tweed was thoroughly washed in a running stream and dried on the heather, exposed to the sun and wind for several days until perfectly clean. The women kneaded and pushed the cloth round and round the table with song after song ... When it was thought to be sufficiently shrunk and the feel of the texture right, one would measure the length with her third finger. If not yet shrunk enough they would give it another song ... (Shaw, 1939: 6)

The musical tradition of the *waulking* song is brought into Act II, where a semi-chorus of three women comment on what is happening in the Act. But the main focus of this act is the disappearance of the husband into a fairy knoll. Fairy knolls are in the raised beaches of the West side of the Hebrides, where, now and again, there are little green hillocks in what is know as the Machair land. In writing an act located beside one of these knolls, Weir had to consider how she would repre-sent the sound of fairy singing. To do this, she set substantial passages of Gaelic for chorus. The texts were created from the combination of chants of the *Carmina Gadelica*. The reason for the choice of short, Gaelic texts was in order to differ-entiate human from fairy worlds. Weir felt that Gaelic has 'a kind of misty, dreamy atmosphere. Characteristically of the language we hear a lot of very long vowels but not many consonants, and it has a rather static quality, which is quite right for a story which suggests that time stands still for twenty years ... ' (Weir, 1996).

Act III, 'The stranger' makes use of a well-known myth of the Western Isles, that of the *each-uisge*, or 'water horse', described again in Shaw:

The *each-uisge*, as he is called, becomes a handsome young man at night and he comes about the house to court pretty girls. At daylight he changes into a savage horse that drags his victim into the loch. He has a weakness which results in his being recognised. He likes to have his head rubbed, and while his sweetheart puts her fingers through his hair she feels the sand and the bits of water-weed and so knows who her lover is. (Shaw, 1939: 11)

This act focuses on the daughter's attempt to outwit the devil – who here has water-horse features – and who, in disguise, attempts to woo the young woman. Unlike Ireland, whose obsession with the Channel Islands was spread across many years, Weir's fascination with the Western Isles, specifically South Uist, was focused in one particular period of her life, occupying the years 1987–90. The urge to connect with the remote island of South Uist was a literary one, with Weir drawn to the place through its folk traditions, hence her extensive use of elements of folk music in her compositions.

Andrew Hugill and His Island Symphony

The third of the case studies in this chapter is a large-scale work by the composer Andrew Hugill (*b.* 1957), currently Professor of Music at De Montfort University, Leicester, UK. His approach differs from that of Weir in that his *Island Symphony* was composed in 1995 in direct response to an actual landscape. And different again from that of Ireland in that, in accordance with his work with music technology, the symphony weaves the recorded physical sounds of the island into a complex electronic web.

The *Island Symphony* was commissioned by South West Arts and Cornwall County Council, written as a response to the tiny St George's Island, Cornwall, home at the time of writing to two women, Babs and Evelyn Atkins, now bequeathed to the Cornwall Wildlife Trust to be preserved as a nature reserve. The Atkins sisters purchased the island in 1964, after seeing it from the mainland and falling in love with it:

> Below ... was the sea shimmering in the early morning sunlight, but what riveted my gaze in spellbound astonishment was what I thought at first must be a mirage. There ... rising like a lost Atlantis out of the mist, was an island. Tender and green in the soft morning light it looked infinitely alluring as the mists melted in the rays of the rising sun ... Rising gracefully to the sky it looked like the tip of a submerged mountain. (Atkins, 1976: 33)

After some time living in isolation the island was opened to vistors. Hugill first visited St George's when on holiday in Cornwall. While staying in Looe, like Atkins, he had caught a glimpse of the island from the mainland, and took a day trip to the place. According to Hugill, 'At the time, I was composing a piece called *The Way Things Are*, which was proving rather difficult to complete, and I took the manuscripts with me just in case I had any ideas during the day. Once I set foot on the Island a remarkable thing happened: the piece "wrote itself" in a couple of hours' (Hugill, 1995).

After mentioning this to the Atkins sisters, they asked him to return, and to write an *Island Symphony*. Hugill worked on the piece while seated at the window of an eighteenth-century stone cottage, one of only a few houses on the island, which is one mile in circumference. The reason for the choice of an electroacoustic piece was in order to allow the work to be performed (initially, at least) in situ, on the island, and the composer therefore decided to mix natural, sampled and synthesized sounds. There is also a purely orchestral version of the work. With such a varied palette of sounds available, he felt that he could create a 'map' of the island, in all its diversity. One further aspect of this decision that he particularly liked was that it turned the workstation and the composer into a compositional 'island'. Hugill describes the work thus:

> *Island Symphony* has four movements, and attempts to map out the island in four different ways and through four different compositional approaches. The word Symphony is used in its etymological sense of 'sounding together', but the four movement scheme is a quite conscious echo of the classical Symphonic structure and my piece does have a sense of organic growth and the opposition of modalities.
>
> Island Symphony was created on an Apple Macintosh LC475 computer, with an additional 2.1 gigabyte hard disk (continuous data flow). Two software programmes were used: CuBase Audio, for sequencing; and Digidesign's SoundTools for audio editing. The samples were stored on a Roland S-760 sampler and were loaded from three main sources: Roland's CD-ROM sample libraries; Synclavier's CD-ROM sample libraries; digital recordings made by the composer, both in the field and downloaded from Internet sites. A Yamaha SY35 synthesizer was used as the controlling keyboard and for some sounds, and the master tape was recorded on to a Casio DA-7 Digital Audio Tape recorder. Monitoring was through a home hi-fi system, and this whole workstation represents a fairly portable 'home set-up', rather than a fully-fledged 'studio'. (Hugill, 1995)

The first movement of the symphony examines the island as a physical object. Firstly, it takes the silhouette of the location, as seen from the shore, as a graph of density over time, and a walk round the island as a means of constructing a sound narrative. Secondly, the inlets and outlets of the island's shoreline are translated into alternating and duration-varying 'in-breaths' and 'out-breaths', which dominate the overall sound of the movement. This effect is created by wind and brass players fingering particular notes and then inhaling silently through the instruments, with random key clacks added at intervals, but also through the inclusion of sampled human breaths.

Thirdly, there is a series of soundscapes intended to represent the various environments encountered during a brisk walk around the island (which, for Hugill, takes 19 minutes), and the movement is correspondingly nearly 19 minutes in duration. One of the most striking features of the island's appearance is the 'extreme proximity of wildly contrasting landscapes, for example: at the highest point one is on the edge of a rugged cliff, complete with seabirds; a turn and a couple of paces then plunges one into a forest, with woodland flora and fauna' (Hugill, 1995). The music reflects this, moving often quite abruptly from one sound world to another. For example, a section in which the strings are given 'irregular knocking on body of instrument', against the sampled sounds of waves of pebbles, gives way to blocks of wind textures, passages in which a solo viola meanders over string glissandi and full orchestra playing spiky staccato. The main musical material of the movement consists of rapid scale and arpeggio patterns. There is a constant sense of ebb and flow – the surrounding water – and despite the inclusion of specific detail, the overall impression is of a wash of sound.

While the first movement aims to capture the sounds of the island as a whole, the second focuses on one aspect of one part of the place. The island has a long history of being inhabited. At its highest point, overlooking the English Channel to the south and the Cornish coast to the north, a few carved stones are all that remains of a medieval chapel. The island was called Lammana during the thirteenth century, and was a retreat for Benedictine monks. Augustinian monks based in Launceston laid claim to the island too, and a dispute arose that had to be settled by the Pope himself. The island has also been known as St Michael's.

Below the chapel are caves, in which the wind echoes, sounding at times 'almost like an echo of distant singing' (Hugill, 1995). Movement 2: *Ten Little Middle Ages*, takes the medieval history of the chapel as its starting point. In his book *Travels in Hyperreality,* Umberto Eco describes ten versions of the middle ages, which appear almost as historical echoes in modern film, literature and thought. These *Ten Little Middle Ages* include *ironical revisitation* (for instance using pastiche of twelfth-century compositional techniques) and the *expectation of the Millennium.* Correspondingly the second movement is a set of ten variations on a medieval theme, each variation suggested by one of Eco's descriptions. The movement opens with a short theme, based on a lament by Peter Abelard entitled *Planctus David*, composed in Brittany (appropriately for the medieval context of this movement) in the twelfth century. The presentation of the theme is as a modal viola melody over a drone. The variations are then as shown in Table 10.1.

Thus this movement has a historical basis, taking as its starting point the island chapel, and using Eco's ideas both as a way of considering the island and as a means of structuring a theme and variations.

The third movement is a short, pastoral response to the sights and sounds of the island, with its cliff walks, wooded areas, beaches and daffodils already in bloom as early as Christmas. As with the first movement, the different aspects of the island are evoked through changing soundscapes, but here the emphasis is very much on percussion timbres, with the opening rapid muffled timpani strokes a prevalent feature, and other pervasive sounds such as bamboo wind chimes, crotales, Burmese gong and vibes.

The fourth and last movement, called *People and Buildings*, is, as its title suggests, a synthesis of aspects of the island's people and buildings. There are only a few buildings on the island, probably the most significant of which is the island's generator, a diesel engine built to supply the island's electricity, described thus by Evelyn Atkins:

Table 10.1 Variations in the second movement of Hugill's *Island Symphony*

1. Pretext	The modality and drone feature are developed as a pseudo medieval dance, giving way to a brief, richer orchestral section, described by Hugill as an 'operatic interlude'.
2. Barbarism	Melodramatic film pastiche, exploiting 'oriental' winding woodwind melodies over drones and tam tams.
3. Ironical Revisitation	A different sort of pastiche, this time of the compositional technique of the composers of the school of Notre Dame, distorted.
4. Romanticism	This is Eco's 'computers in the dungeon', a version of contemporary representations of stormy castles and space battles. As in the first movement of the symphony, airy sounds are exploited.
5. Philosophie Perennis	A densely-textured variation, based on the techniques of change-ringing, with the sounds of the bells prominent and sampled bird song interwoven.
6. National Identities	Fragments of the national anthems of ninety-five countries are woven around the theme. These are presented alphabetically, starting with Albania, and are all marked on the score.
7. Decadentism	This returns to the medieval dance element, but in a darker version, dissolving quickly into eight complex figurations.
8. Philological Reconstruction	Complex, dissonant figurations.
9. Tradition	This is the 'St George's Island Chorale'.
10. Expectation of the Millennium	A rapid three-time variation containing 1,000 notes. Described by Hugill as a millennium, which is 'both the medieval one and the one which faces us today'.

… of all the fascinating things we saw the one that rivetted our attention was the generator building. The front part of this housed a diesel engine for generating A.C. electricity. A doorway led to another room at the rear. This was about forty feet by twenty feet, one wall of which was lined with a row of large glass accumulators. Concrete blocks supported heavy wooden beams which ran the entire length of the room, and, apart from gangways, filled all available floor space. (Atkins, 1976: 43)

Hugill's fourth movement is founded on the recorded sound of this generator, with which it opens, and develops a busy riff made from the initials of the sisters who owned the island, Babs and Evelyn Atkins: B-A-B-S (Bb, A, Bb, Eb) and E-E-A (Eb, Eb, A). (B=B flat, and S=E flat, in German notation.)

Hugill's *Island Symphony* is a synthesis of the real, lived and experienced aspects of a particular island, an experiment in creating a type of traditional four-movement symphony from a mixture of sounds. Thus there is the equivalent of the sonata-form first movement – here the 'map' of the island, a second movement theme and variations, a third movement and a fast and furious finale, harnessing the energies and actual noises of the island. Weir's island is a literary island, part of her own Scottish heritage, and Ireland's a backward glance, a repository of memories. It is with a reference to retrospection that I want to end the chapter. For Ireland, and indeed for many of the composers who wrote 'island' pieces, nostalgia and memory are major factors in the creation of their compositions. To conclude, here is the final paragraph from Muriel Spark's island novel, *Robinson*, in which she writes:

> And now, perhaps it is because the island is passing out of sight that it rises so high in my thoughts. Even while the journal brings before me the events of which I have written, they are transformed, there is undoubtedly a sea-change, so that the island resembles a locality of childhood, both dangerous and lyrical ... And sometimes when I am walking down the King's Road or sipping my espresso in the morning – feeling, not old exactly, but fussy and adult – and chance to remember the island, immediately all things are possible. (Spark, 1978: 162)

References

Atkins, E. A. (1976), *We Bought An Island,* London: Coronet Books, Harrap.

Ballantyne, R. M. (1857), *The Coral Island,* London: T. Nelson.

Barrie, J.M. (1988, first ed. 1911), *Peter Pan,* London: Puffin Books.

Blake, Q. (2000), *The Laureate's Party,* London: Red Fox.

Blyton, E. (2000) [1947], *Five on Kirrin Island Again,* London: Hodder & Stoughton.

Campbell, J. F. (1994, first published 1860–2), *Popular Tales of the West Highlands,* Edinburgh: Birlinn Ltd.

Carmichael, A. (1994, first publ. 1900), *Carmina Gadelica,* Edinburgh: Floris Books.

Defoe, D. (1719), *Robinson Crusoe,* London: W.Taylor.

Eco, U. (1986), *Travels in Hyperreality,* New York: Harcourt, Brace & Co.

Griffith, P. (1990), Review of *The Vanishing Bridegroom,* in *The Times,* 19 October.

Hugill, A. (1995), Sleeve notes for the *Island Symphony.* Rubble Records.

Ireland, J. personal correspondence in the John Ireland Trust and the British Library (*Gb:Lbm,* Add.ms 60535/6)

Lawrence, D. H. (1928), 'The Man Who Loved Islands', in *The Woman Who Rode Away and Other Stories,* New York: Knopf.

Ransome, A. (1930), *Swallows and Amazons,* London: J. Cape.

Shaw, Margaret Fay (1939), *Folk Songs and Folk Lore of South Uist,* Oxford: Oxford University Press.
Spark, M. (1978, first ed. 1958), *Robinson.* Harmondsworth: Penguin Books.
Stevenson, R. L. (1883), *Treasure Island,* London: Dean.
Weir, J. (1996), Interview with Fiona Richards, 4 October 1996, South Uist. Used in part in an Open University television programme to support the Arts course A103, TV22, 'Myth and Music', first broadcast in 1998.

Recommended Listening

John Ireland
The Forgotten Rite, LSO / Hickox. Chandos 8994. 1991.
Sarnia, John Lenehan (piano). Naxos 8.553700. 1995. Eric Parkin (piano). Chandos 9250. 1994.
The island spell, John Lenehan (piano). Naxos 8.553889. 1996. Eric Parkin (piano). Chandos 9056. 1992

Judith Weir
Distance and Enchantment, Domus. Collins Classics CD14532.
Songs from the Exotic, Tapestry. BML 012

Andrew Hugill
Island Symphony, Rubble Records. 1995.
http://www.mti.dmu.ac.uk/~hugill/island/attiesmap.html (this site includes the natural sounds of St George's island, a virtual tour and many photographs).

Index

global cultural economy, 3
global musical economy, 3
Gomes, Eduardo Sa, 159
Grecian Lad, A (piano piece), 203
Guilbault, Jocelyne, 15–16
Guillermo Tell (song), 78

Haiteny (Drought) (song), 58–9
Hawaii, 11–12, 15, 25n18, 59
Homer, 5
Hoopi, Sol, 59
Ho, Yu, 103, 104
Hugill, Andrew, 21–2, 200, 207–11
hybridity, 1, 142, 144

Ibiza, 7, 20, 123–36
Idagi, Richard, 20–1, 139–51 passim
identity narrative, 138–51
Ikhwani Safaa (club), 22, 173–97
    passim, 192n4, 192n11
Imaginary Cuba (CD), 14
Inji (village), Chindo, 100, 110
Insula, 4–5, 24n4
Intagible Cultural Assets, 19, 99–121
    passim
International Journal of Island Affairs,
    4, 24n8
Iraklion, 69–71
Ireland, John, 22–3, 200, 201–4
Island Blues (CD), 13, 26n27
Island Spell, The (piano piece), 23,
    201–2
Island Symphony, 23, 200, 207–11

Jamaica, 14
Jaojoby, 53, 54
jineterism, 85, 90–4, 96n16, 96n20

Kaluli (people), 24–5n13
Kanggangsullae, 110–11
Kidumbak, 180–2, 188
Kigalawa (song), 183–4

Kijiti (song), 185
kinship, 33, 67, 71
Kraftwerk, 124
Kulthum, Umm, 177, 179

La Charanga Habanera, 87–8, 92
Laswell, Bill, 14, 26n29
Leach, Edmund, 8
lemur, 52, 56
London Missionary Society, 142
Los Van Van, 84, 86, 88, 96n18
Love in Sea Express (song), 22, 188,
    194n33
lyra (music), 18, 68–75

Mabo Decision, 145
Madagascar, 6, 14, 17, 51–64
Madagascar: A World Out of Time
    (CD), 26–7n30, 51
Malinowski, Bronislaw, 8
Mandrora Mantsilany (song), 17,
    51–64 passim
Manuel, Peter, 16
marae (ritual area), 32, 35, 37, 45
Marley, Bob, 141
Maxwell Davies, Sir Peter, 200
Merina (people), 60–1
mining, 55–6
Moe, Tal, 15
Moses Miracle, 111–12
Moundákis, Kostas, 70
music business, 7, 69–74, 79
musicians, 2, 6–7, 14, 15, 18, 20, 21,
    65–75, 80–97, 104, 107, 154, 156,
    162, 164, 167, 173, 176
myth, 1

National Carnival Commission, 163
National Center for Korean Traditional
    Performing Arts, The, 20, 112,
    115n27
nationalism, 1